박문각의 합격 노하우와
편입에 특화된 커리큘럼

편입의 마스터
박문각 편입 영어

실전 문법

Grammar

합격기준 박문각 편입

홍준기 편저

PMG 박문각

머리말
PREFACE

〈실전 문법〉은 순수 예상문제로 구성된 책이다. 다른 교재들과 다르게 기출문제들을 분석하여, 최신의 경향을 파악하고 시험의 방향을 예측하여 비슷한 수준으로 실전을 대비하고자 만들었다. 그런 생각으로 만들다 보니 일부 문제는 어렵기도 하고, 또 일부 문제는 자주 접하지 못한 유형도 있을 수 있겠지만, 실전 대비 가장 근접한 예상문제로 만든 장점이 있다.

〈실전 문법〉에 수록된 문제의 개수가 많지 않은 것은, 많은 문제보다도 하나의 문제라도 정확히 아는 것이 더 중요하다는 생각에서 출발하였기 때문이다. 박문각의 편입 영어 시리즈를 꾸준히 공부한 학생들은 알겠지만, 〈필수 문법〉에서 400문제, 〈유형 문법 600제〉에서 600문제, 〈기출 문법 700제〉에서 700문제를 이미 풀었기 때문에, 본 책에서 실전 300문제까지 푼다면 총 2,000문제를 푼 것이고 결코 적지 않은 양이다. 여기에 더해 각종 모의고사와 최신 기출문제를 풀 것이므로, 이를 체계적으로 반복한다면 시험에서 좋은 성과를 거둘 것이다.

이 책은 실전 대비용 교재이므로 문법 이론에 관한 정리하지 않았다. 이론적 토대 없이 문제만 푸는 것은 올바른 학습은 아니기 때문에 혹시 문법 이론에 대한 학습이 필요하면 필수문법으로 정리해야 한다. 시간이 부족하다면 필요한 부분만 발췌해서 이론을 살펴보는 것도 좋다. 이론을 알긴 하지만 적용이 안 되면 〈유형 문법 600제〉를, 다양한 기출 문제를 풀고 싶다면 〈기출 문법 700제〉를 풀어 보길 권한다.

실전에서는 내가 자주 틀리는 부분을 파악하여 메꿔 나가는 것이 점수를 올리는 지름길이기 때문이다. 문법의 왕도는 없지만, 저자는 반복학습의 중요성을 다시 강조하고 싶다. 문법 문제는 새로운 것을 틀리는 것이 아니라 알고 있지만 확신이 없어서 틀리거나, 아는 내용은 당연하다고 제쳐놓기 때문에 틀리는 경우가 비일비재하다. 기본에 충실하고, 어려운 문제를 접하게 되면 예외적인 사항에 집중하지 말고 기본적인 사항부터 제대로 확인하길 바란다.

이 책을 만드는 데는 언제나처럼 홍정현 교수님이 많은 도움을 주었다. 저자가 문제를 만들고 홍정현 교수님이 해설 작업을 담당해 주었다. 어려운 작업인데 항상 최선을 다 해줘 감사할 따름이다. 이 책으로 공부하는 학생들에게 밝은 미래가 펼쳐지길 진심으로 기원한다.

2020년 9월

홍준기

편입 문법 학습법 GUIDE

1 문법은 영어학습의 기본이다.

문법은 글을 읽을 수 있는 틀을 제시해 주는 과목이다. 문법이 안 되지만 독해는 된다거나, 문법은 되지만 독해는 안 된다거나 하는 경우는 거의 없다. 왜냐하면 문법의 토대 없이는 어휘의 뜻을 나열하는 데 불과하기 때문이다. 그러므로 영어 학습을 시작하는 데 있어서 문법은 기본이며, 편입시험에 있어서도 그 기본 발판이 된다.

2 문법의 올바른 학습방법론

1. 문법용어를 숙지하고 문장의 구조를 파악하라.

문법의 세부적인 내용을 공부하기에 앞서, 먼저 그 용어의 의미를 파악하는 것이 급선무이다. 문법용어를 몰라서 의사소통이 되지 않는 경우가 허다하다. 문법용어에 대해 숙지했다면 이제는 문장의 구조를 파악해 보아야 한다. 크게 주어, 동사, 목적어, 보어와 수식어를 판단하는 힘을 길러야 한다. 복잡한 문장의 구조를 분석하라는 것이 아니고, 단문 구조의 기본적인 틀을 익히라는 것이다. 그런 기본적인 연습을 하면 머릿속에 서서히 주어가 될 수 있는 성분은 명사를 기본으로 한다는 식의 나름의 틀이 형성되어 갈 것이다.

2. 문법의 기본적인 틀을 세워 나간다.

문장의 규칙은 문법은 8품사 가운데도 동사를 기본으로 한다. 이러한 동사의 활용을 이해하기 위하여 동사의 종류와 시제를 공부하고, 동사 역할과 다른 품사의 기능을 함께 하는 동사에 준하는 to부정사, 동명사, 분사 등을 익히게 된다. 또 주체와 객체의 관계를 염두에 둔 수동태와 능동태를 익히고, 발생하지 않은 일에 대해서 나타내기 위하여 가정법을 공부한다. 더불어 동사의 어감을 보충해주는 조동사 역시 동사와 관련지어 다루게 된다. 이렇게 동사는 다양한 쓰임을 바탕으로 문법의 핵을 이루고 있다.

이렇게 동사에 대한 학습이 끝나면 개별 품사를 익히게 된다. 주어를 구성하는 명사와 대명사, 명사 앞에 붙는 관사, 명사를 대신하는 대명사와 접속사의 기능을 하는 관계대명사, 명사를 수식하며 보어의 역할도 하는 형용사, 동사와 형용사를 수식하는 부사, 명사 앞에 위치하는 전치사, 단어와 단어, 문장과 문장 간의 관계의 관계를 설정해주는 접속사 등이 품사의 전부이다.

이후에 이러한 문법을 바탕으로 주요 구문을 학습하게 되는데, 부정구문, 비교구문, 무생물주어구문, 도치나 생략 등 특수구문 등을 공부한다. 이렇게 하면 문법의 전반적인 틀이 완성이 되며, 전체를 한눈에 아우를 수 있는 자신의 문법 틀이 갖추어진다.

3. 단원별 문제를 중심으로 이론을 재정비해야 한다.

문법의 기본이론에 대한 학습을 마쳤다면 단원별로 문제를 풀면서 정리해 나간다. 이렇게 단원별로 풀다 보면 단원에 의거해 푸니 어려운 문제도 단원을 인지하고 푸는 단점도 있지만, 스스로 익힌 문법의 틀을 확고히 다져 보는 계기가 된다. 문제를 풀면서 부족한 부분은 다시 이론으로 넘어가 이론을 공고히 하면서 문제를 통하여 빠진 부분이 메워지게 된다. 이론만을 볼 때는 안다고 생각하고 쉽게 여겼던 것들도 막상 문제를 접하게 되면 확실히 답을 고르기 어려운 부분들이 있기 때문이다.

4. 단원별이 아닌 종합문제를 실전처럼 풀어봐야 한다.

어느 정도의 학습이 끝났다면 이제는 실전처럼 종합적으로 문제를 풀 단계이다. 단원별로 풀 때는 쉽게 풀었던 것들도 섞어서 출제되면 약점을 보이게 마련이다. 그러므로 실전을 위한 연습으로 꼭 필요한 단계이다. 여기서 기출문제를 풀면서 그간 출제의 핵은 무엇이고, 최근의 변한 경향은 어떠한지를 함께 파악해 나가야 한다. 이런 과정에서 문법 각 단원 간의 내용이 유기적으로 혼합되면서 체계화된다. 이 때 자신의 부족한 부분을 파악하게 되면서 다시 부족한 이론을 메워주는 것이 필요하다. 예를 들어 분사를 개별적으로 학습하고 문제를 풀 때는 몰랐지만, 접속사와 섞어 나오는 문제를 접한 후에 자신이 접속사에 대한 이해가 부족했다는 등의 느낌이 올 것이며, 이때가 바로 깨달음을 통한 문법의 완벽한 체계 구성을 위한 최종단계가 된다.

5. 최신의 출제경향을 대비한 예상문제를 풀어야 한다.

문법도 출제경향이 있다. 이에 맞춰서 당대의 경향에 맞춘 문법을 학습하고 때때로 부족한 이론에 대해서 다시 틈틈이 보충하면 된다. 이 시기가 되면 학교별로 특수한 유형에도 대비하여야 한다. 예를 들어 서강대와 이화여대에서는 최근 구두법에 대한 문제가 출제되고 있으며, 중앙대의 경우 No Error 문제가 출제된다. 이런 부분을 연습해 두어야 한다.

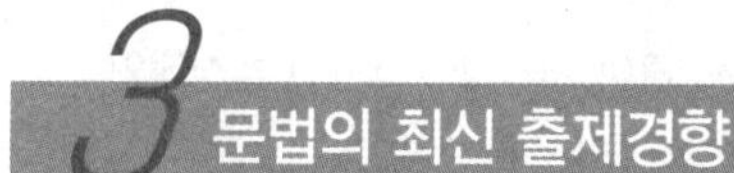

1. 문법 문제의 다양화를 들 수 있다.

중앙대에서 문법문제에서 기존의 틀을 깨고 No Error 문제를 출제하고, 서강대에서는 구두법에 관한 문제를 묻고 있는데, 이는 전형적인 SAT 유형의 문제로 문법을 위한 문법의 형태가 아닌 실용영어로 활용할 수 있는 문법으로 변하고 있다는 것이다.

2. 문법에서 인용하고 있는 문장이 어렵다.

문법문제로 인용하는 문장들의 길이가 길고, 문장 구조가 어려워지고 있다. 이는 밑줄만을 보고 답을 고르기가 쉽지 않고 해석을 통하여 풀어야 하는 문제가 늘어나고 있다는 것이다. 예를 들어 이화여대나 한양대를 비롯한 많은 대학들이 문법 문제를 장문으로 출제하고 있는데, 이 또한 글의 해독능력을 바탕으로 문법을 묻고 있다는 증거이다.

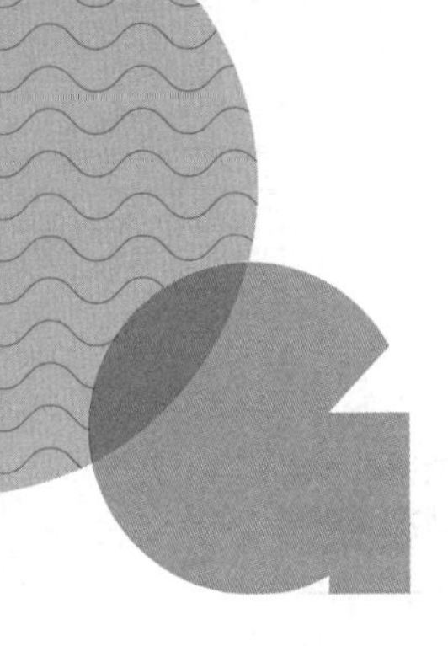

이 책의 구성과 특징
FOREWORD

01 실전모의고사

Answer p.74

[01~06] Choose the one that could best complete each of the following sentences.

01 **The test can identify Alzheimer's disease long before the patient starts __________ the symptoms — before he/she even knows he/she has got Alzheimer's.**
① before long the patient started having
② long before the patient starts having
③ before long the patient starts to have
④ long before the patent started to have

02 **Two pedestrians walking toward each other on a narrow sidewalk will seldom, __________, make eye contact to more effectively negotiate the tight passage.**
① if so ② if any
③ if ever ④ if possible

03 **He added that even if one is rich but is not healthy, then he __________ enjoy the money that he has.**
① will cannot ② will be able to
③ would be able to ④ will not be able to

04 **You are in control, the option is yours, you can either play live games or download them, and choose whichever you like from one of the many you can find on the website — __________ I have listed above.**
① neither of which ② none of which
③ wherever ④ some of which

12 ▪ 박문각편입 실전 문법

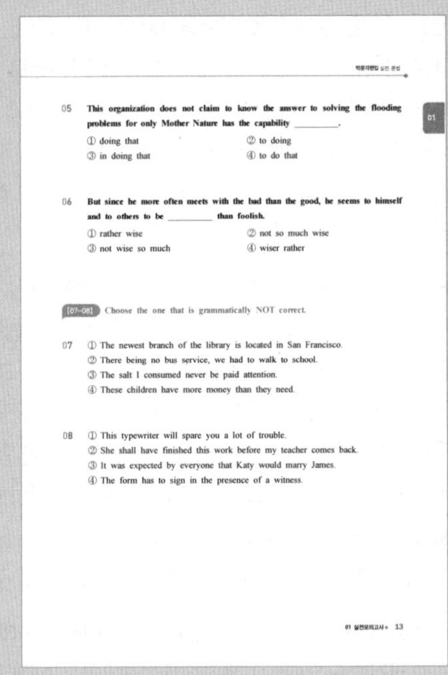
박문각편입 실전 문법

01

05 **This organization does not claim to know the answer to solving the flooding problems for only Mother Nature has the capability __________.**
① doing that ② to doing
③ in doing that ④ to do that

06 **But since he more often meets with the bad than the good, he seems to himself and to others to be __________ than foolish.**
① rather wise ② not so much wise
③ not wise so much ④ wiser rather

[07~08] Choose the one that is grammatically NOT correct.

07 ① The newest branch of the library is located in San Francisco.
② There being no bus service, we had to walk to school.
③ The salt I consumed never be paid attention.
④ These children have more money than they need.

08 ① This typewriter will spare you a lot of trouble.
② She shall have finished this work before my teacher comes back.
③ It was expected by everyone that Katy would marry James.
④ The form has to sign in the presence of a witness.

01 실전모의고사 ▪ 13

❶ 실전 대비 완벽한 예상문제

최신 기출문제를 철저히 분석하여 어느 학교라도 시험에 대비할 수 있게 구성하였다. 지문의 소재도 다양하게 구성하여 시사적인 내용과 추상적인 내용도 함께 문제화하여 여러 학교의 경향에 만전을 기할 수 있도록 구성하였다.

❷ 마무리에 적합한 종합적 문제 구성

단원별이 아닌 종합 형태의 구성이고, 실제 출제 빈도를 고려하여 문제를 수록하였다. 만약 특정 단원에서 어려움을 느낀다면, 〈필수 문법〉의 이론을 한 번 확인해 보길 권한다.

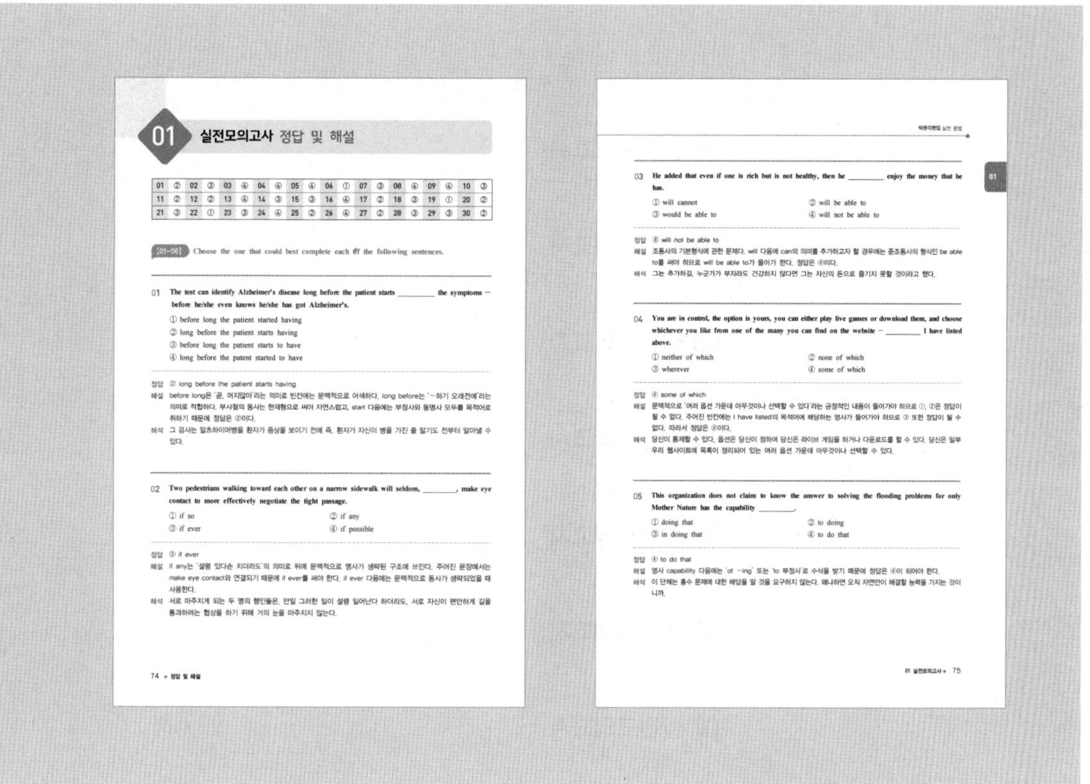

01 실전모의고사 정답 및 해설

01	②	02	③	03	④	04	④	05	④	06	①	07	③	08	④	09	④	10	③
11	②	12	②	13	④	14	③	15	③	16	④	17	②	18	③	19	①	20	②
21	③	22	①	23	③	24	④	25	②	26	④	27	②	28	③	29	③	30	②

[01-06] Choose the one that could best complete each of the following sentences.

01 **The test can identify Alzheimer's disease long before the patient starts ________ the symptoms – before he/she even knows he/she has got Alzheimer's.**

① before long the patient started having
② long before the patient starts having
③ before long the patient starts to have
④ long before the patent started to have

정답 ② long before the patient starts having
해설 before long은 '곧, 머지않아'라는 의미로 빈칸에는 문맥적으로 어색하다. long before는 '~하기 오래전에'라는 의미로 적합하다. 부사절의 동사는 현재형으로 써야 자연스럽고, start 다음에는 부정사와 동명사 모두를 목적어로 취하기 때문에 정답은 ②이다.
해석 그 검사는 알츠하이머병을 환자가 증상을 보이기 전에 즉, 환자가 자신이 병을 가진 줄 알기도 전부터 알아낼 수 있다.

02 **Two pedestrians walking toward each other on a narrow sidewalk will seldom, ________, make eye contact to more effectively negotiate the tight passage.**

① if so ② if any
③ if ever ④ if possible

정답 ③ if ever
해설 if any는 '설령 있다손 치더라도'의 의미로 뒤에 문맥적으로 명사가 생략된 구조에 쓰인다. 주어진 문장에서는 make eye contact와 연결되기 때문에 if ever를 써야 한다. if ever 다음에는 문맥적으로 동사가 생략되었을 때 사용한다.
해석 서로 마주치게 되는 두 명의 행인들은, 만일 그러한 일이 설령 일어난다 하더라도, 서로 자신이 편안하게 길을 통과하려는 협상을 하기 위해 거의 눈을 마주치지 않는다.

74 • 정답 및 해설

박문각편입 실전 문법

03 **He added that even if one is rich but is not healthy, then he ________ enjoy the money that he has.**

① will cannot ② will be able to
③ would be able to ④ will not be able to

정답 ④ will not be able to
해설 조동사의 기본형식에 관한 문제다. will 다음에 can의 의미를 추가하고자 할 경우에는 준조동사의 형식인 be able to를 써야 하므로 will be able to가 들어가 한다. 정답은 ④이다.
해석 그는 추가하길, 누군가가 부자라도 건강하지 않다면 그는 자신의 돈으로 즐기지 못할 것이라고 했다.

04 **You are in control, the option is yours, you can either play live games or download them, and choose whichever you like from one of the many you can find on the website – ________ I have listed above.**

① neither of which ② none of which
③ wherever ④ some of which

정답 ④ some of which
해설 문맥적으로 '여러 옵션 가운데 아무것이나 선택할 수 있다'라는 긍정적인 내용이 들어가야 하므로 ①, ②은 정답이 될 수 없다. 주어진 빈칸에는 I have listed의 목적어에 해당하는 명사가 들어가야 하므로 ③ 또한 정답이 될 수 없다. 따라서 정답은 ④이다.
해석 당신이 통제할 수 있다. 옵션은 당신이 정하여 당신은 라이브 게임을 하거나 다운로드를 할 수 있다. 당신은 일부 우리 웹사이트에 목록이 정리되어 있는 여러 옵션 가운데 아무것이나 선택할 수 있다.

05 **This organization does not claim to know the answer to solving the flooding problems for only Mother Nature has the capability ________.**

① doing that ② to doing
③ in doing that ④ to do that

정답 ④ to do that
해설 명사 capability 다음에는 'of ~ing' 또는 'to 부정사'로 수식을 받기 때문에 정답은 ④이 되어야 한다.
해석 이 단체는 홍수 문제에 대한 해답을 알 것을 요구하지 않는다. 왜냐하면 오직 자연만이 해결할 능력을 가지는 것이니까.

01 실전모의고사 • 75

③ 각 문제에 대해 최적화된 해설

문법 이론을 장황하게 나열하기보다 핵심을 지적하는 방식으로 해설을 달았다. 어려운 문장들이 꽤 들어 있어 해석에 어려움을 겪을 수 있어, 특히 해석에 신경을 썼다. 처음 보는 문장을 접할 때 제대로 글을 이해하면 문법 문제의 경우에도 반은 푼 것과 다름없기 때문이다.

④ 조금 긴 실전문제를 10회에 나누어 배치

학교에 따라서 실전에서는 약간 긴 문장들이나, 두 문장이 하나의 문제로 나오기도 한다. 그런 학교들에 당황하지 않도록 긴 문제들을 상당수 만들어 두었으니, 한양대나 이화여대 등의 편입시험에 대한 충분한 연습이 될 것이다.

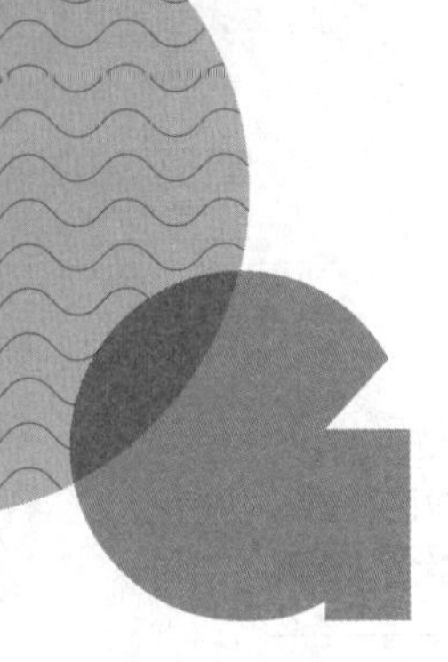

차례
CONTENTS

박문각 편입

실전 문법

TEST

01–10

실전 모의고사

01 실전모의고사

Answer p.74

[01-06] Choose the one that could best complete each of the following sentences.

01 **The test can identify Alzheimer's disease long before the patient starts __________ the symptoms – before he/she even knows he/she has got Alzheimer's.**

① before long the patient started having
② long before the patient starts having
③ before long the patient starts to have
④ long before the patent started to have

02 **Two pedestrians walking toward each other on a narrow sidewalk will seldom, __________, make eye contact to more effectively negotiate the tight passage.**

① if so
② if any
③ if ever
④ if possible

03 **He added that even if one is rich but is not healthy, then he __________ enjoy the money that he has.**

① will cannot
② will be able to
③ would be able to
④ will not be able to

04 **You are in control, the option is yours, you can either play live games or download them, and choose whichever you like from one of the many you can find on the website – __________ I have listed above.**

① neither of which
② none of which
③ wherever
④ some of which

05 **This organization does not claim to know the answer to solving the flooding problems for only Mother Nature has the capability __________.**

① doing that
② to doing
③ in doing that
④ to do that

06 **But since he more often meets with the bad than the good, he seems to himself and to others to be __________ than foolish.**

① rather wise
② not so much wise
③ not wise so much
④ wiser rather

[07–08] **Choose the one that is grammatically NOT correct.**

07
① The newest branch of the library is located in San Francisco.
② There being no bus service, we had to walk to school.
③ The salt I consumed never be paid attention.
④ These children have more money than they need.

08
① This typewriter will spare you a lot of trouble.
② She shall have finished this work before my teacher comes back.
③ It was expected by everyone that Katy would marry James.
④ The form has to sign in the presence of a witness.

[09-30] Choose the one that makes the sentence grammatically INCORRECT.

09 We must by all means avoid ① overthrowing all of them, lest we should help the enemy ② become more united and ③ land ourselves in an ④ isolating position.

10 The changes ① are alarming scientists and environmentalists, because they ② far exceed the rate ③ that computer models of climate change ④ predict the Arctic ice will melt as a result of global warming.

11 A thing about Capers and his career ① is when he left the Carolina Panthers a lot of people were questioning his passion, ② said this guy is not a passionate sort, he is not able to instill the type of emotion and enthusiasm in his team. ④ No error.

12 Elizabeth is slightly taller, slimmer and ① with more healthier, rosier cheeks. Katy has a rounder face and a ② noticeable paler complexion. But look closer and you can see similarities. They have the same shaped eyes, ③ though not the same colour. ④ No error.

13 ① Unlike many countries, the United States has ② few federal policies for working parents. One is the Family and Medical Leave Act of 1993, ③ which provides workers at companies of a certain size ④ in 12 weeks of unpaid leave.

14 Similarly, ① permission to appeal was granted by the Supreme Court that ② had denied defendant's motion to compel the plaintiff's parents to ③ submit to an examination before trial and provide medical authorizations on the ground that the medical information ④ privileged.

15 I didn't have to wait for ① long before my cafe latte and egg & bacon were served. The egg and bacon roll can certainly ② be had ③ for its half price elsewhere. It was warm and crusty and tasty, but that was about it. The cafe latte came with a heart-shaped latte art, and though ④ inferior to Campos Coffee, was still a pretty good cup.

16 My best friend and I recently started college together ① as roommates. One weekend we went away with some friends, including a guy I liked. The next thing I know my friend is holding his hand and dancing with him. I ② tried not to let it bother me because I know she ③ would never do anything ④ hurting me.

17 It may be more than two centuries ① since he died but his ability to spark controversy remains undimmed. A typical example now is of fragmented approach ② to honor his memory. A furious row has broken out over plans to ③ only partially restore a monument to him. ④ No error.

18 It has not recovered well ① this past winter − ice extent for every month since September 2015 has been far below average. And "② it's been so warm in the Arctic ③ that the ice has grown this winter is ④ probably rather thin", Professor Peter Wadhams of Cambridge University explains.

19 The carbon footprint shows ① how many greenhouse gases a product creates. The primary footprint ② measures the direct CO2 amounts from the whole life cycle of a product. CO2 ③ emissions are created not only from making products but also from ④ maintaining and destroying them.

20 Public anger is growing in China ① following last week's deadly explosions at a warehouse in the northern port city of Tianjin. Officials there announced the death toll ② continues to raise : 114 ③ are confirmed dead and 70 others ④ are still missing.

21 Ask me what my favorite sports movie is and you're in for a long wait. There are, in my opinion, ① too many great sports movies out there to choose just one. I could maybe pick a favorite one for ② each sport, but ③ no one that stands out above all the others. ④ No matter what sport the movie is about, the plot is usually the same.

22 ① Most all intelligent creatures, ② be they parrots, sharks or human beings, are vertebrates. This is ③ inconvenient for anyone ④ trying to understand the nature of intelligence.

23 A Criminal Court, for instance, will issue a gag order ① on the media if the judge ② believes that potential jurors in a future trial will be influenced ③ on the media reporting or speculation ④ on the early stages of a case.

24 If you're tired of hearing about millennials, you ① might want to revisit your old friends at MTV. The ② youth-aimed cable network, known for making radical shifts in its programming every few years, is already ③ turning its attention to Generation Z, loosely defined ④ people born from the late 1990s to the present.

25 The driver of any vehicle ① involved in an accident ② results in the death of any person shall immediately stop ③ such vehicle at the scene of the accident or as ④ close thereto as possible.

26 Francis Bacon is one of the important ① thinkers of the Scientific Revolution of the 17th century. Although Bacon was neither a mathematician ② nor an experimental scientist, he ③ exerted great influence on his contemporary by introducing ④ a method on which science is based observation and experimentation.

27 In a burglary trial, the defendant's actions after he entered the house ① can be evidence used to determine if he had the intent to commit a crime at the time of entry. For example, if a defendant ② entered the house and committed criminal sexual conduct (CSC), the jury could find him guilty of burglary even though there ③ may not have been ④ any specific evidence that at the time he entered the house he intended to commit CSC.

28 After a certain length of time living in fear with ① no guarantees about any facet of everyday life, any sort of government is ② preferable to none. Would you trade a government that stones adulterers ③ with the ability to walk to the store safely? For most, the answer ④ becomes absolutely. A repressive regime claiming religious credibility is fast forming and therefore perfectly placed to take over in an unstable situation.

29 Pasta's ethnic roots have been long debated. Many theories ① have been put forward, some notably far-fetched. An enduring myth, based on the writings of the 13th-century explorer Marco Polo, that pasta was brought to Italy from China, ② rose from a misinterpretation of a famous passage in Polo's Travels. ③ In them, Polo mentions a tree from which something like pasta was made. It was probably the sago palm, ④ which produces a starchy food that resembles, but is not pasta.

30 Just thinking that a particular brand's products are especially effective may have a kind of placebo effect, researchers have found. In ① a series of studies, participants received nearly identical tools for skill tests in golf and math. The only difference : Half of the putters bore Nike labels, while half of the earplug sets given to test takers ② was said to have been made by 3M. Those who thought they were using a Nike putter indeed ③ needed fewer putts, on average, to sink a ball, and participants who thought they had 3M earplugs during the math test answered more questions correctly. It was also found that those with the lowest initial confidence in their abilities seemed ④ to gain the most from the subtle upgrade.

02 실전모의고사

Answer p.86

[01-06] Choose the one that could best complete each of the following sentences.

01 __________ I was part of this nonsense was not lost on me, and at times it troubled me beyond mere embarrassment.

① What ② The fact
③ That ④ Whether

02 She was so captivated by it that she went home and finished a project in one night that __________ span the full four-week program.

① are supposed to ② supposed to
③ was supposed to ④ will be supposed to

03 His weight hit 220 ; he felt and looked like a blimp. One night, the company nurse invited him to __________ his blood pressure tested.

① having been ② have
③ have had ④ having

04 To make the United States more competitive, he said he __________ a fair tax that __________ income tax and the payroll tax system.

① would push … would get rid of
② would push … got rid of
③ would push … would have gotten rid of
④ pushed … would get rid of

05 **__________ her before I encountered her music, I would not have been surprised at how intelligently humorous her works are.**

① Having been met ② Had I met
③ If I hadn't met ④ If I met

06 **Your wedding will be more than just ______________, perfectly color-coordinated flowers, and an awesome reception.**

① the most beautiful imaginable dress
② the most beautiful and imaginable dress
③ the beautiful dress most imaginable
④ the most beautiful dress imaginable

[07-08] Choose the one that is grammatically NOT correct.

07 ① The same thing, happening in wartime, would amount to disaster.
② If he had listened to me, he would not have failed.
③ If the sun was to collide with the moon, what would become of the earth?
④ If he had worked hard in his school days, he would succeed now.

08 ① Once you come in, you cannot get out without permission.
② If he were to be president, he would make a drastic reform.
③ A famous scientist found that most stars were bigger than the sun.
④ He wishes to resign on the ground that his health is failing.

[09-30] Choose the one that makes the sentence grammatically INCORRECT.

09 ① The native Italians refuse to speak ② an ounce of ③ its language ④ to foreigners for fear that we should butcher their romantic language.

10 The Clemson House offers several living options for undergraduate students. Each room or apartment ① houses ② two to four students and has a private bath. As with the apartment complexes, ③ little, ④ if any, freshmen are assigned to the Clemson House.

11 ① Even though you'll find plenty to do in Vancouver, there are ② nearby destinations definitely worth a look. ③ Among the must-sees ④ is Vancouver Island, with historic Victoria and Butchart Gardens, Whistler, and the North Shore, with Grouse Mountain.

12 Although the session had its successes, lawmakers agree ① more work is needed and they will spend ② their off time on researching local ③ constituents' needs in preparation for the 2007 session. ④ No error.

13 Each footprint ① is made up of three massive toes – each one at least one and ② a half time as big as my foot. That makes them the biggest dinosaur prints ③ ever found in Scotland. And Dr Clark says they are significant, because they are still in the original strata of rock ④ where they were formed.

14 Truthfully, ten years ago, I didn't care much about community. My dream was to win a lot of money ① to help my own family. ② Little I know, so many families right here in Atchison are less fortunate ③ than my own. ④ There is poverty, molestation, addictions and many other types of violence and crime.

15 I could not feel any heat off the light, just coldness. It didn't have a shine ① nor a brightness to it. Just ② a glow to it. After standing there for just like a minute or so, one of my cousins couldn't take the fear ③ no longer, so we started to run back towards the cross roads and ④ it followed us.

16 The underlying premise of the prior opinion, it ① seems to me, is that, under the Constitution, the mere absence of ② a prohibition against an asserted power, plus the abstract reasonableness of its use, ③ is enough ④ to be established the existence of the power. I think this is erroneous.

17 When the Impressionists first ① tried to show their work people ② were warned to stay away from it ③ for fear of endangering their health and sanity. Pregnant women in particular were exhorted to steer clear of its influences ④ lest should they miscarry.

18 Influenza, commonly ① called the flu, is always caused ② by virus. Antibiotics will not help, unless the person develops a secondary bacterial infection. The symptoms ③ usually occur abruptly. Many people will develop a cough, ④ which is usually dry and can be severe, and chest pain.

19 The ① low performing schools that we hear about are not the fault of the teachers. There are many ② factors involved, and a majority of the problems begin at home. ③ Some of the factors are : gangs, language, discipline, single parent home environment, respect for themselves, etc. Let's support our educators and not ④ blame on the teachers.

20 ① There must be no big trees and buildings around fish ponds ② for fear that they should shade the sunlight and block the blowing of the winds. It's beneficial to ③ the raising of water temperature of fish ponds and the growth of plankton and the improvement of D.O. conditions. ④ No error.

21 The government will probably intervene ① <u>if it will see</u> unfair discrimination against competitors or censorship. If the Googles of the world win, the network owners will ② <u>undoubtedly</u> figure out ③ <u>some other way</u> to raise prices. And the government will ④ <u>surely</u> intervene.

22 If other nations were as far ① <u>inferior to us</u>, as we are willing to imagine, their condition would evidently tend to ② <u>decay and extermination</u>. ③ <u>Without regard to</u> the inferior orders of being, both animal and vegetable, it seems to be a law of nature ④ <u>to gradually decline</u>, and at last cease to exist.

23 Disaster can strike quickly and without warning, make a plan. During an emergency, the more ① <u>planned you have</u> ② <u>ahead of time</u>, the calmer you and your family will be. ③ <u>These six steps</u> will help you through the process : Talk, Plan, Learn, Check Supplies, Tell, Practice.

24 O'Neill is ① <u>the Homer of</u> 20th-century American dramatists. Tennessee Williams, Arthur Miller, and Edward Albee follow ② <u>in wake</u> and none took the exploration of tragedy in a familiar American setting further ③ <u>than he did</u>. And of all his plays, nothing is more extreme or more achieved than ④ <u>this one</u>.

25 I ① <u>strongly encourage</u> the School Committee, town safety officers, and state agencies to develop ② <u>a well thought out</u> policy that is good for the long term and is practically and economically sensible and fair. First and foremost, ③ <u>these mean</u> protecting the safety of our children, as well as drivers ④ <u>through and around town</u>.

26 Naturally, this family event had me thinking about my own plans for retirement, which, ① until a few years ago, were practically non-existent. In fact, I ② enjoy writing for a living and ③ run my own business so much that I don't ever plan to retire ④ as such. Instead, I see retirement as a gradual transition from full-time writing to working as and when it suits me.

27 They do ① not so much as know dice, or any such foolish and mischievous games. They have, however, two sorts of games ② not unlike our chess ; the one is between several numbers, in which one number, ③ as it was, consumes another ; the other ④ resembles a battle between the virtues and the vices.

28 However, you cannot do it ① better than other people if they have talent and you do not. Hard work will not make up for raw ability if the people with raw ability are ② applying themselves. If by chance they are all lazy, you may have ③ a chance to being the best. So, find your raw talent, then work hard and you'll be ④ better than the competitors.

29 ① With this goal in mind, should you now sell your A fund because the stock market is hitting new highs and put the money into the B fund? The stock market is seductive. It is good at setting investors up for a fall. It can make you ② giddy with the thought of your new wealth. It can also ③ make you depressed as you contemplate how much money you would have made ④ if only you invested differently at the right moment.

30 Since both science and technology are ① blessed words in our contemporary vocabulary, some may be happy at the notions, first, that, ② viewed historically, modern science is an extrapolation of natural theology and, second, ③ that modern technology is at least partly to be explained as an occidental realization of the Christian dogma of ④ man's transcendence, and rightful mastery over nature.

03 실전모의고사

Answer p.97

[01-06] Choose the one that could best complete each of the following sentences.

01 Not a single word __________ except as I wrote. But how is that, I hear someone say ; did you write without knowing what it was that you were writing?

① I read ② did read
③ I read ④ did I read

02 Several other Munch paintings have recently been stolen : six years ago, another well-known masterpiece, The Vampire, __________ from the Munch Museum in Oslo, but was later recovered, as was a lithograph, Madonna, which disappeared in 1990.

① was robbed ② was lost
③ was stolen ④ have been stolen

03 As a fellow veteran of Kerry's generation, I received his remarks as a Vietnam-era flashback. Back __________, it was common to say, "Study hard or you might go to Vietnam." That's because we had something then that young people don't have to contend with now : a military draft.

① in 1960's ② in the 1960
③ in the 1960s ④ in 1960s

04 One thing you have to remember is __________ the declination changes significantly, so you'll need to know __________ it is this year.

① that ··· which ② what ··· what
③ what ··· that ④ that ··· what

05 **I love a girl and she also loves me but she is __________ and had an ex-boyfriend with whom she says its not possible for us to continue.**

① senior to 4 years ② 4 years younger than me
③ older than I for 4 years ④ 4 years senior to me

06 **If you drink alcoholic beverages, ______________ (no more than one drink a day for women, and no more than two drinks a day for men).**

① in moderation do so ② in moderation so do
③ so will do in moderation ④ do so in moderation

[07–08] Choose the one that is grammatically NOT correct.

07 ① The picture hidden in the archives for 40 years was found.
② Some diseases can be prevented by proper vaccination.
③ She felt the call of God and decided to devote her life to help others.
④ You are supposed to refrain from smoking in this room.

08 ① We don't want to get too deeply involved with those people.
② What would become of your family if you would be killed in an accident?
③ On a fine morning, you can see a beautiful sunrise from here.
④ James wanted to make a good impression at a job interview.

[09-30] **Choose the one that makes the sentence grammatically INCORRECT.**

09 ① At the other side, I could ② vague see a fat figure that, ③ pipe in mouth, sat behind the shining ④ little panes and snowy curtain.

10 So he went ① a little distance toward cabin and listened once more. Evidently some people were making ② a great deal of noise in cabin. As soon as he ③ has realized this, he ④ returned to his house. He entered and blurted out to his grandmother, "Some people in cabin really seem to be very happy."

11 This is a book for educators. Those who have chosen ① to be educators are generally ② dedicating to students. But, sometimes we don't quite understand ③ what we are seeing. We hope this book will help educators ④ make sense of the many patterns and behaviors that we see.

12 Finally, as I did last week, ask ① the audience which one they would rather give up ② than keep it — their browser, or ③ all the rest of their desktop applications? (Unanimously, they'd all give up the latter without a blink.) All these trends show a ④ slow upgrade appetite.

13 ① All the strategies in the world won't have impact ② if employees understand how to integrate them into their daily activities. Communication with customers, a focus on relevant offers and the ability ③ to solve problems ④ are attributes every employee should possess in order to facilitate the creation of brand loyalty.

14 If you ① attend to Oxford University, you can ② go and see your college nurse (limited hours each week at most colleges), or visit the medical practice that ③ takes care of your college. Find out more ④ on the Oxford University Health and Welfare pages.

15 I felt that there are ① too many people on this earth. I like ② life and living, and I ③ prefer to rich living and good life. Or analogously, quality than quantity. However, this is not the case. Look at people on the streets, stupids and ④ have nots and uglies with their children.

16 Computers, fax machines, the Internet, cell phones, e-mail – from the viewpoint of business owners, these are the ① keys to success in today's world of hyper-competitive, 24-hour capitalism. But as the pace of work ② quicken, growing numbers of workers ③ are being pushed to the limits and are feeling ④ stressed out too much.

17 Chronic fatigue syndrome (CFS) is ① a condition that ② causes extreme tiredness. People with CFS are so tired that they are unable to carry on normal activities ③ for a period of at least six months. They also have other symptoms, ④ such pain as in the joints and muscles, headaches, and sore throat.

18 A high percentage of cloned monkey embryos that look healthy ① is really a "gallery of horrors" deep within, says a researcher at Advanced Cell Technology, the company that last month ② published the first paper on cloned human embryos. This could mean that there is ③ something unique about primate eggs that will make cloning monkeys or people ④ far more difficult than cloning other animals.

19 ① Because of its small size, this dictionary is not, and can't be, as ② comprehensively as large dictionaries. However, it ③ does surprisingly manage to define the vast majority of words that even medical students/professionals will encounter. Moreover, the definitions are clear and concise with good technical depth, but still ④ reasonably understandable for laymen.

20 Although ① track and field have considerably higher participation numbers, its ratio of championship qualifiers to total participants ② is higher than any other individual-team championship. While there were more than 18,000 male and female participants ③ in Division I track and field in 2013-14, only one out of 23 women and one out of 24 men ④ participated in the outdoor championships.

21 Employees with military service of more than 30 days but ① not more than 180 days must submit an application for reemployment no later than ② 14 days following completion of service (or within the next calendar day that application becomes possible when application within that period is impossible or unreasonable through ③ no fault of the employee). ④ No error.

22 As one of the few who boarded the aircraft at Gatwick 30 years ago ① bound for Naples, I was asked by the Advertiser's sports desk, ② four of them were not even born then - for my memories of the Town's cup-winning performance. It may be hard for these 20-something lads ③ to believe, but I was ④ even younger in 1970.

23 The feelings ① associated with loneliness feed on themselves — the more lonely you feel, ② the harder this is to take steps to break out of loneliness. However, feeling lonely is a phase and does not have to be a constant way of being. ③ As with changing any patterns of behaviour, it may take effort and commitment ④ to begin to move out of feeling lonely.

24 William Faulkner ① summed up his life as a writer in his Nobel Prize acceptance speech in 1949. It ② had been, he said, "a life's work in the agony and sweat of the human spirit, not for glory and least of ③ all profit, but to create out of the materials of the human spirit ④ something which did not exist before."

25 A path that not only led to a film ① being made of his wildly inventive script but also to receive generous investments from abroad ② were purely a coincidence. But they really ③ latched on to it in a way that is unique even in film making. It's such ④ an honor they would do that for me.

26 Incentives typically range in value from $4 to $50, per survey or focus group, ① depended upon the length of the questionnaire and the time ② it takes to complete it. Simply ③ filling out surveys for money, participants in online focus groups ④ generally receive more than $25.

27 Darren and Vicky Hewitt, from Hartlepool, ① were stranded for around 18 hours and were forced to endure 60ft waves ② crashing over their yacht. They hailed those who rescued them ③ as "true heroes." From Spain, Darren, 31, told the us : "If the yacht had gone over abruptly we ④ would have left in the sea, 50 miles off the shore."

28 Although he had ① little hands-on experience with the extensive special-effects work ② an X-Men movie requires, Ratner says the six months he spent preparing Spiderman taught him more than he realized. "In that process of preparing Spiderman, I worked with animatics and ③ visual effect supervisors and artists, so I had an idea ④ of how it works," he says.

29 From the opening moments, we understand the authority that ① rests in Don Corleone (Marlon Brando). That he is a powerful man ② is as explicit as the fact that he wields ③ that power mercifully, within the context of the murder and mayhem that naturally ④ go with his territory. The Don is the head of a renegade organization, and, yes, he's a criminal with politicians in his pocket. But he has integrity.

30 Beware, though : If your baby seems good as gold, this may be the calm before the storm! He ① may have absorbed drugs from your system or at the very least ② is probably tired from squeezing his way through the birth canal, even if you had natural childbirth. He's not quite himself ③ yet, but, as you will read in the pages that follow, his real temperament ④ will be emerged soon.

04 실전모의고사

Answer p.108

[01-06] Choose the one that could best complete each of the following sentences.

01 **__________ was Jim wise and diligent, he was deeply egalitarian and his commitment to equality showed in everything he did, including our work together.**

① Never ② At least
③ Not only ④ Neither

02 **You are moving way too fast. I think you need to slow down a little bit or you __________ just when the goal line is right in front of you.**

① will get exhausted
② exhausted
③ got exhausted
④ have been exhausted

03 **She is __________ when she creates a work of art, __________ sketching a drawing, writing a poem, or composing a musical theme on her guitar or piano.**

① the happiest – whether it will be
② happiest – should it be
③ happiest – whether it be
④ the happiest – whether it was

04 **Now, __________ a single mother at home and a director outside home makes her as busy as a bee, yet she seems to enjoy her new way of life very much.**

① acting ② act such as
③ acting as ④ be acting

05 **Far bigger cuts in greenhouse gas emissions could be needed to prevent dangerous climate change than __________.**

① previous thought
② thought previously
③ previous thoughts
④ none of the above

06 **One result was that Southern civilians probably had to ____________________ during the war than Northern civilians did.**

① make real more sacrifices
② make more real sacrifices
③ making real sacrifices more
④ making sacrifices much real

[07–08] Choose the one that is grammatically NOT correct.

07
① Some are like volcanoes in that they pose no risk to us.
② You might have heard fire safety is important.
③ The policeman saw the suspected man enter the building.
④ You ought not make a noise in the museum.

08
① Man is no more than a reed, the weakest in nature.
② Barbara was not so young as I expected.
③ He studied harder because his master praised him.
④ This dictionary is even more useful than that.

[09-30] Choose the one that makes the sentence grammatically INCORRECT.

09 I know the subject fairly well because I ① have been studying it for long time, so far, I ② have read about three textbooks that ③ are related to. ④ No error.

10 There are no clues ① as to who he is or what he does, but it is clear by the man's ② fixed stare ③ that he symbolizes : Self-respect ④ in the face of persecution.

11 ① Speaking on BBC Radio 4's Today programme, Dr James said : "We're trying to sort of mimic what normal physiology ② would like." "It's just connecting ③ all the three components together so that they can talk to each other and then work in a way that ④ delivers insulin in a physiological manner."

12 "Children ① will only work if they're motivated and they'll only ② motivate if they're interested. They are all intelligent creatures. The experience has to be interesting and entertaining. Why on earth ③ shouldn't education be a pleasure?" ④ No error.

13 Our vision is ① to create a green, sustainable urban village, built ② by and for ourselves using ③ mostly donated and/or recycled materials, solar and wind power, composting toilets, and ④ grow our own organic food in our gardens and on our farm. To read more about our vision, please see our website.

14 Injury is the worst thing that can happen to a pitcher. It ① has well documented that Jackson's numbers in Triple A are partly ② due to that. Recently it was revealed that he ③ has had a little arm trouble (very minor) throughout the year that prevented him from going out and throwing at 100% ④ every start.

15 Orta lives alone, ① having no knowledge of who she is, where she came from, or even ② who are her real parents. But one fateful night, the Empire and the Dragonmares ③ come tearing through the valley, destroying anything — and anyone — that gets in their way. They ④ make for Orta's tower, and break through the walls.

16 Do you ① have trouble finding enough time to study? Do you frequently find yourself rushing to places, missing deadlines, feeling you ② have insufficient time for relaxation and personal relationships, or having a general sense ③ of overwhelming? Do you realize that you probably have ④ as many as 70 hours of available time each week?

17 As well read as I am, I have only read a fraction of even ① English language literature, and ② much less other tongues, but my own inner pattern detection system is ③ as close to flawless in sniffing out clichés as ④ anything could be.

18 The tragedy of the commons is a term ① coining to describe the way that human populations overuse and undermaintain common resources, ② leading to their destruction. The evidence of the trend is everywhere, from our over-fished oceans, polluted air and ③ spendthrift use of fossil fuels to the ④ unloved public spaces and graffiti-covered buildings in many cities.

19 Both books cover topics like Participatory Design (in that instance, in quite similar ways too). But Crabtree ① essentially just sketches in the sorts of things ② you would have to do. While he ③ does discuss what each technique involves and gives some illustrations, it's doubtful ④ if a reader could then go away and try the techniques out.

20 If you can't ① make it through a 40-minute Fringe show without snacking, ② skip the show and just go for dinner—because when you try to eat a snack with a crinkly wrapper quietly, it ends up ③ being much louder and, therefore, much more ④ annoyed to the rest of us who snacked ahead.

21 None of the men ① dared speak. They could only stare as the bubble floated a few feet off the dirty floor. After a few seconds, Rip shook off his wonder and charged her, ② having had enough and being too ignorant ③ to recognize the true danger. Kevin, ④ the smarter of the three, shouted a warning too late.

22 ① Compared with placebo, kava extract is an effective symptomatic treatment for anxiety although, ② at present, the size of the effect seems small. The effect lacks robustness and is ③ based on a relatively small sample. The data available from the reviewed studies suggest that kava ④ be relatively safe for short-term treatment (1 to 24 weeks), although more information is required.

23 Now Friedman probably knows exactly how much unemployment ① this will cause. He probably knows how many people ② will lose their homes. He probably knows how many kids won't be able to ③ go to the college. He probably knows something of the social unrest that ④ could happen if the U.S. economy is hit with $100/barrel oil.

24 The publish/subscribe model of podcasting ① is a version of push technology, ② in that the information provider chooses ③ to offer which files in a feed and the subscriber chooses among available feed channels. While the user is not "pulling" individual files from the Web, there is a strong "pull" aspect in that the receiver is free to ④ subscribe to a vast array of channels.

25 Because the river deposits more silt closer to its banks, the riverbed ① itself has been built up ② so little that the river's surface is actually higher than the surrounding land at about 11 feet above sea level. Only the natural levee along its banks is higher than the river's surface, ③ and since the levee is only a foot or two higher than the river's surface, the river is naturally ④ prone to overflow.

26 Employees quite often ① kid themselves that a job change is a logical affair. Not true, especially at middle to senior levels. While the prospective employee has made a logical choice, his heart may "still not be there". He might look for something that ② appeals to his heart. When that happens, he ③ swept away. Comfort, emotional fit, the feel good factor are ④ all very important.

27 The more yellow a banana is, ① the sweet it will taste. Bananas are fully ripened when brown spots appear on the peel. These bananas have a ② softer texture and are very sweet. The next time you and your family are at the grocery store, ③ buy two bunches of bananas—a bunch of yellow bananas to eat immediately and a bunch of ④ green-tipped bananas that will be ready to eat in 2-3 days!

28 The warmer air over the land expands and becomes ① lighter. This creates a low pressure situation. The air over water is cooler and denser (heavier), ② than the land air and this creates a high pressure situation. The high pressure air over the water pushes into the low pressure area on the land. The air ③ moved in from the water toward the land pushes the lighter land air up and out of its way. This movement is ④ what causes a sea breeze.

29 I was surprised at how ① influentially George Washington has been on all the presidents after him. The language they use in inaugural addresses and State of the Union messages ② still has Washingtonian echoes. I was surprised at how shy ③ certain of our Founding Fathers were about public speaking, even though they were gifted writers : Jefferson ④ in particular, and Madison even more.

30 This much I can declare of the Persians ① with entire certain, from my own actual knowledge. There is another custom which is spoken ② of with reserve, and not openly, concerning their dead. ③ It is said that the body of a male Persian is never buried, until it has been torn either by a dog or a bird of prey. That the Magi have this custom ④ is beyond a doubt, for they practice it without any concealment.

05 실전모의고사

Answer p.119

[01-06] Choose the one that could best complete each of the following sentences.

01 **Unwilling to lose his filberts, and yet unable to withdraw his hand, ______________ and bitterly lamented his disappointment.**

① tears were in his eyes
② that tears were in his eyes
③ he burst into tears
④ it burst into tears

02 **He offers problem-solving guidance by way of narrative biography, ______________ his extensive experience in defining and tackling tough problems.**

① he described
② described
③ being described
④ describing

03 **He only worked the harder, concentrating upon his business those extra hours ______________ instead.**

① when another sort of home-life would have claimed
② that another sort of home-life would have been claimed
③ which another sort of home-life would have claimed
④ whose another sort of home-life would have been claimed

04 **Perhaps no other city in the world is so misunderstood as Las Vegas. Although "Sin City," as it is commonly called, __________ for about 50 years, it has left an indelible impression on the American consciousness.**

① was only around
② has only been around
③ had only been around
④ only has been around

05 **The summit was a key step towards realizing the plans, ______________ were merely investing with a view to a rapid £60m flotation.**

① eased fears that the hedge fund owners
② it eased fears which the hedge fund owners
③ easing fears that the hedge fund owners
④ easing fears what the hedge fund owners

06 **If you experience the same thing as I __________ now several times, I can guarantee you that __________ the battery completely will not help.**

① have had … charging　　② had … to charge
③ had had … charging　　④ have … to charge

[07-08] **Choose the one that is grammatically NOT correct.**

07 ① Our teacher taught us that water boils at 100℃.
② Statistics shows that the population of the city has increased.
③ Neither of them has succeeded in the test.
④ The school is stricter about grades than it used to be.

08 ① The DMZ extends about two hundred kilometers from east to west.
② Katherine always looks her best in a dress of that color.
③ The temperature's rising by about three degrees a week.
④ The carrots are my favorite vegetable.

[09-30] **Choose the one that makes the sentence grammatically INCORRECT.**

09 ① Paying for primary care ② by hour would be ③ better for both doctors and patients, and it ④ would return a measure of rationality to our health care system.

10 In order that people may be happy in their work, ① three these things ② are needed : They must be ③ fit for it. They must not do too much of it. And they must have a sense of success ④ in it. – John Ruskin

11 I am sure everybody is ① aware that the government's tough regulations to ban driving while you are ② on the phone, but ③ to my surprise, yesterday as I was coming back from post office, guess ④ what I saw?

12 "The total cost of manufacturing in China is not ① as cheap as it might appear to be", says Mr Howard. Shipping costs ② have been rising, containers are expensive and ③ staffs have to be maintained in ④ both countries to manage the operation. It is also difficult to react quickly if the market changes.

13 She tapped him ① on his shoulder and asked ② if he remembered her ③ from previous brief ④ encounters when she'd told him about the photo project.

14 He was also struck by ① a lack of awareness among clients about the extent ② at which in-house lawyers offer ③ advice on business matters, as well ④ as on legal issues.

15 For decades it was ① no more than a whispered rumour in the corridors of Soviet medicine but now ② a team of doctors claim to have proved ③ that Lenin, communism's greatest icon, ④ dying of syphilis.

16 A body ② pulled from Stockton Deep Water Channel late Thursday was believed to be ② those of an elderly longshoreman who appeared ③ to have been driving a truck that plunged into ④ the water.

17 ① All other holidays are in a more or less degree ② connected with conflicts and battles of man's prowess over man, of strife and ③ discord for greed and power, of glories ④ are achieved by one nation over another.

18 ① Considering that the ② existing international conventions, recommendations and resolutions ③ concerned cultural and natural property demonstrate the importance, for all the peoples of the world, of ④ safeguarding this unique and irreplaceable property.

19 The collection is ① made from 100% organic cotton ② grown in Paraguay and is the brainchild of two sisters ③ risen in South America. The natural color of the cotton that enhances the handmade quality of all their knits is a bit of a quiet respite from all the colors.

20 This minor point is important since it ① demonstrated to me that you miss small but significant facts and ② read into things that are not there, things that you want to see. Since you ③ have done this here and in other places in our discussion, I suspect that you have also done it in ④ determining to believe there is no God.

21 One attempt at a solution has already ① been hinted at in the process of defining the paradox. The notion that the linguistic term 'heap' is vague ② begs the question of whether or not further elaboration of our ③ existing language, or the inclusion of a meta-language, ④ removing the vagueness.

22 Just a quick tip for ① those of you who might unexpectedly encounter the danger fruit this weekend : if the peach tastes funny, ② stop eating it right away — even if the odd smell you think you smell ③ go away each time to attempt to confirm it. Not at all. ④ No error.

23 The arrest was made Wednesday evening when a detective located Derrick Larue White ① walking near the Cabell County Courthouse. The man was ordered ② to stop, but did not comply. A foot chase then ③ was ensued, and he was arrested. He ④ was charged with felony first-degree robbery and misdemeanor fleeing on foot.

24 Like his father, Bell was a ① noted speaker and involved in numerous scientific and philanthropic ② association. He was ③ founder of the American Association to promote the Teaching of Speech to the Deaf, and for a time he served as ④ president of the National Geographic Society. He was appointed a Regent of the Smithsonian Institution in 1898.

25 The transfer of heat and water vapor from the ocean to the air above it ① depends on a disequilibrium at the interface of the water and the air. Within about ② a millimeter of the water, air temperature ③ is close to the surface water, and the air is nearly ④ saturated with water vapor.

26 The twentieth century has produced books of power not only in science and in politics ① but also philosophy and literature. However, ② this being an age of specialization, we often find that the influential ideas contained in these books have first been propounded or ③ mentioned in theses and papers for experts before reaching the layman. The popular magazine articles and the ④ works of interpretation come last.

27 Education if it is ① to be adapted to our modern needs must fit young people ② to understanding the problems raised by the situation. The ③ imparting of knowledge in education has always had two objects : on the one hand, to give skill ; and on the other, to give a vaguer thing which we may call ④ wisdom.

28 How ① much of the observed difference in contraceptive use between the two countries can be explained by differences in the quality of the national programs? Although we can not directly answer this question ② with these data, we argue that extra-programmatic factors must also be significant because the improvements in the Kenyan program, dated around the mid-1980's, ③ could have had enough time to be exclusively responsible for the sharp use differences observed by 1988-1989, when ④ the data were gathered.

29 In a recent study on family and family values, Americans ① were asked of their definition of the family. ② Only 22 percent thought a family was "a group of people related by blood, marriage or adoption." The definition ③ preferred by 74 percent was much broader. A family, ④ the majority felt, was "a group of people who love and care for one another."

30 Despite all the controversy, GM crops ① are spreading rapidly : in 2004 the area sown with them increased by 20%. Even though it faces considerable pressure from European customers, Brazil has lifted ② its ban on GM soy, and is getting ready to ③ dispense its other restrictions ; European customers are now free to choose whether to eat GM foods, or pay more for the old-fashioned kind. In Britain, at least, it seems inevitable that ④ bio-engineered crops will become commonplace.

06 실전모의고사

Answer p.131

[01-06] Choose the one that could best complete each of the following sentences.

01 **A licensee who changes the place __________ shall notify the Council of such change of address within 7 days.**

① which he lives in ② in that he lives
③ where he lives at ④ that he lives

02 **I studied in a private university with the help of a 50% scholarship and now I am willing to continue my studies but I __________ enough money to do so.**

① did not have ② will not have
③ had not had ④ do not have

03 **Substantial numbers of drivers say that it is completely unacceptable to drive 15 mph over the speed limit on freeways, yet admit __________ that in the past month.**

① had done ② to have done
③ doing ④ having done

04 **The most daring thing about the room is the pricing, but a lot of people don't mind paying ______________ to taste something truly outstanding.**

① double the price usual ② the usual double price
③ usual double the price ④ double the usual price

05 **It is the same with design ; it's _________ to have a hint unobtrusively available __________ to ask your audience to memorize and track everything on the site.**

① prefer ··· rather
② more ··· than
③ just as ··· so
④ better ··· than

06 **Botanists are not sure where the fist plant was grown or even ________________.**

① what plant was
② what plant it was
③ it was what plant
④ what plant was it

[07-08] Choose the one that is grammatically NOT correct.

07 ① The soldier entered into the building occupied by the enemy.
② The children who attend that school receive a good education,
③ Several years ago, he was badly off, but he is now better off than he used to be.
④ By our next anniversary, we will have been married for 5 years.

08 ① You had better be on time, or we will leave without you.
② I overslept this morning because I didn't set my alarm clock.
③ I'm disappointed not to have been invited to the party last night.
④ I don't like the movies, most of them are imported from America.

[09-30] Choose the one that makes the sentence grammatically INCORRECT.

09 In closing let me say that I trust you may learn to love all the young folks in the story, ① as deep as I have, in introducing them ② to you. Like ③ many a book, it grows more and more interesting as the reader becomes well ④ acquainted with the characters.

10 This information ① described below is designed as ② a guide only. It does not take the place of ③ immediately emergency medical attention. If you have ④ any doubts, call your doctor or 911 for emergency medical services right away.

11 ① Although the combination of formal learning and informal learning already ② takes place at MIT, the relationship between them is sometimes undervalued in the way we think about education. The two ③ often treated as separate, perhaps because they ④ tend to take place in different physical spaces and times, and they often involve different groups of people.

12 Man must find peace, tranquility, happiness, unity, love, and ① every good quality within his own life, within his own innermost heart. Only a person who does ② that can understand the difficulties, the pain, and the misery of others. ③ A man of wise will know this, understand this, and rectify ④ his own mistakes. Then he can help others.

13 As a post-script, I do wish someone ① would have the kindness to stretch-print those ② speeded-up action scenes, which only look ludicrous to modern eyes. If these films can be "colourised," they can be ③ restored to a more naturalistic speed. ④ No Error.

14 ① Once you have the basics (i. e. – how to construct a simple sentence), try to use them ② as much as possible. Instead of just saying "two" and pointing at the bananas, ③ learn to say "I'd like to buy two bunches of bananas," and then practice ④ to say it.

15 It is said that "Necessity is the Mother of Invention." If we need something, there is always a creative person around ① to invent. Where would our world be today without ② all of the millions of inventions that people use everyday? Quite often they ③ are put to use without a thought about their history, creation, or the imagination of the person who first had ④ the initiative to invent.

16 I saw Scott in concert on a Yoga Cruise and was just ① stunned by his playing. He is ② an Einstein on the guitar. At first his concert was ③ very unusual that I was disoriented and later I realized that it was because I had become so disconnected with nature and the inner music of the earth ④ that resides all around us.

17 ① For the time of the Chou Dynasty (11th-3rd Century BCE), there was a man named Lao Lai-tzu, who was ② by nature extremely filial. He took care of both his parents and ③ provided for them with the choicest delicacies. After he himself ④ turned seventy, he never spoke about his age.

18 The orbit of ① the new dwarf planet is even more eccentric than ② Pluto. Pluto moves from 30 to 50 times the sun-earth distance over its 250 year orbit, ③ while the new planet ④ moves from 38 to 97 times the sun-earth distance over its 560 year orbit.

19 When someone uses ① a stolen card and gets away with it, the bank refuses the charges, and so it is the store that ② gets ripped off. The store then finds ways to make up that loss – adding a bit of extra profit to all of their merchandise that we all ③ end up to pay. The same applies ④ to shoplifting, etc. All retails stores have built-in charges into their prices to cover for these kinds of losses.

20 Why ① <u>was it that</u> the most talented women at the firm I worked for seemed to disappear shortly after the birth of their first or ② <u>second child</u>? And how was it that ③ <u>all the rising stars</u> at that firm were men, and ④ <u>those who</u> were dads, nearly all had stay-at-home wives?

21 Charlie Chaplin is extremely amorous and ① <u>he is difficult</u> to go without romantic relationships for very long. When he ② <u>is attracted to</u> someone, Charlie Chaplin pursues them very ardently and sometimes ③ <u>comes on</u> too strong. Doing creative work or artistic work can also satisfy ④ <u>the very strong desire</u> for love and beauty that Charlie feels.

22 The city of Montreal ① <u>lies</u> in the east of Canada, just 50 miles ② <u>north</u> of the border with the USA. It has a total population of 3.3 million and ③ <u>situated</u> on an island in the Saint Lawrence River and ④ <u>on</u> its adjacent shores.

23 Moreover, of the various efforts ① <u>made on</u> the improvement of university education, ② <u>those which</u> are unique and superior have been selected and broadly <u>publicized</u>. This way, universities are able to use the efforts of other universities as ③ <u>a reference to</u> promote the revitalization of ④ <u>higher education</u>.

24 Up the hill from this location ① <u>was</u> a village built by the North British Railway for the railway employees. Employees had to travel by train to go shopping and ② <u>attended</u> church as there ③ <u>were</u> no roads to the location. In the 'v' of the junction at the south end of the station was a signalbox ④ <u>lying</u> between the lines to Carlisle and Hexham.

25 Ziegler looks at the ① <u>increasing</u> corporate conflicts and legal restrictions ② <u>to be</u> imposed ③ <u>on free speech</u>, particularly when it comes ④ <u>to political speech</u>.

26 An ear is the organ used by a human or an animal ① <u>to detect</u> sound waves. The term may refer to the entire system responsible for collection and ② <u>early processing</u> of sound, or merely the ③ <u>external-visibly</u> part. Not all animals have ears in the same part of the body. Audition is the scientific name ④ <u>for the sense</u> of hearing.

27 Her husband, Frank Foster, who ① <u>died in</u> June 1996, left ② <u>little her</u> money, and he had no life insurance. But in April 1999, Mrs. Foster said, she ③ <u>received</u> more than $200,000 in the settlement of a lawsuit ④ <u>brought</u> when her mother died in "horrible conditions" in a Wylie nursing home.

28 She remembered her mother ① <u>mainlining with</u> a dirty needle injecting its discolored point into a dirtier thigh. She remembered her mother as ② <u>a drunken lady</u> who refused to cook a meal ③ <u>to her children</u> or wash either their clothes or ④ <u>them or herself</u>.

29 Of the 19 ① <u>alleging</u> hijackers identified by the FBI, at least six turned up ② <u>alive</u> after the attack. The FBI's identifications included names, photographs, and, in several cases, other personal details — ③ <u>all of which</u> matched the six persons who ④ <u>surfaced after</u> the attack to proclaim their innocence.

30 Next week, the incredible heat across the Southwest, especially Southern California, ① <u>ease</u> just a bit Monday and ② <u>into</u> Tuesday. A strengthening, onshore flow ③ <u>will begin</u> to cool the immediate coast. Thunderstorms will also retreat ④ <u>back toward</u> the east as more stable air pushes in from the west.

07 실전모의고사

Answer p.142

[01-06] Choose the one that could best complete each of the following sentences.

01 **He did not know who was saying these things to him nor did he know what it meant __________ back home.**

① him coming ② for him to come
③ for his coming ④ he would come

02 **Upon arriving in Tucson one could hardly miss how __________, sort of in perpetual drought.**

① a desert city may be dry ② may a desert city be dry
③ dry a desert city can be ④ a desert city dry may be

03 **However, if Shawn __________ to Alabama, he would owe the company an extra 50 percent to buy the contract out.**

① were to return ② was to return
③ is to return ④ were returned

04 **He doesn't believe in God, but __________ occasionally because he believes everyone should grapple with key moral questions in life.**

① go to church ② went to church
③ goes to church ④ goes to the church

05 **Such is life in an Internet age ; an age that __________ the way the reporters had approached the Watergate investigation had it occurred today.**

① would be greatly changed
② would greatly change
③ would have greatly changed
④ would have been greatly changed

06 **Any student may enter college provided that the _________ requirements have been met : The student must have a 2.00 cumulative ___________ average and must demonstrate the ability to complete total requirements within nine semesters.**

① following … grade-point
② following … grade-pointed
③ followed … grade-point
④ followed … grade-pointed

[07-08] **Choose the one that is grammatically NOT correct.**

07 ① Kevin delivered a speech and was asked many questions afterwards.
② The doctor who examined the patient was very gentle.
③ The news that the candidate was elected president was shocked.
④ When will the media and other powerful elements in our society stop insisting that thinness is the ideal?

08 ① The students learned that the French Revolution broke out in 1789.
② Cities themselves generate heat from a lot of sources, including motor vehicles.
③ Helen was most intelligent of all the students.
④ If there is a fire in your home, you must stay close to the floor and leave the building immediately.

[09-30] Choose the one that makes the sentence grammatically INCORRECT.

09 The fabricated document is ① all the more extraordinary because it suggests that local Christian, Muslim and Sikh leaders ② are in support of the casino. In fact, all three faiths ③ explicitly oppose to gambling. ④ No Error.

10 Chomsky's work in the field of linguistics thirty years ago revolutionized the science and in the process ① transformed the field of psychology as well. He argued persuasively that language is an innate ability, ② unique to the human species, ③ that behaviorist learning principles cannot account for. For his work in the field, Chomsky has been called ④ Einstein of linguistics.

11 "You shut the door, then," said the goblin, ① pointing to the door that ② had never been closed, "and I'll wash the pearl." So the little girl ran to close the door, and the goblin began to rub the pearl ; but it only seemed to grow darker. Now the door had been open so long that ③ it was hard to move, and it creaked on its hinges as the little girl ④ trying to close it.

12 I ① remember sitting next to this guy – in his mid-30s – and ② insisting to him that he looked like a Kennedy. He ③ dressed in a suit and I remarked ④ at how uncomfortable he must be.

13 It's clever and does require ① some form of concentration behind it as you need to really pick up clues and what not, especially the really cool English ② they speak throughout the movie. Such as : "Yesterday you were better off than you are today, ③ but this took today for you to realize it. But today ④ has arrived and it's too late."

14 The simplest explanation said that the Earth is round, not flat. Pythagoras noted that the shadow of the Earth ① falling on the Moon during a lunar eclipse was always curved and the amount of the curvature ② was always the same. The only object that always ③ cast a circular shadow regardless of ④ its orientation is a sphere.

15 A revolutionary cancer treatment available and which ① was hailed a "wonder drug" can damage the heart, scientists have warned. Glivec, which is used ② to treat leukaemia and a rare type of ③ the tumour, was the first of a new generation of so-called "magic bullet" cancer drugs. But now the researchers will have it ④ scrutinized for its side effects.

16 He requires that animals ① demonstrated human-like mental abilities in situations ② contrived, or ③ at least observed, by professional researchers. ④ No Error.

17 As Aristotle humorously puts it, "he is ① not the man to bolt and run away, ② swinging his arms." He harbors in his heart a certain noble scorn for the impertinence of aggressive wickedness and ③ in the pomp and pride of evil powers. He is not easily excited. He will meddle only with big things, and with ④ little things as they bear on big things.

18 ① Whoever should imagine that I have intended to write a panegyric would be strangely mistaken, and on reading this book he will perceive that such was not my design ; nor ② it has been my object to advocate any form of government in particular, for I am ③ of the opinion that absolute perfection ④is rarely to be found in any system of laws.

19 In high school, students may not have received comments on language problems, or they may have received only ① global remarks such as "you ② need keep working on your grammar." In order to help students ③ continue to acquire academic English and to correct patterns of error that may persist in their writing, they need ④ structured help.

20 Justified force, ① <u>if used</u>, should directly and intentionally target only the guilty, and the means ② <u>used should be</u> such as to avoid harm to others so far as possible. Michael Walzer has it right, I believe, in arguing that the moral principles governing the use of ③ <u>force implication</u> a special care to protect innocent parties from "collateral damage" due to force ④ <u>aimed at</u> the guilty.

21 Global Dimming is a phenomenon ① <u>that's been</u> on the increase over the past 100 years. Basically, particles of pollution ② <u>are thrown up</u> into the atmosphere and block the sun. But that's not all — they also collect water molecules ③ <u>around them</u> in clouds, causing clouds to mirror-back the sunlight out into space. ④ <u>No Error</u>.

22 OSU has received ① <u>$1.5 million</u> grant from the prestigious Howard Hughes Medical Institute ② <u>to bolster</u> science education at all grade levels throughout the state. This grant will provide many young Oregonians with ③ <u>experiences</u> that will propel them into careers as scientists, which ④ <u>is</u> good for Oregon and the nation.

23 Jack Hubbard ① <u>has been involved</u> in print and broadcast journalism for more than four decades. He has been ② <u>associate director</u> at the Stanford News Service since 1992, and oversees news issues for broadcasters, ③ <u>including</u> live television and radio feeds, ④ <u>coordinated</u> live events and news conferences, and daily coverage of the university.

24 The administration has been hiding ① <u>to the extent that</u> most Americans are not aware of just how dire it is and how ② <u>many progresses</u> has been made. They keep talking about how the Iraqi army ③ <u>is doing</u> much better and taking over responsibilities, but for the most part ④ <u>that's</u> not true.

25 So far scientists have not found a way ① <u>to determine</u> the exact age of the Earth directly from Earth rocks because Earth's oldest rocks have ② <u>recycled and destroyed</u> by the process of plate tectonics. If there ③ <u>are</u> any of Earth's primordial rocks left in their original state, they have ④ <u>not yet</u> been found.

26 After dealing with far ① <u>too much water</u>, southern Louisianans must now cope with far too little : In the century that records ② <u>have been</u> kept, the region has never been so dry. The drought started in April of last year, and since then only hurricanes Katrina and Rita ③ <u>overfilled</u> rain gauges. Despite devastating flooding, climatologists worry Louisiana ④ <u>is</u> on the verge of exceptional drought conditions.

27 We ① <u>stayed at</u> the Atlantis and everything there was very expensive. The water activities were fun though. The island was absolutely ② <u>breathtaking</u> and was the most relaxing place that I ③ <u>have ever been</u>. A little tip is that there ④ <u>is</u> a strip of shops right of the grounds of the Atlantis with an excellent pizza place, and it is cheap!

28 When Boulanger's daughter crashed his car, ① <u>an</u> initial police report determined that she was at fault. In his capacity as ② <u>police chief</u>, Boulanger ordered ③ <u>the second</u> investigation, which determined that his daughter was not at fault in ④ <u>the crash</u>.

29 Attacking Iran would ① <u>height</u> the risks to American and coalition forces inside Iraq. ② <u>What if</u> one hundred thousand Iranian volunteers ③ <u>came across</u> the border? They were going to come to Iraq before, but ④ <u>didn't</u>.

30 This was striking, the researchers added, especially ① <u>given</u> that past research has shown aggression, misfortune and other negative thoughts tend ③ <u>to weigh</u> prominently even in healthy people's dreams. Yet the sleep disorder patients were no more violent in real life than ③ <u>ordinary</u>, the researchers wrote, and some past reports have suggested they may be even ④ <u>little</u> so.

08 실전모의고사

Answer p.153

[01-06] Choose the one that could best complete each of the following sentences.

01 **Man cannot live alone, __________ he live confined within the four walls of his close-knit family.**

① or can ② nor
③ and ④ nor can

02 **No High Fructose Corn Syrup : If you prefer your coffee __________, our white chocolate powder and natural caramel are a great option.**

① to be sweetened ② sweetened
③ being sweetened ④ that is sweetened

03 **For the first thing which a scholar should bear in mind is that a book __________ for mere amusement.**

① ought to not be read ② not ought to be read
③ ought to be not read ④ ought not to be read

04 **There was a man who checked out of a hotel, and after he went out, he realized that he __________ his umbrella so he went back inside.**

① had been forgotten ② forgot
③ had forgotten ④ has forgotten

05 **As you walk toward the maintenance shop, you will ______________ and see light gray smoke coming from the window.**

① something burning smell ② smell burning something
③ burning smell something ④ smell something burning

06 **Most causes of infection (bacteria and viruses) are quite fragile and only able to survive in ____________________________.**

① a temperature range very narrowly
② a very narrow temperature range
③ a range very narrowly temperature
④ a very narrow range temperature

[07–08] Choose the one that is grammatically NOT correct.

07 ① When I opened the window, a bird flew into the room.
② Everyone was amazed at the change in his appearance.
③ We will reach for the top of the mountain in five minutes.
④ Light from the nearest star has been traveling for 4 years.

08

08 ① Tom wondered where Jane was. He had not seen her from their quarrel.
② I had intended to leave the party before midnight.
③ Whether he graduated from a college or not doesn't matter.
④ If we are willing to open our minds and listen and learn, we may be able to overcome our ignorance.

[09–30] Choose the one that makes the sentence grammatically INCORRECT.

09 My weekly workout ① consists in jogging ② two to four kilometers two to three times a week. During summer, I run on the beach and swim. In the winter months, my jog ③ takes me around Sydney's Centennial Park. I also change my routine and run on the weekends during summer. ④ No Error.

10 ① The reason why difference in profession ② makes one feel worlds apart and two of a trade can ③ never agree ④ due to a lack of mutual understanding.

11 We walked out and ① checked everything out, but I'm not going to write about ② all that right now ③ because of I want to do a photo diary ④ in a day or two.

12 Neither of the books ① is laden with heavy technical or academic jargon, and the essays flow together ② quite smoothly. Going Green may appeal to ③ wider audience, with lots of photographs, uncrowded pages, and large print captions in the wide margins — ④ somewhat of a coffee table book for activists.

13 If it ① is to the user that I address my anger, as he as well as I ② am motivated by anger. It is ③ all the fault of anger — I should ④ be angry at that.

14 As a conclusion, I ① would say that this camp have brought me to further steps ② to understanding more about people and culture in Korea. The Korean are very ③ warm hospitable people. I enjoyed very much and ④ wish to have more opportunities to visit Korea again in the near future.

15 It ① is aimed to create no useless or expensive tastes. Plain living and high thinking ② is the right formula for educational work. In all the work and living at Hampton, the idea is to surround the students with influences that shall stimulate self-respect, and that shall develop the higher and better nature by a practical ④ recognition for it.

16 The only major conflict that ① existed was the rivalry of the Hellenes and Iranians over economic and strategic advantage. There was no feeling of intense cultural rivalry ② at all, and no ③ resort in religious propaganda. Each had ④ its own unique cultural tradition.

17 "My children, this is ① the last lesson I shall give you. The order has come from Berlin to ② teach only Germans in the schools of Alsace and Lorraine. The new master ③ comes tomorrow. This is your last French lesson. I want you to ④ be very attentive."

18 If ① you've read the bargain notebook Labs over the previous ② few pages and decided to buy one, you'll no doubt be thinking of extras ③ to add to the order. But before you simply put the suggested accessories in your basket on the supplier's website, ④ take while to browse our own recommendations.

19 Tea becomes a meditation for the senses. ① Listen for the gentle sounds of the ② water boiling in the kettle and observe the graceful dance of rising steam. Admire the beauty of the ③ teawares and the wonder of the leaves as they slowly unfurl to release their green, golden, or amber liquor. Delight in the ④ comforting warmth and texture of the cup in your hands, as you inhale the fragrant aroma and savor the delicate flavors.

20 There's four different ① kind of fundamental forces, ② but as we will see later some of them have been unified and it's thought that they are ③ all the same force only in different "modes", but for the sake ④ of simplicity we will first talk about them as different forces.

21 A significant number ① go into computer science ; but other philosophy students pursue careers in a great range of fields, ② business and medicine to writing, arts administration, publishing, and so on. Experience shows that students who choose to study philosophy do not, in any way, jeopardize ③ their chances for success after college, however success ④ might be defined.

22 A new study helps to explain why smokers tend to have ① <u>boozier</u> nights out than non-smokers. The work, done in rats, shows that a heavy dose of nicotine can cut blood-alcohol levels ② <u>in half</u>. If cigarettes similarly ③ <u>lowers</u> intoxication in people, it could mean that smokers need to drink more than non-smokers ④ <u>to get the same</u> buzz.

23 It seems plausible, then, given the knowledge at hand and a chain of inference ① <u>which</u> in retrospect at least appears ② <u>straightforward</u> Archimedes could have suspected the universality of gravitation. But could he have demonstrated it? I think he ③ <u>could</u>, with the help of some ④tools and reasoning.

24 Students are encouraged to refer ① <u>back to</u> these guidelines while they are running their experiments to understand how to deal with any difficulties they might encounter and ② <u>how to</u> interpret their results. We have also included some hints on ③ <u>how to</u> present these results in a competition once the projects ④ <u>complete</u>.

25 We might hypothetically possess ourselves of every technological ① <u>resource</u> on the North American continent, but ② <u>as long as</u> our language is inadequate, our vision remains formless, our thinking and feeling ③ <u>are</u> still running in the old cycles, our process may be revolutionary but not ④ <u>transformation</u>.

26 We ought to show gratitude to others and ① <u>held</u> accountable for our conduct. We should seek justice, equity. We should manifest tolerance, ② <u>be</u> cooperative, seek to negotiate any differences ③ <u>peacefully</u>, and work out compromises whenever ④ <u>possible</u>.

27 If ① for any reason you must limit your visit to a very short time, call your host in advance to explain. That might sound like, "② I'd loved to be there for the entire party, but I ③ promised to pick my brother up at the airport. Would you mind if I stop ④ by for a few minutes?" Generally, a stay should be at least 30 minutes.

28 Does this suggest that we ① do no longer prepare clinical specialists or ② advanced practice nurses in master's programs? No. It ③ does suggest that there be increased opportunities for nurses to pursue ④ preparation as educators.

29 We agree that we ① should find diplomatic solutions to the problem as far as Iran is concerned. I strongly encourage the Iranian government ② respond positively and constructively to the proposal ③ presented by the international community. We also discussed the situation in Iraq. We would ④ very much like to see a strong role for the UN in Iraq.

30 It's been 11 months ① that Hurricane Katrina devastated the Gulf States. Students at Nazareth College ② didn't need to go very far to help families ③ devastated by Hurricane Katrina. For months, they ④ have been building a home for one lucky family in Mississippi, right here on campus.

09 실전모의고사

Answer p.164

[01-06] Choose the one that could best complete each of the following sentences.

01 __________ a week off, I'd go back to the Two Bunch Palms Resort and Spa in the desert.

① If I have ② If I have had
③ What I would have ④ If I had

02 Ever __________ nationalized in 1969, banks have been playing a major role in the socio-economic life of the country.

① because they were ② since they were
③ after they were ④ when they were

03 Jeremy Clarkson's popularity is hardly surprising, __________ that he transformed Top Gear from a traditional information programme to one filled with supercars, stunts and humour.

① being considered ② considered
③ considering ④ our considering

04 Who is the cause of this fear and this feeling of insecurity? It is certain __________ everyone would announce, "Not I, but he is the cause." A very interesting position indeed! And this is the culture __________ we have attained in the sunlit midday of this century.

① what … to which ② that … to which
③ what … of which ④ which … which

05 **Generally speaking, video download sites __________ themselves with respect to image quality — although things are clearly improving in that area.**

① had to prove ② have yet to prove
③ have been proved ④ have to prove

06 **Not only __________ too small to be seen with a light microscope, they also cannot be detected through _______ biological activity, except ________ it occurs in conjunction with other organisms.**

① are viruses — their — as ② are viruses — its — that
③ is virus — their — that ④ virus is — its — as

[07-08] Choose the one that is grammatically NOT correct.

07 ① I closed the door quietly because she was still sleeping.
② The form has to be signed in the presence of a witness.
③ People were waiting at the airport, hoping to see the politician arriving.
④ It will not be long till mother comes back from America

08 ① We postponed our trip because the weather was bad.
② More often words add to help make the meaning of a sentence clear.
③ He is a man of few words, but when he does speak, he is very eloquent.
④ We have been playing soccer since early this morning.

[09-30] Choose the one that makes the sentence grammatically INCORRECT.

09 John Keats's mother, brother, and good friend Richard Woodhouse all ① died of tuberculosis, ② which was then termed "consumption." He long suspected that he had ③ the disease himself, and when on February 3, 1820, he had a severe hemorrhage of the lungs, he knew that he ④ could not survive from another English winter.

10 If you ① currently have a pair of glasses that ② is a comfortable fit, then read the numbers from the arm and choose a frame from our selection with the dimensions that closely ③ match to the ones that you have. You can then be confident ④ that the glasses that you order will fit nicely!

11 One person who boarded the train in New York ① refused to accept his seat assignment, as he was not facing in the direction that the train ② was going in. I offered to ③ exchange a seat with him, but he wouldn't have ④ any of that. He was eventually put in a forward-facing seat by himself in the last row of seats at the end of the car.

12 'Romeo and Juliet' is thought to ① have been written in 1595 or 1596. The story was adapted by Shakespeare but it is his version that ② was known by old and young the world over. It is a tragic story of ③ forbidden love. The whole episode of Romeo and Juliet's meeting, falling in love, marriage, and tragic end, ④ takes place within five days.

13 We asked Barbara for her suggestions a year ① before putting our house on the market. This gave us adequate time to have the house painted and the landscaping ② perfected. We followed her suggestions in every detail. We accepted ③ a good, strong offer six days after the house was on the market. Barbara and her assistant David are extremely efficient and ④ calmly under pressure. Barbara knows the market and knows how to sell.

14 The eagle ① represents freedom. Living ② as it is on the tops of lofty mountains, amid the solitary grandeur of Nature, it has unlimited freedom, whether with strong pinions ③ it sweeps into the valleys below, or ④ upward into the boundless spaces beyond.

15 ① Briefly spoken, this formation has a dual dimension : of course we have to learn, and to acquire knowledge, ability, ② know-how, as they say. In this sense Europe, and in the last decades America, ③ have done a lot, and that's important for the advancement of strategy in this game. ④ No Error.

16 ① Talking of music, I recently ② read that you tend to ③ listen to your favorite record of the moment over and over again ④ on weeks or even months.

17 ① Until about 60 years ago, most New Zealand stamps still had a picture of ② the King's or Queen's head. Except for the colour and price of the stamp, they all looked the same. Today, New Zealand stamps are all very different – ③ showing animals, cars, ships, flowers, birds, pretty scenes, famous people, and more. ④ No Error.

18 I myself am an Indian, but I ① have never lived in India. I do have the utmost respect for my fellow Indians, but I am an American first and foremost. This is my home, I ② was raised here all my life. There is ③ not more annoying than getting on a call and talking with someone who cannot communicate clearly. I have family members with the accent, but ④ nothing compared to this. I can't even understand them!

19 ① Any child can do a puzzle, ② given the right support. Puzzles build spatial awareness and logical thinking, and reinforce concepts ③ such as letters, numbers, shapes and themes. ④ No Error.

20 But back ① <u>in early 1930</u>, Walt had another matter to ② <u>attend to</u> : the creation of the comic strip after Iwerks' departure. At first Walt was content to ③ <u>continue scripting</u> it and assigning the art to Win Smith. However, Walt's focus ④ <u>has always been</u> in animation and Smith was soon assigned with the scripting as well.

21 I ① <u>think generally</u> that it's good for the country when at least one house ② <u>majority is</u> opposite the president because it provides a check on ③ <u>the more extreme</u> decisions. Your example of the Supreme Court is ④ <u>a good one</u>. It's one thing to appoint a moderate justice, even one who leans conservative. It's a completely different thing to appoint an ultra-conservative justice.

22 Unlike most domestic-abuse incidents, this one ① <u>wasn't taken</u> place in the home. It's sad to say, but if a guy ② <u>beats</u> his wife within the confines of his home, it ③ <u>is up to</u> the wife to press charges – and that ④ <u>rarely</u> occurs.

23 Why don't we fix our textbooks? In case you haven't noticed, this is the year we are finally going to start ① <u>improving</u> American high schools, where progress in ② <u>rising</u> achievement has been as slow as a teenager's response to a request that he ③ <u>clean</u> his room. The government has put ④ <u>fixing</u> high schools at the top of their to-do lists, but it never happened so far.

24 Let's key both the minimum wage and Congressional and other Federal ① <u>salaries</u> to per-capital gross domestic product. ② <u>Otherwise</u> the sheer competence of the federal government will continue ③ <u>to be diminished</u> over time as the talent ④ <u>drains out to</u> the private sector.

25 What problems are caused by thumb-sucking? ① <u>Prolonging</u> thumb-sucking can lead to dental, speech, and self-image problems. In rare cases, thumb-sucking after age 5 is ② <u>a response</u> to an emotional problem or ③ <u>other disorder</u>, such as anxiety. Children with this type of problem need ④ <u>to be evaluated</u> by a health professional.

26 As many as 80 Tibetans have been reported ① <u>wounded</u> in a clash with the Chinese authorities over China's anti-Dalai Lama campaign. Witnesses reported ② <u>seeing</u> two trucks of ③ <u>badly</u> beaten Tibetans, ④ <u>main</u> monks and nuns, arriving at a hospital in Lhasa, the Tibetan capital.

27 While it is impossible to ① <u>objectively</u> determine the greatest film of all time, it is possible to discuss the films that have been regarded ② <u>the greatest ever</u>. The important criterion for ③ <u>inclusion</u> in this article is that the film is the "greatest" by some specific ④ <u>criterion</u> or indicator

28 ① <u>The third</u> of the lessons in England's secondary schools ② <u>are being taught</u> by people who do not have degrees in the subject they ③ <u>are teaching</u>, an official survey indicates. And ④ <u>almost</u> a fifth of lessons are taught by people with no qualification in the subject.

29 We may, in future, use an outside advertising company ① <u>to display</u> ads on our site. These ads may contain cookies. While we use cookies in ② <u>other parts of</u> our Web site, cookies received with banner ads ③ <u>will be collected</u> by our ad company, and we do not ④ <u>have access in</u> this information.

30 What crops ① <u>are seen</u> from Kansas highways 50 years from now may still be in doubt. Global warming is shifting some species permanently ② <u>north</u> and changing migration patterns for ③ <u>others</u>, altering Kansas' ④ <u>wildlife</u>.

10 실전모의고사

Answer p.175

[01-06] Choose the one that could best complete each of the following sentences.

01 **In Gurgaon, for instance, transformers routinely blow out because of heavy loads. Voltage fluctuations damage electrical appliances of all sorts. __________, many take for themselves.**

① That the state cannot provide efficiently
② The state cannot provide efficiently and
③ What the state cannot provide efficiently
④ The state cannot provide them efficiently and

02 **After rocking or feeding baby to sleep in your arms, lie down with your sleeping baby next to you and nestle close to her ________ she is sound asleep.**

① unless ② as long as
③ until ④ otherwise

03 **It depicts several New York police officers ________ on the front steps of the main Pace building and a ________ student being aided by two other people.**

① stood … wounded ② standing … wounded
③ stood … wounding ④ standing … wounding

04 **Probably one of the best overall forms of exercise is swimming, ________ it does not stress the joints as much as running does.**

① while ② likewise
③ because ④ unless

05 **I __________ see relationships among variables such as ethnicity, poverty, special education, time of day, and the location of the offense.**

① am anxious about ② was anxious to
③ am anxious to ④ am anxiety to

06 **Some of the questions that scholars ask seem to the world to be scarcely worth asking, let alone answering. They ask questions __________ for you and me to understand without years of explanation.**

① too minute and specialized
② so minute and specializing
③ so minute and specialized
④ too minute and specializing

[07-08] Choose the one that is grammatically NOT correct.

07 ① They believe Pat to win.
② John regrets Bacon to be real author.
③ They want Pat to win.
④ I hope for your having a happy summer.

08 ① It is not necessary to bring a lunch for hiking tomorrow.
② It is necessary that the patient exercise more regularly.
③ She is necessary to come to school earlier than others.
④ Money is absolutely necessary to carry out this plan.
⑤ Is it necessary for me to go?

[09-30] **Choose the one that makes the sentence grammatically INCORRECT.**

09 It is natural ① for children to first show some sort of denial that the situation really ② happened. Fears, worries or nightmares are ③ commonly following a trauma. Sleep disturbances or eating difficulties may happen. ④ No Error.

10 ① Nothing worthwhile is achieved through absent effort, which is why I ② emphasize on mental preparation for the task at hand. I provide ③ merely the roadmap ; it's your obligation to initiate, continue, and ④ complete the journey. Destiny is yours ; seize the moment, and GOD BLESS!

11 She thought of her life ① being shaken by a man — ② comparable to a small rain drop — who she ③ had never spoken. She laughed at herself thinking how silly she was to still hope that she will meet him. She decided she would put him out of her mind and life. She decided she ④ wouldn't let him affect her life so much.

12 "In Europe," said Thomas Jefferson, "the object is to make the most of their land, labor ① being abundant ; here it is to ② make the most of our labor, land being abundant." These contrasting models of economic growth ③ resulted in various cultural and industrial differences at this time. It was in America, therefore, that the great advances in nineteenth-century agricultural machinery ④ first came.

13 ① Besides giving a general information on ② what is forensic science and why one should study forensic science, this website also talks about the further course of study ③ for those of you still at school or college and ④ is interested in taking up forensics as a career. And, for this purpose the site provides a list of universities that offer courses in forensic science and specialization in various branches.

14 Italian ① has always had a distinctive dialect for each city, since the cities were up until recently ② city-states. A well-known Italian dictum has it that the best spoken Italian is lingua toscana in bocca romana. The Romans are known ③ by speaking clearly and distinctly, while the Tuscan dialect is the closest existing dialect to Dante's ④ now-standard Italian.

15 Don't let the dogs and cats ① impacted by Hurricane Katrina ② forgotten. You can read more about the rescue efforts, ③ donate money and learn how you ④ can help out at The Humane Society of the United States website.

16 I wish I ① had a toy guide like this to browse through when my daughter was younger. The trouble with a lot of toys is that some are fads and ② some are genuinely great for little people development. We've tried to steer ③ clear of the fad toys and recommend ones that we really think are fun to play ④ with and educational too.

17 All you need ① to make is a so-called argument by analogy, he says. If X has these 10 characteristics and Y has nine of them, chances ② are Y also has the tenth. From a philosophical perspective, you end up ③ to treat farmed fish as if you knew for certain they experienced pain, despite the lack of ④ scientific proof.

18 I know that he and the whole House will want Ministers to give ① top priority to dealing with the practical day-to-day issues, which may help us ② in bringing the epidemic to an end. I regret that he ③ repeated what has occasionally been heard from Opposition Members about the bad ④ handling of the outbreak.

19 Young people, particularly the 49 percent of ① 18-to-29-year-olds who live in rural and inner city communities and have no college experience, ② and don't suffer from lack of interest in politics. It's because there is lack of access. We try not to push positions. But we build an infrastructure that allows people, who ④ would not otherwise have the opportunity, ④ to engage in genuine, active dialogue with civic leaders.

10

20 We have ① much in common. We share a history ② as nations of the New World. We ③ were founded by empires but grew up as free democracies. We are united by geography. And we ④ share common vision for our hemisphere in the 21st century.

21 Mideast diplomats will be pressing Syria ① to stop backing Hezbollah. As the guerrillas fired more deadly rockets onto Israel's ② third-largest city Sunday, things have worsened. Israel faced ③ tougher-than-expected ground battles and ④ bombard targets in southern Lebanon.

22 Breathing ozone can trigger ① variety of health problems including chest pain, coughing, throat irritation, and congestion. It can ② worsen bronchitis, emphysema, and asthma. "Bad" ozone also can reduce lung function and ③ inflame the linings of the lungs. Repeated exposure may permanently ④ scar lung tissue.

23 She suffered from severe emotional disturbance, the most remarkable symptom ① which was compulsive stealing from the home, the staff, other children and from families ② that would take her ③ in for brief home stays. However, she was able to overcome these difficulties and is now pursuing her goal of working with the disabled and ④ is engaged to get married.

24 He was noted ① as being crossed and disagreeable because he was not happy, and he was not happy because he wanted to ② go down the mountain and visit the big world below and his father ③ wouldn't let him. No one paid any attention to Kiki Aru, because he didn't ④ amount to anything, anyway.

25 The utilization of ① state-of-the-art Internet technology ② is allowing thousands more Americans to engage in public policy debates on ③ the most pressing issues of today. ④ With an advent of the virtual dialogue, citizens are infinitely closer to the policy issues that affect their lives.

26 ① <u>Many as</u> 1,200 people die a day in violence in the Democratic Republic of Congo and more than ② <u>half of them</u> are children. The United Nation's children's fund UNICEF reports ③ <u>will have publicized</u> that more children under the age of five die in the war-battered African nation each year than ④ <u>do</u> in China, which has a population 23 times larger, it said in a report.

27 If the reviewer feels ① <u>unqualified</u> to review a part of a patch, they can ② <u>delegate</u> part of the review to another party who ③ <u>needs</u> not be a blessed reviewer. If the reviewer feels unqualified to review any of the patch, and feels there is a better ④ <u>blessed</u> reviewer, they should attempt to notify a better reviewer.

28 American investigators ① <u>were given</u> the first name and telephone number of one of the Sept. 11 ② <u>hijackers</u> two and a half years before the attacks ③ <u>on</u> New York and Washington, but the United States appears ④ <u>to fail</u> to pursue the lead aggressively, American and German officials say.

29 Landfills take up valuable space and emit methane, a potent greenhouse gas ; and ① <u>although</u> incinerators are not as ② <u>polluted</u> as they once were, they still produce noxious ④ <u>emissions</u>, so people dislike ④ <u>having them around</u>.

30 Harmful bacteria can survive ① <u>for</u> as long as 24 hours on computer keyboards, a study released yesterday showed, ② <u>highlighting</u> what could be a growing threat as hospitals increase investment in technology. The study carried out at Northwestern Memorial Hospital in Chicago found that keyboards can contaminate the fingers, ③ <u>bare</u> or gloved, of a nurse or ④ <u>doctor</u>, who could then transfer bacteria to patients.

MEMO

박문각의 합격 노하우와
편입에 특화된 커리큘럼

편입의 마스터
박문각 편입 영어

실전 문법

Grammar
정답 및 해설

합격기준 박문각 편입

홍준기 편저

PMG 박문각

01 실전모의고사 정답 및 해설

01	②	02	③	03	④	04	④	05	④	06	①	07	③	08	④	09	④	10	③
11	②	12	②	13	④	14	③	15	③	16	④	17	②	18	③	19	①	20	②
21	③	22	①	23	③	24	④	25	②	26	④	27	②	28	③	29	③	30	②

[01-06] Choose the one that could best complete each of the following sentences.

---

01 **The test can identify Alzheimer's disease long before the patient starts ________ the symptoms – before he/she even knows he/she has got Alzheimer's.**

① before long the patient started having
② long before the patient starts having
③ before long the patient starts to have
④ long before the patent started to have

정답 ② long before the patient starts having

해설 before long은 '곧, 머지않아'라는 의미로 빈칸에는 문맥적으로 어색하다. long before는 '~하기 오래전에'라는 의미로 적합하다. 부사절의 동사는 현재형으로 써야 자연스럽고, start 다음에는 부정사와 동명사 모두를 목적어로 취하기 때문에 정답은 ②이다.

해석 그 검사는 알츠하이머병을 환자가 증상을 보이기 전에 즉, 환자가 자신이 병을 가진 줄 알기도 전부터 알아낼 수 있다.

---

02 **Two pedestrians walking toward each other on a narrow sidewalk will seldom, ________, make eye contact to more effectively negotiate the tight passage.**

① if so
② if any
③ if ever
④ if possible

정답 ③ if ever

해설 if any는 '설령 있다손 치더라도'의 의미로 뒤에 문맥적으로 명사가 생략된 구조에 쓰인다. 주어진 문장에서는 make eye contact와 연결되기 때문에 if ever를 써야 한다. if ever 다음에는 문맥적으로 동사가 생략되었을 때 사용한다.

해석 서로 마주치게 되는 두 명의 행인들은, 만일 그러한 일이 설령 일어난다 하더라도, 서로 자신이 편안하게 길을 통과하려는 협상을 하기 위해 거의 눈을 마주치지 않는다.

03 **He added that even if one is rich but is not healthy, then he __________ enjoy the money that he has.**

① will cannot
② will be able to
③ would be able to
④ will not be able to

정답 ④ will not be able to
해설 조동사의 기본형식에 관한 문제다. will 다음에 can의 의미를 추가하고자 할 경우에는 준조동사의 형식인 be able to를 써야 하므로 will be able to가 들어가 한다. 정답은 ④이다.
해석 그는 추가하길, 누군가가 부자라도 건강하지 않다면 그는 자신의 돈으로 즐기지 못할 것이라고 했다.

04 **You are in control, the option is yours, you can either play live games or download them, and choose whichever you like from one of the many you can find on the website – __________ I have listed above.**

① neither of which
② none of which
③ wherever
④ some of which

정답 ④ some of which
해설 문맥적으로 '여러 옵션 가운데 아무것이나 선택할 수 있다'라는 긍정적인 내용이 들어가야 하므로 ①, ②은 정답이 될 수 없다. 주어진 빈칸에는 I have listed의 목적어에 해당하는 명사가 들어가야 하므로 ③ 또한 정답이 될 수 없다. 따라서 정답은 ④이다.
해석 당신이 통제할 수 있다, 옵션은 당신이 정하며 당신은 라이브 게임을 하거나 다운로드를 할 수 있다. 당신은 일부 우리 웹사이트에 목록이 정리되어 있는 여러 옵션 가운데 아무것이나 선택할 수 있다.

05 **This organization does not claim to know the answer to solving the flooding problems for only Mother Nature has the capability __________.**

① doing that
② to doing
③ in doing that
④ to do that

정답 ④ to do that
해설 명사 capability 다음에는 'of ~ing' 또는 'to 부정사'로 수식을 받기 때문에 정답은 ④이 되어야 한다.
해석 이 단체는 홍수 문제에 대한 해답을 알 것을 요구하지 않는다. 왜냐하면 오직 자연만이 해결할 능력을 가지는 것이니까.

06 **But since he more often meets with the bad than the good, he seems to himself and to others to be ________ than foolish.**

① rather wise
② not so much wise
③ not wise so much
④ wiser rather

정답 ① rather wise

해설 먼저 'not so much A as B'라는 형식으로 써야 하는데 빈칸 뒤에는 than이 나와야 하기 때문에 ②, ③은 정답이 될 수 없다. 동일인 사람이나 사물에서 비교를 나타낼 경우에는 형용사의 음절의 수와 관계없이 무조건 more를 써서 'more wise than foolish'를 쓸 수 있다. 그렇지 않을 경우에는 ①처럼 'rather wise than foolish'를 쓸 수 있다.

해석 그러나 그가 좋은 것보다는 나쁜 것을 더 많이 만나는 관계로 그는 그에게나 다른 사람들에게나 바보보다는 현명한 것처럼 비춰졌다.

[07-08] Choose the one that is grammatically NOT correct.

07 ① The newest branch of the library is located in San Francisco.
② There being no bus service, we had to walk to school.
③ The salt I consumed never be paid attention.
④ These children have more money than they need.

정답 ③ The sugar I consumed was never paid attention to.

해설 pay attention to 다음에 목적어를 취하기 때문에 수동태가 될 경우에는 'be paid attention to'라는 형식을 써야 한다. 그리고 never는 조동사가 아니라 부사이기 때문에 never be라는 형식에도 오류가 있다.

해석 ① 그 도서관 분점은 샌프란시스코에 위치하고 있다.
② 버스 편이 없었기 때문에 우리는 학교에 걸어가야만 했다.
③ 나는 내가 섭취하는 염분에 대해 주의를 기울이지 않았다.
④ 이 어린이들은 그들이 필요로 하는 것보다 더 많은 돈을 가지고 있다.

08 ① This typewriter will spare you a lot of trouble.
② She shall have finished this work before my teacher comes back.
③ It was expected by everyone that Katy would marry James.
④ The form has to sign in the presence of a witness.

정답 ④ has to sign ⇨ has to be signed

해설 주어인 The form은 사물이기 때문에 '서명되다'라는 수동태의 형식이 와야 한다. 따라서 능동형의 has to sign을 has to be signed로 고쳐야 한다.

해석 ① 이 타자기 덕으로 당신은 수고를 많이 덜게 될 것이다.
② 그녀는 선생님이 돌아오시기 전에 이 일을 끝마쳐 버리게 될 것이다.
③ 모든 사람은 Katy가 James와 결혼할 거라고 기대했다.
④ 그 서류는 증인이 있는 가운데 서명되어야 한다.

[09-30] Choose the one that makes the sentence grammatically INCORRECT.

---

09 We must by all means avoid ① <u>overthrowing</u> all of them, lest we should help the enemy ② <u>become</u> more united and ③ <u>land</u> ourselves in an ④ <u>isolating</u> position.

정답 ④ isolating ⇨ isolated

해설 ④에서는 '고립된, 격리된'이라는 의미로 수식해야 하므로 isolating을 isolated로 고친다. 다음과 같은 예를 보면 쉽게 알 수 있다. 'an isolated house(외딴집), an isolated patient(격리 환자)'

해석 우리는 어떤 경우에도 그들을 완전히 전복시키지 말아야 한다. 만일 그렇게 된다면 우리는 적을 도와 그들이 보다 단결하게 되고 우리는 고립된 상황에 봉착하게 된다.

---

10 The changes ① <u>are alarming</u> scientists and environmentalists, because they ② <u>far exceed</u> the rate ③ <u>that</u> computer models of climate change ④ <u>predict</u> the Arctic ice will melt as a result of global warming.

정답 ③ that ⇨ at which

해설 'the rate that ~'에서 that의 기능이 무엇인지 살펴보아야 한다. that은 the rate를 선행사로 하는 주격 관계대명사인지 목적격 관계대명사인지 알 수가 있다. 먼저 주격도 아니고 그렇다고 predict의 목적격도 아니다. 마지막 남은 '동격'의 that 또한 아니다. 의미상 성립하지 못하기 때문이다. 선행사 the rate는 뒤의 문장에서는 전치사와 함께 부사구로 쓰였던 것으로 판단해 볼 수가 있다. 뒤의 문장구조는 다음과 같다. computer models predict that the Arctic ice will melt as a result of global warming <u>at the rate</u>.에서 the rate가 앞의 문장과 공통된 부분이며 전치사 at의 목적격이므로 which가 되어 전치사 at과 함께 앞으로 이동한 것이어야 하므로 at which가 문법적으로 옳다.

해석 그 변화들은 과학자들과 환경론자들에게 경각심을 주고 있다. 이 변화들이 지구 온난화의 결과로 북극 얼음이 녹을 수 있는 예측 비율을 훨씬 넘고 있기 때문이다.

11 A thing about Capers and his career ① is when he left the Carolina Panthers a lot of people were questioning his passion, ② said this guy is not a passionate sort, he is not able to instill the type of emotion and enthusiasm in his team. ④ No error.

정답 ② said ⇨ saying

해설 when 부사절 다음에 이어지는 주절은 'he is not able to instill ~' 부분이다. 그러므로 ② 부분은 과거형 동사가 아니라 현재분사형인 saying이 와야 한다.

해석 Capers와 그의 경력에 관해 특이한 것은 그가 Carolina Panters를 떠났을 때 많은 사람들이 이 사람은 열정적인 타입이 아니다, 그는 자신의 팀에게 감정과 열정을 불어넣을 수 있는 사람이 아니라는 식으로 말하며 그의 열정에 대해 의문을 가졌다는 점이다.

12 Elizabeth is slightly taller, slimmer and ① with more healthier, rosier cheeks. Katy has a rounder face and a ② noticeable paler complexion. But look closer and you can see similarities. They have the same shaped eyes, ③ though not the same colour. ④ No error.

정답 ② noticeable ⇨ noticeably

해설 형용사 비교급인 paler를 수식하는 품사는 부사가 되어야 하므로 ②의 noticeable을 noticeably로 바꿔야 한다. ③은 though they don't have the same colour의 생략형으로 'though not'이 된 것이므로 문법적으로 오류가 없다.

해석 Elizabeth는 약간 더 키가 크고 말랐으며, 건강해 보이는 장밋빛의 볼을 가지고 있다. Katy는 둥그런 얼굴에 창백한 안색을 보였다. 하지만 가까이 보면 비슷함을 볼 수 있다. 같은 색깔은 아니지만 그들은 같은 모양의 눈을 가지고 있었다.

13 ① Unlike many countries, the United States has ② few federal policies for working parents. One is the Family and Medical Leave Act of 1993, ③ which provides workers at companies of a certain size ④ in 12 weeks of unpaid leave.

정답 ④ in ⇨ with

해설 동사 provide에 관한 용법이다. provide는 3형식 동사로 'provide + 사람 + with + 사물'로 써야 하며 'provide + 사물 + for/to 사람'의 형식으로도 쓸 수 있다. 따라서 ④의 전치사 in을 with로 써야 한다.

해석 많은 국가들과는 달리 미국은 일하는 부모들을 위한 연방정책이 거의 없지만 '1993년 가족 및 의료 휴가법'에 따라 일정 규모의 회사들은 당사 근로자들에게 12주의 무급휴가를 제공하고 있다.

14 Similarly, ① permission to appeal was granted by the Supreme Court that ② had denied defendant's motion to compel the plaintiff's parents to ③ submit to an examination before trial and provide medical authorizations on the ground that the medical information ④ privileged.

정답 ③ privileged ⇨ was privileged

해설 동사 privilege는 '~에게 특권을 주다'라는 타동사로 쓰인다. 또한, on the ground that 구조 다음에는 '주어 + 동사'가 와야 한다. 동사 privilege는 자동사로 쓰인 것이 아니기 때문에 'was privileged'의 수동태 형식으로 써야 하므로 정답은 ③이다.

해석 유사하게, 피고가 원고의 부모에게 재판 전에 검진자료를 제출하고 의학적 검증을 받으라는 신청을 의료정보는 개인적 권한이라는 근거로 기각했던 그 대법원에 의해 상고가 허락되었다.

15 I didn't have to wait for ① long before my cafe latte and egg & bacon were served. The egg and bacon roll can certainly ② be had ③ for its half price elsewhere. It was warm and crusty and tasty, but that was about it. The cafe latte came with a heart-shaped latte art, and though ④ inferior to Campos Coffee, was still a pretty good cup.

정답 ③ for its half price ⇨ for half its price

해설 half는 전치한정사로 어순에 있어 소유격 앞에 와야 한다. ③의 its half price는 half its price로 써야 한다. ④의 inferior는 '–ior은 라틴어 비교급'을 나타내고 than 대신에 to를 쓰기 때문에 맞는 표현이다.

해석 나의 카페라테와 계란베이컨말이가 나오기까지 많이 기다리지 않아도 되었다. 계란베이컨말이는 다른 곳에서 절반 가격에 먹을 수 있었다. 그것은 따뜻했고 바삭했으며 맛있었지만 그뿐이었다. 카페라테는 하트 모양의 거품으로 나왔다. 그리고 Campos Coffee보다는 못했지만 여전히 괜찮은 커피였다.

16 My best friend and I recently started college together ① as roommates. One weekend we went away with some friends, including a guy I liked. The next thing I know my friend is holding his hand and dancing with him. I ② tried not to let it bother me because I know she ③ would never do anything ④ hurting me.

정답 ④ hurting me ⇨ to hurt me

해설 현재분사형이 후치 수식으로 명사를 수식할 수 있지만, 의미적으로 '~할'이라는 의미로 수식할 경우에는 보통 to부정사를 쓴다. 의미적으로 '나를 아프게 하고 있는 것'이 아니라 '나를 아프게 할 어떤 것'이 되어야 하므로 정답은 ④이다.

해석 나와 내 가장 친한 친구는 최근 대학 룸메이트로 만났다. 며칠 전 주말에 내가 좋아하는 남자와 친구 몇 명과 놀러 간 적이 있었다. 그때 내가 본 건 내 친구가 그의 손을 잡고 춤을 추고 있는 것이다. 나는 내 친구가 나를 아프게 하지 않을 것이라는 걸 알고 있기 때문에 신경 쓰지 않으려 했다.

17 It may be more than two centuries ① since he died but his ability to spark controversy remains undimmed. A typical example now is of fragmented approach ② to honor his memory. A furious row has broken out over plans to ③ only partially restore a monument to him. ④ No error.

정답 ② to honor ⇨ to honoring

해설 'of fragmented approach'에서 approach는 명사로 쓰였다. 뒤에 쓰인 to는 부정사가 아니라 전치사이므로 ②의 to honor를 to honoring으로 써야 한다. ③에서 only partially는 부사로 뒤에 부정사의 동사적 의미를 수식하는 분리부정사로 문법적으로 오류가 없다.

해석 그가 죽은 지 200년이 지났을 것이지만 그의 논란을 일으키는 능력은 아직도 꺼지지 않았다. 전형적인 사례는 바로 지금으로 그를 기리기 위한 방식에 대한 분열된 의견들이다. 부분적으로만 기념비를 세우는 것에 대해 치열한 논란이 일고 있다.

18 It has not recovered well ① this past winter – ice extent for every month since September 2015 has been far below average. And "② it's been so warm in the Arctic ③ that the ice has grown this winter is ④ probably rather thin", Professor Peter Wadhams of Cambridge University explains.

정답 ③ that the ice ⇨ that the ice that

해설 ③의 that은 'so ~ that' 용법의 that이므로 문법적 오류가 없으나, 'has grown this winter' 부분 뒤에 is의 주어는 the ice가 되기 때문에 the ice 다음에는 주격 관계대명사 that이 하나 더 필요하다.

해석 과거 겨울 동안 제대로 회복이 되지 않았다. 얼음의 규모가 2015년 9월 이후 평균 이하로 떨어졌다. 그리고 북극의 온도가 너무 따뜻해져 올 겨울의 얼음 역시 다소 얇을 것이라고 케임브리지 대학의 피터 와담 교수는 설명했다.

19 The carbon footprint shows ① how many greenhouse gases a product creates. The primary footprint ② measures the direct CO2 amounts from the whole life cycle of a product. CO2 ③ emissions are created not only from making products but also from ④ maintaining and destroying them.

정답 ① how many ⇨ how much

해설 밑줄 친 ①의 문장을 정치된 문장으로 분석해 보자. A product creates greenhouse gases ________.가 된다. 빈칸에는 '부사'로 한 상품이 이산화탄소를 얼마나 '많이' 배출하느냐가 되기 때문에 many가 아니라 much에 해당되는 내용이 들어가야 한다는 것을 알 수 있다. 따라서 shows의 목적어로 의문사절이 올 경우 how many가 아니라 'how much + 목적어 + 주어 + 타동사'의 구조가 되어야 한다.

해석 탄소발자국은 한 상품이 얼마나 많은 온실가스를 배출하는지를 보여준다. 1차 탄소발자국은 한 상품을 사용하고 폐기할 때까지 방출되는 이산화탄소의 양을 측정한다. 이산화탄소는 상품을 제조하면서 유지하고 폐기할 때까지 배출된다.

20 Public anger is growing in China ① following last week's deadly explosions at a warehouse in the northern port city of Tianjin. Officials there announced the death toll ② continues to raise : 114 ③ are confirmed dead and 70 others ④ are still missing.

정답 ② continues to raise ⇨ continues to rise

해설 '수가 증가하고 있다'를 표현하기 위해서는 raise 타동사가 아니라 자동사 rise가 쓰여야 하므로 정답은 ②이 된다. ③ 114는 의미적으로 114 persons이므로 복수형 동사 are가 쓰인 것이 맞고 'confirm + O + dead(목적어가 죽은 것으로 확인하다)'의 수동형으로 맞게 쓰였다.

해석 중국 북부 톈진항의 한 창고에서 지난주 초대형 폭발사고가 발생한 후 국민들의 분노가 커지고 있다. 그곳의 관리들은 사망자가 계속 증가할 것이며 현재까지 114명이 숨지고 70명이 실종됐다고 발표했다.

21 Ask me what my favorite sports movie is and you're in for a long wait. There are, in my opinion, ① too many great sports movies out there to choose just one. I could maybe pick a favorite one for ② each sport, but ③ no one that stands out above all the others. ④ No matter what sport the movie is about, the plot is usually the same.

정답 ③ no one ⇨ not one

해설 'not A but B'의 형식과 의미적으로 같은 형식은 'B, but not A'가 된다. 문맥적으로 ③ 부분은 '고를 수 있는 것이 아니다'가 되기 때문에 but not one이 되어야 한다. 이때 one은 a favorite one을 의미하는 부정대명사로 쓰였다.

해석 나에게 내가 가장 좋아하는 스포츠 영화가 뭔지 물어본다면 당신은 오랫동안 기다려야 할 것이다. 내 생각에 좋은 스포츠 영화가 너무 많아 하나를 고르기가 어렵다. 나는 아마 각 스포츠마다 하나씩 좋은 영화를 고를 수 있겠지만 그중 가장 뛰어난 것을 고를 수는 없다. 영화가 어떤 스포츠에 관련된 것이든지 간에 각본은 대개 같다.

22 ① Most all intelligent creatures, ② be they parrots, sharks or human beings, are vertebrates. This is ③ inconvenient for anyone ④ trying to understand the nature of intelligence.

정답 ① Most all ⇨ Almost all

해설 most는 형용사로 쓰일 경우 all을 수식할 수가 없다. 전치한정사로 쓰인 all을 수식하기 위해서는 부사가 되어야 하기 때문이다. 따라서 most를 almost로 바꿔야 문법적으로 옳은 표현이 된다.
②의 문장 구조에 '동사원형'이 온 이유는 '양보 구문'일 경우 '접속사가 생략되면 동사원형 + 주어 + 나머지 성분이 오는 구조를 취하기 때문이다.

해석 거의 대부분 지능을 가진 생물은 앵무새든, 상어든, 인간이든지 모두 척추동물이다. 이것은 지능의 본질을 이해하려고 하는 사람에게는 불편한 현실이다.

23 A Criminal Court, for instance, will issue a gag order ① on the media if the judge ② believes that potential jurors in a future trial will be influenced ③ on the media reporting or speculation ④ on the early stages of a case.

정답 ③ on ⇨ by

해설 주어진 문장에서 ③ 앞에 쓰인 동사 influence는 '~에게 영향을 미치다'라는 의미로 타동사 용법으로 쓰였다. 따라서 수동태가 될 경우에는 전치사 on을 수반하지 않는다. influence가 명사로 쓰일 경우에는 전치사 on을 수반한다.

해석 예를 들어 형사법정에서 판사가 생각하기에 앞으로 잠재적인 배심원이 될 사람들이 사건 초기 단계에서 언론 보도나 추측 보도로 인해 영향을 받을 것 같다면 언론매체에 함구령을 내릴 수 있다.

24 If you're tired of hearing about millennials, you ① might want to revisit your old friends at MTV. The ② youth-aimed cable network, known for making radical shifts in its programming every few years, is already ③ turning its attention to Generation Z, loosely defined ④ people born from the late 1990s to the present.

정답 ④ people born ⇨ as people born

해설 Generation Z와 동격을 이루고 있는 부분이 바로 'loosely defined ~'가 된다. 동사 define은 'define A as B'로 5형식으로 분석되는 형식을 갖추기 때문에 'loosely defined as people who were born from ~'으로 써야 올바른 문장이 된다.

해석 밀레니엄 세대에 관한 이야기를 듣는 데 지쳤다면 아마도 당신은 MTV에서 옛 연예인들을 다시 보고 싶을지 모른다. MTV는 몇 년마다 프로그램을 대폭 개편하는 것으로 알려진 청소년층을 대상으로 하는 케이블 네트워크 방송이지만 현재는 이미 Z세대를 겨냥하고 있다. Z세대란 대략 1990년대 후반부터 지금까지 태어난 사람들로 정의되는 세대다.

25 The driver of any vehicle ① involved in an accident ② results in the death of any person shall immediately stop ③ such vehicle at the scene of the accident or as ④ close thereto as possible.

정답 ② results in ⇨ resulting in

해설 involved는 과거분사로 맞는 어법이며, 본동사는 shall immediately stop이 되어야 하므로 ②의 results를 resulting으로 고쳐 accident를 수식하게 해야 한다.

해석 누군가가 사망하게 되는 결과를 초래하는 사고에 관련된 차량의 운전자는 그 현장이나 또는 될 수 있는 한 그 곳에 가까운 곳에서 즉시 자신의 차량을 즉시 멈추게 해야 한다.

26 Francis Bacon is one of the important ① <u>thinkers of the Scientific Revolution</u> of the 17th century. Although Bacon was neither a mathematician ② <u>nor an experimental scientist</u>, he ③ <u>exerted great influence on</u> his contemporary by introducing ④ <u>a method on which science is based</u> observation and experimentation.

정답 ④ a method on which science is based ⇨ a method in which science is based on

해설 a method in which까지 '그 방법으로'라는 의미로 뒤의 문장에 쓰일 부사를 만들었다. 그 다음에는 완전한 문장이 나와도 된다는 것을 생각하자. 주어로 science 동사 is based가 나왔으나 그 다음 observation 이하의 명사를 만났다. 그럼 on이라는 전치사가 필요하지 않을까? 단순히 뒤의 is based가 있다고 on which를 외우는 습관은 아무런 소용이 없다. a method on which S + be based로 끝나버리면 물론 on which가 맞겠다.

해석 프랜시스 베이컨은 17세기의 과학혁명의 중요한 철학자들 중 한 사람이다. 베이컨은 수학자나 실험적 과학자는 아니지만, 동시대에 과학이 관찰과 실험에 근거하는 방식을 도입함으로써 동시대인들에게 커다란 영향을 미쳤다.

27 In a burglary trial, the defendant's actions after he entered the house ① <u>can be evidence</u> used to determine if he had the intent to commit a crime at the time of entry. For example, if a defendant ② <u>entered the house</u> and committed criminal sexual conduct (CSC), the jury could find him guilty of burglary even though there ③ <u>may not have been</u> ④ <u>any specific evidence</u> that at the time he entered the house he intended to commit CSC.

정답 ② entered the house ⇨ entered a house

해설 '들어가다'라는 의미로 동사 enter를 쓸 경우에는 전치사 into를 쓰지 않는 점에서는 문법적으로 맞다. 하지만 뒤에 정관사가 올바르게 쓰였는지를 따져봐야 한다. For example, 다음에는 '지칭되지 않는' 일반적 사례를 진술하기 때문에 the house가 아니라 a house가 되어야 하므로 정답은 ②이다.

해석 강도죄에 대한 재판에서 피고의 주거침입 이후의 행동은 피고가 침입 시점에서 범죄를 저지를 의향이 있었는지에 대한 판단 증거가 될 수 있다. 예를 들어 피고가 주거침입을 한 후 성적 범행을 저질렀다면 그가 침입 시 성범죄를 저지를 의도가 있었다는 별다른 증거가 없더라도 배심원들은 그가 강도죄를 저지를 것으로 본다.

28 After a certain length of time living in fear with ① <u>no guarantees</u> about any facet of everyday life, any sort of government is ② <u>preferable to none</u>. Would you trade a government that stones adulterers ③ <u>with the ability</u> to walk to the store safely? For most, the answer ④ <u>becomes absolutely</u>. A repressive regime claiming religious credibility is fast forming and therefore perfectly placed to take over in an unstable situation.

정답 ③ with the ability ⇨ for the ability

해설 'a government that stones adulterers' 이 부분은 trade의 목적어에 해당한다. 전체적 문맥적으로 'trade A for B(A와 B를 교환하다, 바꾸다)'가 자연스럽기 때문에 ③의 전치사 with를 for로 수정해야 한다.

해석 일정 기간 동안 일상에서 어떤 보장되지 않는 두려움에서 살고 난 이후라면 어떤 정부도 없는 것보다는 낫다. 당신은 가게까지 안전하게 가는 것 때문에 간통죄를 지은 자에게 돌을 던져 죽게 하는 정부를 택하겠는가? 대부분 당연하다고 대답할 것이다. 종교적 믿음을 강조하는 강압적인 정부들은 급속히 틀을 갖추고 불안한 상황에서 정부의 자리를 차지하게 된다.

---

29 Pasta's ethnic roots have been long debated. Many theories ① <u>have been put forward</u>, some notably far-fetched. An enduring myth, based on the writings of the 13th-century explorer Marco Polo, that pasta was brought to Italy from China, ② <u>rose from</u> a misinterpretation of a famous passage in Polo's Travels. ③ <u>In them</u>, Polo mentions a tree from which something like pasta was made. It was probably the sago palm, ④ <u>which produces</u> a starchy food that resembles, but is not pasta.

정답 ③ In them ⇨ In it

해설 'Polo's Travels'는 책의 제목이다. 지시대명사로 받을 경우에는 복수가 아니라 단수형으로 받아야 하므로 ③의 them을 it으로 수정해야 한다. ②의 주어는 'An enduring myth'으로 자동사의 과거형으로 문법적으로 오류가 없다.

해석 파스타의 민족적 기원에 대해서는 오래 전부터 논쟁이 벌어지고 있다. 수많은 이론이 제시되었고 일부는 특히나 설득력이 없는 이론이다. 13세기의 탐험가 마르코 폴로(Marco Polo)가 남긴 글에 근거하여 파스타가 중국에서 이탈리아로 전해졌다는 내용의 오랫동안 지속되어온 근거 없는 믿음은 마르코 폴로의 "동방견문록(Travels)"에 담긴 유명한 구절을 오독한 데서 기인한다. 동방견문록에서 마르코 폴로는 파스타 같은 것이 나는 나무에 관해 언급했다. 그 나무는 어쩌면 사고야자였을 것으로 보이며, 사고야자에서는 파스타와 비슷한 전분질 음식이 나오는데, 이는 비슷하긴 해도 절대 파스타는 아니다.

30 Just thinking that a particular brand's products are especially effective may have a kind of placebo effect, researchers have found. In ① a series of studies, participants received nearly identical tools for skill tests in golf and math. The only difference : Half of the putters bore Nike labels, while half of the earplug sets given to test takers ② was said to have been made by 3M. Those who thought they were using a Nike putter indeed ③ needed fewer putts, on average, to sink a ball, and participants who thought they had 3M earplugs during the math test answered more questions correctly. It was also found that those with the lowest initial confidence in their abilities seemed ④ to gain the most from the subtle upgrade.

정답 ② was said to ⇨ were said to

해설 'half of the earplug sets'가 주어로 쓰일 경우 수일치는 of 이하의 명사의 수에 따라 결정된다. the earplug sets가 복수형이므로 ②의 was를 were로 써야 맞다. ④의 the most는 명사적 용법으로 쓰였다.

해석 특정 브랜드의 제품이 특히나 효과가 더 좋다는 생각은 어쩌면 일종의 위약효과일 수도 있다고 연구진이 밝혔다. 일련의 연구에서 참가자들은 골프 및 수학 기술을 시험하기 위한 거의 동일한 도구를 수령했다. 유일한 차이점은 골프 퍼터 가운데 반 정도는 나이키 상표가 붙어 있었다는 점이고, 시험을 치르는 사람에게 배부된 귀마개 중에서 반 정도는 3M에서 제조된 것이라고 전해졌다. 나이키에서 만든 퍼터를 사용한다고 생각하던 사람들은 실제로 평균적으로 공을 집어넣기까지 퍼팅 수가 적었고, 자신이 시험 보는 중에 3M에서 만든 귀마개를 쓰고 있다고 생각한 사람은 정답을 더 많이 맞혔다. 또한 자신의 능력에 대한 신뢰가 처음에 가장 낮았던 사람들은 약간의 도구 개선을 통해 가장 큰 성과를 달성한 것으로 보인다.

02 실전모의고사 정답 및 해설

01	③	02	③	03	②	04	①	05	②	06	④	07	③	08	③	09	③	10	③
11	④	12	②	13	②	14	②	15	③	16	④	17	④	18	②	19	④	20	④
21	①	22	③	23	①	24	②	25	③	26	③	27	③	28	③	29	④	30	④

[01-06] Choose the one that could best complete each of the following sentences.

01 **__________ I was part of this nonsense was not lost on me, and at times it troubled me beyond mere embarrassment.**

① What ② The fact
③ That ④ Whether

정답 ③ That

해설 주어진 빈칸에는 was not lost의 주어 역할을 하는 명사절 접속사가 와야 한다. 의미적으로 '~라는 사실'이 와야 하는데 ②은 The fact that이 와야 한다. 따라서 정답은 ③이다.

해석 내가 그 어처구니없는 일에 관련되어 있다는 사실이 마음에서 사라지지 않았으며 한때는 이것이 단순한 부끄러움 이상으로 나를 괴롭혔다.

02 **She was so captivated by it that she went home and finished a project in one night that __________ span the full four-week program.**

① are supposed to ② supposed to
③ was supposed to ④ will be supposed to

정답 ③ was supposed to

해설 동사 suppose는 5형식으로 'suppose + 목적어 + to 부정사'로 쓰거나, 수동태로 'be supposed to ⓥ'의 형식으로 쓴다. 빈칸에는 전체 문장의 시제가 과거이므로 was supposed to가 와야 한다.

해석 그녀는 그것에 너무 매료되어서 집에 가서 4주 기간의 프로그램으로 진행되는 프로젝트를 하루 저녁 만에 끝내고 말았다.

03 **His weight hit 220 ; he felt and looked like a blimp. One night, the company nurse invited him to ________ his blood pressure tested.**

① having been ② have
③ have had ④ having

정답 ② have

해설 빈칸 뒤에 his blood pressure가 목적어, tested가 과거분사형으로 목적격 보어로 쓰였다. 보기 항에 공통적으로 사역동사 have가 쓰인 것으로 보아 정답은 ②이다. to 다음에 to have p.p로 '본동사의 시제보다 그 이전의 시제'를 나타내는 완료 시제를 쓸 필요가 없다.

해석 그의 몸무게가 220 파운드에 도달했다. 그는 뚱보처럼 느꼈고 그렇게 보였다. 어느 날 저녁 회사의 간호사가 그의 혈압을 측정하기 위해 그를 불렀다.

04 **To make the United States more competitive, he said he ________ a fair tax that ________ income tax and the payroll tax system.**

① would push … would get rid of
② would push … got rid of
③ would push … would have gotten rid of
④ pushed … would get rid of

정답 ① would push … would get rid of

해설 'he said' 부분을 단서로 시제 일치를 시키면 되는 문제다. 과거에서 바라본 미래 시점은 would로 나타내고, 두 번째 빈칸 역시 a fair tax를 선행사로 하는 주격 관계대명사 that 다음에 연결되는 과거에서 바라본 시점의 동사가 와야 하기 때문에 정답은 ①이다.

해석 미국을 보다 경쟁력 있게 하기 위해 그는 소득세와 급여세를 없애는 공정한 세제를 지원할 것이라고 말했다.

05 **________ her before I encountered her music, I would not have been surprised at how intelligently humorous her works are.**

① Having been met ② Had I met
③ If I hadn't met ④ If I met

정답 ② Had I met

해설 주절의 형태가 'I would not have been'이 쓰인 것으로 보아 가정법 과거완료에 해당한다는 것을 알 수 있다. 따라서 빈칸에는 문맥을 고려해서 'If I had met'이 와야 한다. 이때 if가 생략되면 'Had I met'이 되기 때문에 정답은 ②이다.

해석 내가 그녀의 음악을 접하기 전에 그녀를 만났다면 그녀의 지적이며 유머 있는 작업에 대해 그다지 놀라지 않았을 것이다.

06 **Your wedding will be more than just ______________, perfectly color-coordinated flowers, and an awesome reception.**

① the most beautiful imaginable dress
② the most beautiful and imaginable dress
③ the beautiful dress most imaginable
④ the most beautiful dress imaginable

정답 ④ the most beautiful dress imaginable
해설 '최상급의 형용사 + 명사' 다음에 '–ible 또는 –able'로 끝나는 형용사가 수식을 할 경우 원칙적으로 후치 수식을 한다. 보기 항에 ④이 없다면 ①도 정답이 될 수 있지만, 객관식에서는 최선의 답을 선택해야 한다.
해석 당신의 결혼식은 상상할 수 있는 가장 아름다운 드레스, 완벽한 색상의 꽃들, 그리고 훌륭한 리셉션, 그 이상의 것이 될 것이다.

[07–08] **Choose the one that is grammatically NOT correct.**

07 ① The same thing, happening in wartime, would amount to disaster.
② If he had listened to me, he would not have failed.
③ If the sun was to collide with the moon, what would become of the earth?
④ If he had worked hard in his school days, he would succeed now.

정답 ③ was to collide ⇨ were to collide
해설 가정법 미래에서 '전혀 불가능한 일'을 가정하거나 상상할 때는 'if + S + were to V ~, S + 과거형 조동사 + 동사원형 ~.'의 형식을 쓴다. ③의 was를 were로 써야 문법적으로 맞다. ④은 혼합가정법으로 쓰인 문장이다.
해석 ① 이와 같은 일이 만약 전시에 일어난다면 큰 재난이 될 것이다.
② 그가 내 말을 들었더라면 그는 실패하지 않았을 텐데.
③ 태양이 달과 충돌한다면 지구는 어떻게 될까?
④ 그가 학창 시절에 열심히 공부했었더라면, 지금 성공했을 텐데.

08 ① Once you come in, you cannot get out without permission.
② If he were to be president, he would make a drastic reform.
③ A famous scientist found that most stars were bigger than the sun.
④ He wishes to resign on the ground that his health is failing.

정답 ③ were ⇨ are

해설 불변의 진리나 과학적 사실을 언급하는 문장에서는 현재형의 시제가 오므로 ③의 were를 are로 써야 한다. ①의 once는 '일단 ~하면'의 의미로 접속사로 맞게 쓰였다. ②은 가정법 미래의 문장으로 맞게 쓰였다.

해석 ① 일단 들어오면, 너는 허가 없이 나갈 수 없다.
② 만약 그가 대통령이 된다면 그는 과감한 개혁을 취할 것이다.
③ 유명한 과학자가 대부분의 별들이 태양보다 크다는 것을 발견했다.
④ 그는 건강이 나빠지고 있다는 것을 근거로 사임하고 싶어 한다.

[09–30] **Choose the one that makes the sentence grammatically INCORRECT.**

09 ① The native Italians refuse to speak ② an ounce of ③ its language ④ to foreigners for fear that we should butcher their romantic language.

정답 ③ its language ⇨ their language

해설 ③에서는 의미적으로 the native Italians를 지칭해야 하므로 단수형인 its를 their로 수정해야 한다.

해석 본토 이태리인들은 외국인들이 그들의 언어를 망가지게 할 것이라는 두려움에서 그들에게 자신들의 언어를 한마디도 하지 않았다.

10 The Clemson House offers several living options for undergraduate students. Each room or apartment ① houses ② two to four students and has a private bath. As with the apartment complexes, ③ little, ④ if any, freshmen are assigned to the Clemson House.

정답 ③ little ⇨ few

해설 freshmen의 복수 명사를 little로 수식하게 되면 '어린'이라는 의미인데, 문맥적으로는 'few'가 와야 한다. ①의 house는 '수용하다'라는 동사로 쓰였고, ④은 '설령 있다 하더라도'라는 의미로 가정법 관용어구다. 뒤에 if any (freshmen)에서 명사가 의미적으로 생략된 형태이므로 맞는 표현이다.

해석 크림슨하우스(Clemson House)는 학부생들에게 여러 가지 옵션을 제공한다. 개별 방들과 아파트는 2명에서 4명의 학생들이 살게 되며 개별적으로 욕실이 제공된다. 아파트 단지와 마찬가지로 극소수, 만일 있다면, 신입생만이 크림슨하우스에 배정된다.

11 ① Even though you'll find plenty to do in Vancouver, there are ② nearby destinations definitely worth a look. ③ Among the must-sees ④ is Vancouver Island, with historic Victoria and Butchart Gardens, Whistler, and the North Shore, with Grouse Mountain.

정답 ④ is ⇨ are

해설 Among 부사구가 the must-sees까지며, '부사구 + 동사 + 주어'의 형식을 갖는다. 'Vancouver Island, with historic Victoria and Butchart Gardens, Whistler, and the North Shore, with Grouse Mountain.' 이 부분이 주어이므로 ④의 is를 are로 써야 맞다.

해석 비록 당신이 Vancouver에서도 많은 소일거리를 찾을 수 있겠지만 근처에 꼭 가볼 만한 곳들이 있다. 그런 곳 중 하나는 역사적인 Victoria와 Butchart Garden, Whistler가 있는 Vancouver Island와 Grouse Mountain이 있는 North Shore이다.

12 Although the session had its successes, lawmakers agree ① more work is needed and they will spend ② their off time on researching local ③ constituents' needs in preparation for the 2007 session. ④ No error.

정답 ② their off time on ⇨ their off time (in)

해설 'spend + 목적어 + (in) ~ing'의 형식과 'spend + 목적어 + on + 명사'의 구조와 혼동해서는 안 된다. researching은 동명사로 쓰였기 때문에 ②의 전치사 on을 생략하거나 in으로 써야 한다.

해석 비록 이번 회기가 성공적인 면이 있었으나 국회의원들은 더 많은 작업이 필요하다는 데 동의했으며 지역구민들의 요구와 2007년 회기를 준비하는 데 시간을 보낼 것이다.

13 Each footprint ① is made up of three massive toes — each one at least one and ② a half time as big as my foot. That makes them the biggest dinosaur prints ③ ever found in Scotland. And Dr Clark says they are significant, because they are still in the original strata of rock ④ where they were formed.

정답 ② a half time ⇨ a half times

해설 세 배는 three times, 네 배는 four times로 쓴다. 1.5배는 one and a half times를 써야 한다. ②에서 time을 times로 고쳐야 문법적으로 맞는 표현이다. ③은 '부사 + 과거분사'의 형태로 앞의 명사 the biggest dinosaurs prints를 후치 수식한다.

해석 각각의 발자국은 엄청난 크기의 발가락으로 이뤄져 있었다. 각각의 발가락은 적어도 내발의 한 배 반은 되었다. 이는 스코틀랜드에서 가장 큰 공룡 발자국이었다. 클라크 박사는 이것들이 여전히 원래 생성되었던 화석의 계층에 있기 때문에 그 의미하는 바가 크다고 말했다.

14 Truthfully, ten years ago, I didn't care much about community. My dream was to win a lot of money ① to help my own family. ② Little I know, so many families right here in Atchison are less fortunate ③ than my own. ④ There is poverty, molestation, addictions and many other types of violence and crime.

정답 ② Little I know ⇨ Little did I know

해설 준부정어 little이 문두로 나갈 경우에는 '부정어 + 조동사 + 주어 + 동사원형'의 어순을 갖는다. 따라서 ②을 Little did I know로 고쳐야 한다. ④에서는 원칙적으로 뒤에 주어가 복수가 나올 경우에는 are를 쓰는 것이 맞지만, 구어체에는 바로 뒤에 나오는 명사에 수 일치를 시켜 단수를 쓰는 경우도 있다. 확실하게 오류가 있는 보기를 선택해야 하므로 ④보다는 ②을 선택해야 한다.

해석 사실 10년 전, 나는 지역사회에 대해 별 관심이 없었다. 내 목표는 많은 돈을 벌어서 내 가족을 돕는 것이었다. 애치슨의 많은 가족들이 나보다 상황이 나쁘다는 것에 대해서는 거의 몰랐다. 이곳에는 빈곤, 폭행, 중독, 그리고 많은 유형의 폭력과 범죄가 난무하고 있다.

15 I could not feel any heat off the light, just coldness. It didn't have a shine ① nor a brightness to it. Just ② a glow to it. After standing there for just like a minute or so, one of my cousins couldn't take the fear ③ no longer, so we started to run back towards the cross roads and ④ it followed us.

정답 ③ no longer ⇨ any longer

해설 'couldn't take the fear'에 연결되는 부분에서 '더 이상 ~가 아니다'라고 할 경우에는 뒤에 any longer를 써야 한다. 이미 couldn't에 not이 있기 때문에 no longer라고 써서는 안 된다. 'not ~ any longer, not ~ any more'와 같은 표현에 주의해야 한다.

해석 나는 불빛에서 열을 못 느꼈다, 단지 냉기가 있었을 뿐이다. 그것은 반짝이거나 밝지도 않았다. 그냥 빛날 뿐이었다. 한 1분 정도 그곳에 서 있은 후 사촌 하나가 두려움을 견디지 못해 우리는 뒤의 사거리로 달려갔다. 그것은 우리를 쫓아왔다.

16 The underlying premise of the prior opinion, it ① seems to me, is that, under the Constitution, the mere absence of ② a prohibition against an asserted power, plus the abstract reasonableness of its use, ③ is enough ④ to be established the existence of the power. I think this is erroneous.

정답 ④ to be established ⇨ to establish

해설 'the existence of the power'가 명사구로 능동형의 타동사의 목적어 역할을 해야 한다. ④에서 to be established의 수동태가 되어 문법적으로 옳지 않다. 따라서 능동형의 to establish가 되어야 한다.

해석 내게 있어 기존 의견의 기본적인 전제는, 헌법하에서 단순히 권력의 사용에 대한 금지조항이 없는 점(그리고 권력의 사용에 대한 추상적인 근거)이 권력의 존재를 증명할 수 있다는 것이었다. 나는 이것이 실수라고 생각한다.

17 When the Impressionists first ① tried to show their work people ② were warned to stay away from it ③ for fear of endangering their health and sanity. Pregnant women in particular were exhorted to steer clear of its influences ④ lest should they miscarry.

정답 ④ lest should they ⇨ lest they should

해설 lest는 접속사로 lest + 주어 + (should) 동사원형의 형식을 쓴다. lest의 의미가 '~하지 않도록, ~하면 안 되므로'라는 부정적이라 해서 도치를 시키지 않는다. 그러므로 ④의 lest should they를 lest they should로 바꿔야 한다.

해석 인상파들이 처음 자신들의 작업을 보여주려 했을 때 사람들은 건강과 정신을 위협할 수 있다는 이유로 이를 멀리하도록 경고받았었다. 특히 임산부는 그 영향에서 벗어나지 않을 경우 유산의 가능성이 있어 피하도록 권고받았었다.

18 Influenza, commonly ① called the flu, is always caused ② by virus. Antibiotics will not help, unless the person develops a secondary bacterial infection. The symptoms ③ usually occur abruptly. Many people will develop a cough, ④ which is usually dry and can be severe, and chest pain.

정답 ② by virus ⇨ by a virus

해설 명사 virus는 주로 보통명사로 가산명사로 쓰인다. 'be infected with a virus', 'carry a virus'의 표현에서처럼 부정관사를 수반한다. 주어진 문제에서는 독감 바이러스를 설명하는 글이므로 'by a virus'라고 해야 자연스럽다.

해석 독감이라고 불리는 인플루엔자는 항상 바이러스에 의해 생긴다. 2차적 감염이 없다면 항생제는 도움이 안 된다. 증상은 대개 급격히 나타난다. 많은 사람들이 보통 마르고 심한 기침과 가슴 통증을 느낀다.

19 The ① low performing schools that we hear about are not the fault of the teachers. There are many ② factors involved, and a majority of the problems begin at home. ③ Some of the factors are : gangs, language, discipline, single parent home environment, respect for themselves, etc. Let's support our educators and not ④ blame on the teachers.

정답 ④ blame on ⇨ blame 또는 lay blame on

해설 동사 blame은 주로 타동사로 쓰인다. 명사로 쓰일 경우에는 '~을 비난하다'라는 의미로 'lay blame on'이라고 쓴다. 따라서 정답은 ④이다. ②에서 involved의 과거분사가 후치 수식을 하는 경우다. ③에서는 'some of the 복수 명사'의 형식을 잘 지키고 있다.

해석 우리가 듣는 학업성취도가 낮은 학교들의 문제는 선생님들의 문제가 아니다. 많은 원인들이 관련되어 있으며 대다수의 문제들이 집안에서 비롯된다. 원인들 중에는 갱, 언어, 규율, 집안환경, 자신에 대한 존중 등이 있다. 선생님들을 탓하지 말고, 우리 교육자들을 지원하자.

20 ① There must be no big trees and buildings around fish ponds ② for fear that they should shade the sunlight and block the blowing of the winds. It's beneficial to ③ the raising of water temperature of fish ponds and the growth of plankton and the improvement of D.O. conditions. ④ No error.

정답 ④ No error

해설 ①에서는 유도부사 there 다음에 동사가 나왔으며 '~임에 틀림없다'라는 강한 추측을 나타내고 있다. ②은 for fear that은 'lest + 주어 + (should) 동사원형'과 같은 형식으로 '~하는 것이 두려워, ~할까 봐'라는 의미로 쓰인다. 뒤에 주어와 동사가 나와 있기 때문에 'for fear of'가 아니라 'for fear that'이 문법적으로 맞게 쓰였다. ③은 명사 형태로 의미적으로 '~을 올리는 것'이라는 의미로 쓰였다.

해석 햇빛을 막거나 바람이 부는 것을 막을 수 있기 때문에 물고기들이 사는 연못 근처에 큰 나무나 빌딩이 있어선 안 된다. 이것은 연못의 수온을 높이는 데 도움이 되며 플랑크톤의 성장과 D.O. 상태를 향상하는 데 도움이 된다.

21 The government will probably intervene ① if it will see unfair discrimination against competitors or censorship. If the Googles of the world win, the network owners will ② undoubtedly figure out ③ some other way to raise prices. And the government will ④ surely intervene.

정답 ① if it will see ⇨ if it sees

해설 if가 가정법이 아니라 단순조건절로 쓰일 경우에는 if절에 현재형 동사를 쓴다. ①에서 will see를 sees로 써야 한다. 시간, 조건 부사절에서는 현재형이 미래형을 대신한다는 원칙을 떠올리면 된다.

해석 만일 경쟁자나 검열에 있어 불공정한 차별이 발견된다면 정부는 아마도 개입할 것이다. 만일 구글이 이긴다면 네트워 소유자는 여지없이 가격을 높일 방안을 생각해낼 것이다. 그렇다면 정부는 당연히 개입할 것이다.

22 If other nations were as far ① inferior to us, as we are willing to imagine, their condition would evidently tend to ② decay and extermination. ③ Without regard to the inferior orders of being, both animal and vegetable, it seems to be a law of nature ④ to gradually decline, and at last cease to exist.

정답 ③ Without regard to ⇨ With regard to

해설 자연의 법칙으로 서서히 쓰러져 결국 소멸하는 단계로 간다면 문맥적으로 '열등감에 대한 질서'와 관련이 있어야지, 관련이 없어서는 안 된다. ③의 without regard to의 대등적인 표현은 with regard to이므로 항상 전치사에 주의해야 한다.

해석 만일 다른 국가들이 우리가 상상하는 대로 우리보다 열등하다면 그들의 상태는 분명히 소멸하는 쪽으로 향하게 될 것이다. 열등함에 대한 질서와 관련하여, 동물이건 식물이건, 자연의 법칙은 이들을 서서히 쓰러지게 만들어 결국 소멸하게 한다.

23 Disaster can strike quickly and without warning, make a plan. During an emergency, the more ① planned you have ② ahead of time, the calmer you and your family will be. ③ These six steps will help you through the process : Talk, Plan, Learn, Check Supplies, Tell, Practice.

정답 ① planned you have ⇨ you have planned

해설 'the 비교, the 비교'의 형식에 관한 문제다. 'the more planned'에서 the more planned가 뒤에 you have의 목적어 역할을 할 수 없다. the more 부분만 목적어로 쓰여 'the more + you have planned'의 구조가 되어야 하므로 정답은 ①이다.

해석 재난은 소리 없이 빨리 온다. 그러므로 계획을 가지고 있어라. 긴급 상황에서는 당신이 계획을 많이 했을수록 더 차분하게 당신과 당신의 가족이 대처할 수 있다. 다음의 6단계가 도움이 될 것이다 : 대화, 계획, 학습, 장비점검, 보고, 연습.

24 O'Neill is ① the Homer of 20th-century American dramatists. Tennessee Williams, Arthur Miller, and Edward Albee follow ② in wake and none took the exploration of tragedy in a familiar American setting further ③ than he did. And of all his plays, nothing is more extreme or more achieved than ④ this one.

정답 ② in wake ⇨ in his wake

해설 정확한 숙어의 표현을 묻는 문제다. in one's wake가 'in the wake of'의 변형 형태로 '~의 자국을 좇아서, ~을 본떠서, ~에 계속해서, ~의 결과로서'의 의미를 갖는다. 따라서 ②의 in wake를 주어인 O'Neill의 소유격을 써서 in his wake라고 해야 자연스럽다.

해석 O'Neill은 20세기의 Homer라고 할 수 있다. Tennessee Williams, Arthur Miller, Edward Albee가 그의 영향을 받았으며 아무도 미국적인 배경의 비극에 있어 그처럼 발전하지 못했다. 그리고 그의 모든 작품 중 이것보다 더 극단적이고 성공적인 것은 없다.

25 I ① strongly encourage the School Committee, town safety officers, and state agencies to develop ② a well thought out policy that is good for the long term and is practically and economically sensible and fair. First and foremost, ③ these mean protecting the safety of our children, as well as drivers ④ through and around town.

정답 ③ these mean ⇨ this means

해설 앞 문장의 내용을 받는 문장을 쓸 경우 it이나 this를 쓴다. ③의 mean 다음에 protecting의 동명사형이 쓰인 것으로 보아 mean ~ ing은 '~을 의미하다'라는 의미로 맞게 쓰였다. this가 주어일 경우 means로 해야 맞기 때문에 this means로 수정해야 한다.

해석 나는 학교 위원회, 마을 보안관, 주정부 기관에 대해 장기적으로 유리하며 경제적으로 공정하고 이해할 만한 심사숙고한 정책을 낼 것을 제안한다. 최우선적으로 이것은 곧 마을과 마을주변에서 우리 어린이들뿐만 아니라 운전자들의 안전을 보호하는 것이다.

26 Naturally, this family event had me thinking about my own plans for retirement, which, ① until a few years ago, were practically non-existent. In fact, I ② enjoy writing for a living and ③ run my own business so much that I don't ever plan to retire ④ as such. Instead, I see retirement as a gradual transition from full-time writing to working as and when it suits me.

정답 ③ run my own business ⇨ running my own business

해설 enjoy의 목적어로 동명사형 writing이 왔고, and 다음에는 문맥적으로 enjoy와 병치되는 것이 아니라 writing과 병치가 되어야 하므로 ③의 run을 running으로 고쳐야 한다. ④의 as such는 '그것으로서, 그 자체로'라는 의미로 쓰였다. 의미적으로 such는 'the writer'를 지칭한다.

해석 자연스럽게 이번 가족행사는 몇 년 전까지도 없었던 나의 은퇴계획에 대해 생각하도록 했다. 사실 나는 글쓰기 직업을 즐기고 있으며 내 사업도 하고 있어 은퇴라는 생각을 하지 않았다. 대신 은퇴를 풀타임으로 글을 쓰는 것에서 필요할 때에만 쓰는 것으로의 점진적 전화과정으로 보고 있다.

27 They do ① not so much as know dice, or any such foolish and mischievous games. They have, however, two sorts of games ② not unlike our chess ; the one is between several numbers, in which one number, ③ as it was, consumes another ; the other ④ resembles a battle between the virtues and the vices.

정답 ③ as it was ⇨ as it were

해설 '말하자면'이라는 의미로 so to speak와 같은 형식은 as it were로 써야 한다. ③의 was를 were로 고친다. ②의 'not unlike + 목적어'는 결국 'like + 목적어'와 같은 형식이다. ④의 resembles는 타동사로 전치사 없이 목적어를 취한다.

해석 그들은 주사위나 다른 바보 같고 해로운 게임들은 몰랐다. 그러나 그들은 우리의 체스와 비슷한 두 가지의 게임을 알고 있었다. 하나는 여러 숫자 중 하나의 숫자가 다른 숫자를 먹는 것이며 다른 하나는 선과 악의 싸움과 비슷한 것이었다.

28 However, you cannot do it ① better than other people if they have talent and you do not. Hard work will not make up for raw ability if the people with raw ability are ② applying themselves. If by chance they are all lazy, you may have ③ a chance to being the best. So, find your raw talent, then work hard and you'll be ④ better than the competitors.

정답 ③ a chance to ⇨ a chance at 또는 a chance of

해설 명사 chance를 수식하는 형식을 묻는 문제다. 뒤에 to 부정사의 형태로 수식할 수 있는데, ③ 뒤의 being이 쓰인 것으로 보아 전치사 at이나 of가 와야 문법적으로 옳다. ②의 타동사 apply는 재귀대명사를 목적어로 취할 수 있다.

해석 그러나 다른 사람들이 재능을 가지고 있고 당신은 없다면 당신은 그들보다 잘할 수 없습니다. 재능 있는 사람이 노력한다면 당신의 노력은 타고난 능력을 상쇄할 수 없습니다. 우연히 그들이 모두 게으르다면 당신은 최고가 될 가능성이 있습니다. 그러므로 당신의 타고난 재능을 발견하고 열심히 일하시오, 그러면 당신은 경쟁자들보다 뛰어날 것입니다.

29 ① With this goal in mind, should you now sell your A fund because the stock market is hitting new highs and put the money into the B fund? The stock market is seductive. It is good at setting investors up for a fall. It can make you ② giddy with the thought of your new wealth. It can also ③ make you depressed as you contemplate how much money you would have made ④ if only you invested differently at the right moment.

정답 ④ if only you invested ⇨ if only you had invested

해설 'you would have made'의 형식으로 보아 가정법 과거완료인 것을 알 수 있다. 따라서 ④의 invested를 'had invested'로 바꿔야 올바른 if절의 형식이 된다. ②의 giddy는 형용사로 '어지러운, 현기증 나는, 경솔한'의 의미로 동사 make의 목적격 보어 역할을 올바르게 하고 있다.

해석 이러한 목표하에, 지금 주식시장이 고가를 기록하고 있기 때문에 당신은 A 펀드를 팔고 B 펀드에 투자해야 할까요? 주식시장은 유혹적입니다. 투자자들을 실패하도록 하기 좋습니다. 새로운 부를 축적할 수 있다는 생각에 당신을 경솔하게 할 수 있습니다. 만일 당신이 적절한 타이밍에 다르게 투자할 수 있었다면 얼마나 많은 돈을 벌었을까 하는 생각에 이것은 당신을 우울하게 할 수 있습니다.

30 Since both science and technology are ① blessed words in our contemporary vocabulary, some may be happy at the notions, first, that, ② viewed historically, modern science is an extrapolation of natural theology and, second, ③ that modern technology is at least partly to be explained as an occidental realization of the Christian dogma of ④ man's transcendence, and rightful mastery over nature.

정답 ④ man's transcendence ⇨ man's transcendence of

해설 'rightful mastery over nature'의 부분을 보면 명사 mastery와 nature를 연결하는 부분이 전치사 over로 연결되고 있다. 그렇다면 ④의 명사 man's transcendence는 nature와 어떻게 연결되어야 하는지를 생각해야 한다. '인간이 자연을 초월하는 것'이기 때문에 전치사 of가 필요하다는 것을 알 수 있다. 이와 유사한 문제가 이미 기출되었고, 상당히 어려운 문제로 생각했던 출제부분이므로 예상문제를 통해 익혀두자.

해석 과학과 기술은 현대 어휘에서 복 받은 어휘이기 때문에 일부는 첫 번째로 역사적 관점에서 보면 현대과학이 자연신학의 외연이라는 생각 그리고 두 번째로 현대기술은 최소한 부분적으로는 자연에 대한 인간의 초월 및 정당한 지배를 말하는 기독교적 교의의 서양식 실현으로 설명할 수 있다는 생각에 만족할 수도 있다.

03 실전모의고사 정답 및 해설

01	④	02	③	03	③	04	④	05	④	06	④	07	③	08	②	09	②	10	③
11	②	12	④	13	②	14	①	15	③	16	②	17	④	18	①	19	②	20	①
21	④	22	②	23	②	24	③	25	②	26	①	27	④	28	③	29	④	30	④

[01-06] **Choose the one that could best complete each of the following sentences.**

01 **Not a single word __________ except as I wrote. But how is that, I hear someone say ; did you write without knowing what it was that you were writing?**

① I read　　② did read
③ I read　　④ did I read

정답 ④ did I read
해설 문두에 'Not a single word'가 나오고 있다. 부정어를 포함한 목적어 부분이 문두에 올 경우에는 도치현상이 발생하므로 정답은 ④이 된다.
해석 나는 글을 쓸 때를 제외하곤 한 자도 읽지 않았다. 하지만 이것은 어떤가? 누군가가 나에게 "글을 쓸 때 당신이 쓰는 것이 무엇인지 모르면서 쓴 것인가?"라고 물었다.

02 **Several other Munch paintings have recently been stolen : six years ago, another well-known masterpiece, The Vampire, __________ from the Munch Museum in Oslo, but was later recovered, as was a lithograph, Madonna, which disappeared in 1990.**

① was robbed　　② was lost
③ was stolen　　④ have been stolen

정답 ③ was stolen
해설 빈칸 앞의 'The Vampire'는 작품을 일컫는 말로 'rob me of something'의 수동태에서 쓰이는 was robbed를 쓰면 안 된다. 'steal something from somebody'의 수동태 형식으로 되어 있는 ③을 선택해야 한다. 주어는 'another well-known masterpiece'이기 때문이다.
해석 뭉크의 그림들이 이 최근 도난당한 바 있다. 6년 전 유명한 명작인 뱀파이어가 오슬로의 뭉크 박물관에서 도난당한 후 다시 회수되었으며, 1990년에는 석판화 마돈나 역시 사라진 후 다시 찾았었다.

03 **As a fellow veteran of Kerry's generation, I received his remarks as a Vietnam-era flashback. Back __________, it was common to say, "Study hard or you might go to Vietnam." That's because we had something then that young people don't have to contend with now : a military draft.**

① in 1960's
② in the 1960
③ in the 1960s
④ in 1960s

정답 ③ in the 1960s

해설 연도를 나타내는 정확한 표현을 묻는 문제다. in the 1960's 또는 in the 1960s이 올바른 표현이므로 정답은 ③이 된다. 1960년은 'in 1960'이라고 나타내는데 보기 항에는 이러한 표현이 없다.

해석 Kerry 세대의 다른 참전용사들처럼, 나는 그의 말들을 베트남전의 회상으로 이해했다. 1960년대에는 "공부 안 하면 베트남에 간다"라는 말이 유행했었다. 이건 당시 우리가 지금의 젊은이들이 겪지 않아도 되는 무언가를 가지고 있었기 때문이다, 바로 징집.

04 **One thing you have to remember is __________ the declination changes significantly, so you'll need to know __________ it is this year.**

① that … which
② what … what
③ what … that
④ that … what

정답 ④ that … what

해설 첫 번째 빈칸 뒤에 'the declination changes significantly'의 완전한 절이 나오는 것으로 보아 is 다음에 보어 역할을 하는 명사절 접속사 that이 와야 함을 알 수 있다. 두 번째 빈칸에는 it is 다음에 보여 역할을 하는 what이 know의 목적절을 유도해야 하므로 정답은 ④이 된다. which은 선택적 개념에 쓰이지 때문에 ①은 어색하다.

해석 당신이 기억해야 할 하나는 하락세의 변화가 심하다는 점으로 올해는 어느 정도인지를 당신은 알아야 한다.

05 **I love a girl and she also loves me but she is __________ and had an ex-boyfriend with whom she says its not possible for us to continue.**

① senior to 4 years
② 4 years younger than me
③ older than I for 4 years
④ 4 years senior to me

정답 ④ 4 years senior to me

해설 비교단원에서 '나이의 차이'를 정확하게 표현한 문장을 찾는 문제다. '누가 나보다 4살 많다'는 'senior to me by four years' 또는 'older than I by four years'라고 할 수 있다. 아니면 ④처럼 'four years senior to me'로 나타내야 한다. ③에서는 전치사 for를 by로 고친다면 맞는 문장이다.

해석 나는 서로 사랑하는 여자 친구가 있지만 그녀는 나보다 4년 선배이며 우리가 지속될 수 없다고 말하고 있는 전 남자 친구가 있었다.

06 **If you drink alcoholic beverages, ______________ (no more than one drink a day for women, and no more than two drinks a day for men).**

① in moderation do so
② in moderation so do
③ so will do in moderation
④ do so in moderation

정답 ④ do so in moderation

해설 대동사 do의 기능을 묻는 문제다. 주어진 문장에서 문맥적으로 빈칸에는 drink 동사를 대신할 수 있는 대동사가 먼저 와야 하므로 do로 시작하는 ④만이 정답이 될 수 있다. ③에서는 주어가 없어서 정답이 될 수 없다.

해석 만일 당신이 술을 마신다면 마시되 적당히 하라(여자의 경우 하루 한 잔, 남자의 경우 두 잔 이하로).

[07-08] **Choose the one that is grammatically NOT correct.**

07 ① The picture hidden in the archives for 40 years was found.
② Some diseases can be prevented by proper vaccination.
③ She felt the call of God and decided to devote her life to help others.
④ You are supposed to refrain from smoking in this room.

정답 ③ help ⇨ helping

해설 '~에 헌신하다, 전념하다'의 올바른 표현은 'devote + 목적어 + to ~ing'이므로 ③의 to help를 to helping으로 고쳐야 한다. ④의 refrain은 자동사로 뒤에 전치사 from과 함께 '~을 삼가다, 그만두다'라는 의미로 쓰인다.

해석 ① 문서보관소에 40년간 숨겨져 있던 그림이 발견되었다.
② 어떤 질병들은 적절한 백신 접종으로 예방될 수 있다.
③ 그녀는 신의 부름을 느꼈고 평생 동안 남을 돕는 일에 헌신하기로 결심했다.
④ 너는 이 방에서 담배를 피우는 것을 삼가도록 되어 있다.

08 ① We don't want to get too deeply involved with those people.
② What would become of your family if you would be killed in an accident?
③ On a fine morning, you can see a beautiful sunrise from here.
④ James wanted to make a good impression at a job interview.

정답 ② would ⇨ should

해설 if절에 'would + 동사원형'의 형태의 동사부가 쓰일 경우 '주어의 의지'를 나타내는 가정법 미래가 된다. ② 문장에서는 주어의 의지가 아니라 '만일 ~할 경우'의 의미를 나타내야 하기 때문에 조동사 should가 와야 자연스럽다.

해석 ① 우리는 그런 사람들과 깊숙이 관련되길 원치 않는다.
② 만약 네가 사고로 죽게 된다면 너의 가족은 어떻게 되겠는가?
③ 날씨가 좋은 날에, 당신은 여기에서 일출을 볼 수 있다.
④ 제임스는 인터뷰에서 좋은 인상을 주고 싶었다.

[09-30] **Choose the one that makes the sentence grammatically INCORRECT.**

09 ① At the other side, I could ② vague see a fat figure that, ③ pipe in mouth, sat behind the shining ④ little panes and snowy curtain.

정답 ② vague ⇨ vaguely
해설 ② 뒤에 쓰인 see가 could 다음에 와야 하는 동사원형에 해당한다. 동사를 수식하는 품사는 부사가 되어야 하므로 vague를 vaguely로 고쳐야 한다.
해석 다른 쪽으로 나는 어렴풋이 뚱뚱한 사람이 파이프를 물고 빛나는 창유리와 눈 같은 커튼 뒤에 앉아 있는 것을 볼 수 있었다.

10 So he went ① a little distance toward cabin and listened once more. Evidently some people were making ② a great deal of noise in cabin. As soon as he ③ has realized this, he ④ returned to his house. He entered and blurted out to his grandmother, "Some people in cabin really seem to be very happy."

정답 ③ has realized ⇨ had realized 또는 realized
해설 전체 문장의 시제는 과거다. 따라서 ③처럼 현재완료 시제가 쓰인다면 어색한 문장이 된다. 'He entered ~'에서 볼 수 있듯이 현재와 전혀 상관없이 과거 시제로 진술하는 문장이므로 ③을 과거 또는 과거완료의 시제로 써야 문법적으로 옳다.
해석 그래서 그는 오두막 쪽으로 더 다가가 다시 들어보았다. 확실히 몇몇 사람들이 오두막 안에서 큰 소리를 내고 있었다. 그는 이를 확인하자마자 집으로 향했다. 그는 집에 들어서며 그의 할머니에게 "오두막 안에 있는 어떤 사람들은 정말 즐거워 보이네요."라고 말했다.

11 This is a book for educators. Those who have chosen ① to be educators are generally ② dedicating to students. But, sometimes we don't quite understand ③ what we are seeing. We hope this book will help educators ④ make sense of the many patterns and behaviors that we see.

정답 ② dedicating to ⇨ dedicated to
해설 동사 dedicate는 devote와 마찬가지로 'dedicate + 목적어 + to ~ing'의 형식으로 쓰고 수동태는 'be dedicated to ~ing'가 되므로 ②의 dedicating을 dedicated로 고쳐야 한다. ④의 make sense of는 '~을 이해하다'라는 숙어다.
해석 이것은 교육자를 위한 책이다. 교육자가 되려는 사람들은 학생들에게 헌신한다. 하지만 우리는 우리가 보는 것을 잘 모른다. 우리는 이 책이 교육자들에게 우리가 보는 패턴과 행동을 보이도록 했으면 한다.

03

12 Finally, as I did last week, ask ① the audience which one they would rather give up ② than keep it – their browser, or ③ all the rest of their desktop applications? (Unanimously, they'd all give up the latter without a blink.) All these trends show a ④ slow upgrade appetite.

정답 ④ slow ⇨ slowing

해설 형용사 어순에 관한 문제다. '형용사 + 형용사 + 명사'의 어순인 경우 형용사 모두 명사의 의미를 한정하며 어느 하나라도 생략해도 의미적으로 변화가 없어야 한다. 그렇지 않을 경우에는 a slow appetite가 의미적으로 완전한지를 생각해야 한다. 'a slowing appetite'가 맞는 표현이므로 정답은 ④이다.

해석 마지막으로 지난주와 마찬가지로 청중들에게 브라우저나 나머지 데스크톱 애플리케이션 중 어느 것을 포기할 것인지 물어보라. 만장일치로 그들은 눈 하나 깜짝하지 않고 후자를 선택할 것이다. 이러한 모든 추세는 사람들의 업그레이드 욕구가 줄어들고 있음을 보인다.

13 ① All the strategies in the world won't have impact ② if employees understand how to integrate them into their daily activities. Communication with customers, a focus on relevant offers and the ability ③ to solve problems ④ are attributes every employee should possess in order to facilitate the creation of brand loyalty.

정답 ② if ⇨ unless

해설 접속사에 밑줄이 있을 경우, 항상 그 접속사의 기능과 의미를 생각해야 한다. 문맥적으로 if가 아니라 'if ~ not'의 의미를 갖는 unless가 와야 하므로 정답은 ②이다. ④의 주어는 'Communication ~, a focus ~ and the ability ~'가 되므로 are가 맞게 쓰였다.

해석 직원들이 이를 일상적인 활동에 통합시키는 것을 이해하지 못한다면 세상의 어떤 전략도 영향을 미치지 못한다. 브랜드 로열티를 창출하는 것을 촉진하기 위해 모든 직원들이 가져야 할 자질은 고객과의 커뮤니케이션, 관련된 사항에 대한 집중, 그리고 문제해결 능력이다.

14 If you ① attend to Oxford University, you can ② go and see your college nurse (limited hours each week at most colleges), or visit the medical practice that ③ takes care of your college. Find out more ④ on the Oxford University Health and Welfare pages.

정답 ① attend to ⇨ attend

해설 동사 attend가 '~에 참석하다, 출석하다'라는 의미를 가질 경우, 타동사의 용법으로 써야 하므로 ①의 전치사 to를 생략해야 한다.

해석 당신이 Oxford 대학에 다닌다면 대학의 간호사를(대부분 단과대학에서 지정시간이 있음) 찾아가 진찰을 받거나 각 대학을 담당하는 의료원에 갈 수 있다. 보다 자세한 내용은 Oxford 대학 보건 및 후생 웹 사이트를 찾으시오.

15 I felt that there are ① too many people on this earth. I like ② life and living, and I ③ prefer to rich living and good life. Or analogously, quality than quantity. However, this is not the case. Look at people on the streets, stupids and ④ have nots and uglies with their children.

정답 ③ prefer to rich living ⇨ prefer rich living

해설 동사 prefer는 뒤에 명사를 목적어를 취할 수 있다. prefer to ⓥ의 형식과 혼동해서 ③처럼 명사 앞에 전치사 to를 쓰지 않도록 해야 한다. ④의 have nots는 명사로 '가지지 못한 사람들'이라는 의미로 people, stupids와 병치를 이루고 있다.

해석 나는 이 세상에 너무 많은 사람들이 살고 있다는 느낌을 가졌었다. 나는 생명과 인생을 좋아하고 진정한 삶과 훌륭한 인생을 좋아한다. 또는 비유적으로 양보다는 질을 좋아한다. 하지만 이 경우는 다르다. 길거리의 사람들을 보라, 멍청하고 가난하며 못생긴 것들이 아이들까지 데리고 있다.

16 Computers, fax machines, the Internet, cell phones, e-mail – from the viewpoint of business owners, these are the ① keys to success in today's world of hyper-competitive, 24-hour capitalism. But as the pace of work ② quicken, growing numbers of workers ③ are being pushed to the limits and are feeling ④ stressed out too much.

정답 ② quicken ⇨ quickens

해설 형용사 quick의 동사형은 quicken이다. as 다음에 the pace of work가 주어로 사용되었고, 시제는 현재 시제이므로 quickens가 되어야 문법적으로 맞다. ③의 현재진행형의 수동태인 'be being p.p'가 의미적으로나 형식적으로 오류가 없다. ④의 stressed out은 동사 feel의 보어 역할을 한다.

해석 컴퓨터, 팩스, 인터넷, 휴대폰, 이메일 등은 사업가 입장에서는 오늘날 초경쟁, 24시간 자본주의 사회의 성공요인들이다. 하지만 업무속도가 빨라짐에 따라 많은 노동자들이 한계에 직면하고 너무 스트레스를 받는다고 생각하고 있다.

17 Chronic fatigue syndrome (CFS) is ① a condition that ② causes extreme tiredness. People with CFS are so tired that they are unable to carry on normal activities ③ for a period of at least six months. They also have other symptoms, ④ such pain as in the joints and muscles, headaches, and sore throat.

정답 ④ such pain as ⇨ such as pain

해설 other symptoms의 예를 들어 어휘를 나열할 경우에는 'A such as B'와 같이 표현한다. other symptoms such as pain이 되어야 하고 pain을 뒤에서 전치사구 'in the joints and muscles'가 후치 수식하는 구조가 되어야 한다. 결국 pain, headaches, and sore throat으로 연결된다.

해석 만성피로증후군(CFS)은 극단적인 피곤을 부르는 현상이다. CFS에 시달리는 사람들은 너무도 피곤하여 최소 6개월간 정상적인 업무도 하지 못한다. 그들은 다른 증상도 보이는바 관절과 근육의 통증, 두통, 그리고 목감기 등이다.

18 A high percentage of cloned monkey embryos that look healthy ① is really a "gallery of horrors" deep within, says a researcher at Advanced Cell Technology, the company that last month ② published the first paper on cloned human embryos. This could mean that there is ③ something unique about primate eggs that will make cloning monkeys or people ④ far more difficult than cloning other animals.

정답 ① is ⇨ are

해설 percentage 명사가 'a percentage of ~'의 형식으로 쓰여 주어로 올 경우 동사의 수일치는 바로 of 뒤의 명사에 일치시켜야 한다. 'cloned monkey embryos'가 복수이므로 ①의 is를 are로 고쳐야 한다. ③에서는 something을 형용사가 후치 수식하는 경우이고, ④에서는 비교형인 more difficult를 부사 far가 수식하고 있는 형태로 문법적으로 맞게 쓰였다.

해석 건강해 보이는 복제된 원숭이 배아의 대다수가 사실 알고 보면 "공포스런 그림"이라고 지난달 인간복제에 관한 논문을 발표했던 Advanced Cell Technology사의 연구자는 말했다. 이것은 곧 초기 배아 상태에서의 독특한 그 무엇인가가 다른 동물보다 인간이나 원숭이를 복제하기 어렵게 한다는 것을 의미한다.

19 ① Because of its small size, this dictionary is not, and can't be, as ② comprehensively as large dictionaries. However, it ③ does surprisingly manage to define the vast majority of words that even medical students/professionals will encounter. Moreover, the definitions are clear and concise with good technical depth, but still ④ reasonably understandable for laymen.

정답 ② comprehensively ⇨ comprehensive

해설 'this dictionary is not, and can't be' 뒤에 연결될 수 있는 품사는 보어로 형용사가 되어야 한다. ②의 부사형인 comprehensively를 형용사 comprehensive로 써야 한다. ③의 does는 동사를 강조하는 조동사로 쓰였다. ④ 역시 품사의 어순이 맞게 쓰였다. 형용사 understandable은 'the definitions are ~' 뒤에 연결되며 형용사 'clear and concise'와 병치를 이루고 있기 때문이다.

해석 작은 사이즈로 인해 이 사전은 대형사전과 같은 완전성을 가지지 못하고 가질 수도 없다. 그러나 이것은 놀랍게도 의대생이나 전문가들도 찾는 단어들을 잘 관리하고 있다. 게다가 정의가 명확하고 기술적인 수준을 가지면서도 간결하지만 보통사람들에게도 이해가 간다.

20 Although ① track and field have considerably higher participation numbers, its ratio of championship qualifiers to total participants ② is higher than any other individual-team championship. While there were more than 18,000 male and female participants ③ in Division I track and field in 2013-14, only one out of 23 women and one out of 24 men ④ participated in the outdoor championships.

정답 ① track and field have ⇨ track and field has

해설 'track and field'는 '육상'의 의미로 and로 연결되어 있지만 의미적으로 밀접한 관계를 이룰 경우에는 'trial and error'처럼 복수 명사로 취급하지 않고 단수로 취급한다. 그러므로 ①의 동사 have를 has로 써야 문법적으로 맞다.

해석 비록 육상이 많은 참여자 수를 가지고 있지만 참여자 대비 우승자 비율은 다른 어떤 개인 스포츠보다 높다. 2013년과 2014년 18,000명 이상의 남녀 참여자가 Division I에 참가한 반면 23명의 여자 중 한 명, 24명의 남자 중 한 명이 본선에 진출했다.

---

21 Employees with military service of more than 30 days but ① not more than 180 days must submit an application for reemployment no later than ② 14 days following completion of service (or within the next calendar day that application becomes possible when application within that period is impossible or unreasonable through ③ no fault of the employee). ④ No error.

정답 ④ No error

해설 ①의 'not more than + 수사'에서 'not more than'은 at most의 의미를 갖는다. ②의 following은 뒤에 목적어를 수반하며 14 days를 후치 수식하고 있다. ③의 no는 형용사로 명사인 fault를 수식할 수 있다. 따라서 정답은 ④이다.

해석 직원 중 군 경력이 30일 이상 180일 이하인 경우 군복무 종료 후 14일 이내에 재취업 원서를 내야 한다(아니면 기간 중 원서를 내는 것이 직원의 잘못 없이 불가능하거나 불합리할 경우 익일 제출도 가능하다).

---

22 As one of the few who boarded the aircraft at Gatwick 30 years ago ① bound for Naples, I was asked by the Advertiser's sports desk, ② four of them were not even born then — for my memories of the Town's cup-winning performance. It may be hard for these 20-something lads ③ to believe, but I was ④ even younger in 1970.

정답 ② four of them ⇨ four of whom 또는 and four of them

해설 ② 앞에는 'I was asked by'의 형태로 주어와 동사를 갖춘 문장이 왔다. 그러므로 뒤에 were not even born then의 주어가 될 수 있는 부분인 four of them은 접속사 없이 연결될 수 없으므로 and four of them 또는 four of whom의 형태가 되어야 한다.

해석 30년 전 Gatwick에서 Naples로 가기 위해 비행기를 탔던 얼마 안 되는 사람 중 하나로 나는 Advertiser의 스포츠 섹션기자들로부터, 그중 4명은 당시 태어나지도 않았다, Town의 우승 경험을 이야기해 줄 것을 부탁받았다. 아마 이것은 이들 20대 청년들이 믿기 어려울 것이지만 나도 1970년 당시에는 더 어렸었다.

---

23 The feelings ① associated with loneliness feed on themselves — the more lonely you feel, ② the harder this is to take steps to break out of loneliness. However, feeling lonely is a phase and does not have to be a constant way of being. ③ As with changing any patterns of behaviour, it may take effort and commitment ④ to begin to move out of feeling lonely.

정답 ② the harder this is ⇨ the harder it is

해설 'this is to take steps to break out of loneliness'에서 'to take steps ~' 이하가 진주어로 사용되었다. 따라서 가주어 it이 필요한 문장이다. 'it is harder to take steps ~ ' 문장이 원래의 문장이기 때문에 the 비교급을 쓰더라도 'the harder it is to take steps ~'가 되어야 하므로 정답은 ②이다.

해석 외로움과 관련된 감정은 자체적으로 커진다. 외로움이 클수록 외로움에서 벗어나기가 어려워진다. 그러나 외로움을 느끼는 것은 일시적이며 지속적일 필요가 없다. 행동의 변화와 마찬가지로 외로움에서 벗어나는 것은 노력과 책임이 따른다.

---

24 William Faulkner ① summed up his life as a writer in his Nobel Prize acceptance speech in 1949. It ② had been, he said, "a life's work in the agony and sweat of the human spirit, not for glory and least of ③ all profit, but to create out of the materials of the human spirit ④ something which did not exist before."

정답 ③ all profit ⇨ all for profit

해설 'not for glory and'의 표현에서 단서를 찾을 수 있다. 'least of all'은 '~이 아니다, 특히(그중에서도) ~아니다'라는 의미로 쓰였고 'not for glory and all for profit'으로 병치를 이뤄야 한다. 이때 all은 부사로 문법적으로 크게 신경 쓰지 않아도 된다. 'least of all profit'에서 least of all은 부사적 용법으로 쓰기 때문에 profit을 수식할 수 없다. 'I want to hurt you least of all.'에서 'least of all'이 부사적으로 쓰인다는 것을 알 수 있다.

해석 윌리엄 포크너(William Faulkner)는 1949년 노벨문학상 수상 연설에서 작가로서의 자신의 삶을 압축하여 묘사하였다. 포크너에 따르면 자신의 삶은 "인간정신의 고뇌와 땀으로 얼룩지고, 영광을 위해 쓴 것도 아니요, 금전적 이득을 위해 쓴 것은 더욱더 아닌, 다만 인간정신을 소재삼아 여태까지 존재하지 않았던 그 무엇을 창조하고자 썼던, 생애를 바친 하나의 작품"이었다.

---

25 A path that not only led to a film ① being made of his wildly inventive script but also to receive generous investments from abroad ② were purely a coincidence. But they really ③ latched on to it in a way that is unique even in film making. It's such ④ an honor they would do that for me.

정답 ② were ⇨ was

해설 ②의 주어는 A path에 해당한다. 'that not only ~ from abroad'까지가 주격 관계대명사에 해당하는 형용사절이다. 본동사로 단수형이 와야 하기 때문에 ②의 were를 was로 고쳐야 한다. ④에서는 such ~ that + 주어 + 동사 ~의 형식으로 쓴 것인데 이때 that은 생략이 가능하다. an honor 다음에 that이 생략된 구조로 볼 경우 문법적으로 오류가 없다.

해석 몹시 창의적인 대사로 영화를 만들게 하였을 뿐 아니라 해외에서 넉넉한 투자를 받을 수 있게 했던 그 경로는 단순히 우연의 일치였다. 하지만 그들은 영화계에서도 특이할 만큼 일에 몰두하였다. 그들이 나를 위해 일해준다는 것은 내게 영광이다.

26 Incentives typically range in value from $4 to $50, per survey or focus group, ① depended upon the length of the questionnaire and the time ② it takes to complete it. Simply ③ filling out surveys for money, participants in online focus groups ④ generally receive more than $25.

정답 ① depended upon ⇨ depending upon

해설 주어진 문장에서 본동사는 range가 된다. 그러므로 앞 문장은 주어와 동사를 갖춘 문장이고 range의 시제가 현재이므로 과거형 depended가 올 수 없고 의미적으로 현재분사형 분사구문이 와야 하기 때문에 정답은 ①으로 depending on이 되어야 한다.

해석 각 서베이나 중점그룹에 대한 인센티브는 설문지의 길이나 완성하는 데 드는 시간에 따라 일반적으로 4불에서 50불 사이에 있다. 금전적인 목적으로 설문지를 완성하는 온라인 중점그룹의 참여자들은 일반적으로 25불 이상을 받는다.

27 Darren and Vicky Hewitt, from Hartlepool, ① were stranded for around 18 hours and were forced to endure 60ft waves ② crashing over their yacht. They hailed those who rescued them ③ as "true heroes." From Spain, Darren, 31, told the us : "If the yacht had gone over abruptly we ④ would have left in the sea, 50 miles off the shore."

정답 ④ would have left ⇨ would have been left

해설 If the yacht had gone over abruptly에 이어지는 주절은 내용상 '~을 남겨두는 것'이 아니라 '남겨지게 되는 것'이므로 능동형이 아닌 수동형이 와야 하므로 ④의 would have left를 would have been left로 써야 한다. ③의 as는 hail A as B에 연결되므로 맞게 쓰였다.

해석 Hartlepool에서 온 Darren과 Vicky Hewitt은 18시간 동안 밧줄에 묶여 자신의 요트를 덮치는 60피트 이상의 파도를 견뎌내야 했다. 그들은 자신들을 구해준 사람들을 진정한 영웅이라고 칭송했다. 31세의 Darren은 스페인에서 우리에게 보낸 글을 통해 "만일 요트가 갑자기 떠내려갔다면 우리는 육지에서 50마일 이상 떨어진 바다에 남겨지게 될 뻔했다"고 말했다.

28 Although he had ① little hands-on experience with the extensive special-effects work ② an X-Men movie requires, Ratner says the six months he spent preparing Spiderman taught him more than he realized. "In that process of preparing Spiderman, I worked with animatics and ③ visual effect supervisors and artists, so I had an idea ④ of how it works," he says.

정답 ③ visual effect ⇨ visual effects

해설 명사 effect는 가산, 불가산 명사로 모두 쓰일 수 있다. '효과; (법률 등의) 효력; 영향; (약 등의) 효능'을 의미할 때는 가산명사로 쓰일 수 있으며 특히 '영화에서 시각효과, 특수효과'를 나타낼 경우에는 복수형으로 쓰인 것이 보편적이다. 따라서 관용적인 표현으로 ③의 '시각효과'는 visual effect가 아니라 visual effects로 암기해 두는 것이 좋겠다.

해석 비록 X-Men 촬영에 요구되는 폭넓은 특수효과와 관련된 직접적인 경험은 적었지만 Ratner는 그가 스파이더맨을 준비했던 6개월은 생각보다 많은 것을 배우게 했다고 밝혔다. "스파이더맨을 준비하며 애니메이션과 시각효과 전문가들과 일해보아 이것이 어떻게 운영되는지 알고 있다."라고 그는 말했다.

---

29 From the opening moments, we understand the authority that ① rests in Don Corleone (Marlon Brando). That he is a powerful man ② is as explicit as the fact that he wields ③ that power mercifully, within the context of the murder and mayhem that naturally ④ go with his territory. The Don is the head of a renegade organization, and, yes, he's a criminal with politicians in his pocket. But he has integrity.

정답 ④ go with ⇨ goes with

해설 'within the context of the murder and mayhem'의 구조를 살펴보자. ④ 부분에 쓰인 that은 관계대명사로 쓰였다. 선행사는 the context가 되기 때문에 동사는 go가 아니라 goes가 되어야 한다. ③에 쓰인 that은 지시형용사로 명사 power를 수식하고 있다.

해석 오프닝 장면에서 우리는 Don Corleone(Marlon Brando)에 주어진 권한에 대해 이해하게 된다. 바로 그가 영향력을 가진 인물이라는 점은 그가, 자신의 영역에서의 살인, 폭력등과 관련된 힘을 자비롭게 사용한다는 점만큼 명백하다. Don은 반사회 조직의 리더이며 정치인을 등에 업은 범죄인이다. 하지만 그는 성실성을 가지고 있었다.

---

30 Beware, though : If your baby seems good as gold, this may be the calm before the storm! He ① may have absorbed drugs from your system or at the very least ② is probably tired from squeezing his way through the birth canal, even if you had natural childbirth. He's not quite himself ③ yet, but, as you will read in the pages that follow, his real temperament ④ will be emerged soon.

정답 ④ will be emerged soon ⇨ will soon emerge

해설 동사 emerge는 '출현하다, 나타나다'라는 의미로 자동사로 쓰인다. 따라서 'be + p.p'의 형태인 수동태로 쓸 수 없기 때문에 정답은 ④이다.

해석 하지만 조심하라. 아기가 좋아 보인다면 이것은 폭풍전야일 수도 있다. 아기가 당신의 몸에서 약을 흡수하였거나, 자연분만을 하더라도 최소한 밖으로 나오기에 너무 피곤한 경우일 수도 있다. 아기는 아직 자신의 상태가 아니지만, 앞으로 읽게 되듯이 아기의 진정한 기질이 조만간 나올 것이다.

04 실전모의고사 정답 및 해설

01	③	02	①	03	③	04	③	05	②	06	②	07	④	08	③	09	③	10	③
11	②	12	②	13	④	14	①	15	②	16	③	17	②	18	①	19	④	20	④
21	④	22	④	23	③	24	③	25	②	26	③	27	①	28	③	29	①	30	①

[01-06] Choose the one that could best complete each of the following sentences.

01 **__________ was Jim wise and diligent, he was deeply egalitarian and his commitment to equality showed in everything he did, including our work together.**

① Never ② At least
③ Not only ④ Neither

정답 ③ Not only

해설 빈칸 뒤에 나와 있는 'was Jim wise'의 구조로 보아 도치가 된 것을 알 수 있다. 그러므로 빈칸에는 부정어에 해당하는 어구가 나와야 한다. 다시 뒤에 he was deeply가 온 것으로 보아 단순부사가 온다면 두 문장을 연결할 수가 없기 때문에 never, neither는 올 수가 없다. 접속사에 해당하는 상관접속사가 쓰인 ③이 정답이다.

해석 Jim은 현명하고 부지런했을 뿐 아니라 그는 평등주의자이며 평등에 대한 그의 책임감은 우리가 같이 한 일을 포함해 그의 모든 행동에 나타났다.

02 **You are moving way too fast. I think you need to slow down a little bit or you __________ just when the goal line is right in front of you.**

① will get exhausted ② exhausted
③ got exhausted ④ have been exhausted

정답 ① will get exhausted

해설 'when the goal line is right' 부분에서 단서를 먼저 찾을 수 있다. 부사절에서 현재형 동사가 쓰인 경우 주절에는 미래시제가 쓰일 수 있다. 그리고, 'you need to slow down a little bit'에서 문맥적으로 현재이지만 '앞으로 ~할 필요가 있다'는 의미에서 정답은 ①이다.

해석 당신은 너무 빨리 움직이고 있다. 내 생각에는 당신이 늦추지 않으면 나중에 골 라인을 앞두고 지쳐버릴 것 같다.

03 **She is ________ when she creates a work of art, ________ sketching a drawing, writing a poem, or composing a musical theme on her guitar or piano.**

① the happiest – whether it will be
② happiest – should it be
③ happiest – whether it be
④ the happiest – whether it was

정답 ③ happiest – whether it be

해설 최상급이라 할지라도 동일인에서 비교를 할 경우에는 정관사를 생략해야 한다. 첫 번째 빈칸에는 happiest가 와야 한다. 양보절을 나타낼 경우에는 동사원형을 쓰기도 하기 때문에 whether it be가 맞는 표현이다. 따라서 정답은 ③이다.

해석 스케치를 하건, 시를 짓건, 아니면 기타나 피아노의 곡을 쓰건, 그녀는 예술 활동을 할 때 가장 행복해한다.

04 **Now, ________ a single mother at home and a director outside home makes her as busy as a bee, yet she seems to enjoy her new way of life very much.**

① acting
② act such as
③ acting as
④ be acting

정답 ③ acting as

해설 주어진 문장에서 주절은 'yet she seems to enjoy ~' 부분이다. 빈칸에는 '접속사 + 주어 + 동사'가 축약된 분사구문이 올 수 있는 구조다. 이때 빈칸 뒤에 a single mother를 동사 act가 바로 목적어로 취할 경우 의미적으로 자연스럽지 않다. '~로서 역할을 하다'라는 의미가 되어야 하기 때문에 act as의 형태로 연결되어야 하기 때문에 올바른 현재분사형으로 쓰인 ③이 정답이다.

해석 이제 집에서는 남편이 없는 것처럼, 밖에서는 국장의 역할을 하는 것은 그녀를 벌처럼 바쁘게 만들었지만 그녀는 새로운 인생을 매우 즐기는 듯하다.

05 **Far bigger cuts in greenhouse gas emissions could be needed to prevent dangerous climate change than ________.**

① previous thought
② thought previously
③ previous thoughts
④ none of the above

정답 ② thought previously

해설 than 구조 뒤에는 과거분사가 올 수 있다. 이때 '주어와 동사'가 생략된 구조이기 때문이다. 이때 부사의 수식을 받을 수 있기 때문에 정답은 than thought previously로 쓰인 ②이다.

해석 생각보다 심각한 기후변화를 방지하기 위해 보다 많은 그린하우스 가스배출 제재가 이뤄져야 한다.

06 **One result was that Southern civilians probably had to ____________ during the war than Northern civilians did.**

① make real more sacrifices
② make more real sacrifices
③ making real sacrifices more
④ making sacrifices much real

정답 ② make more real sacrifices
해설 make의 3형식 구조와 more의 어순을 묻는 문제다. make의 목적어로 real sacrifices가 오고, 이때 many의 비교급인 more는 어순상 형용사 real보다 먼저 와야 하기 때문에 정답은 ②이다.
해석 하나의 결과는 남부의 시민들이 전쟁기간 동안 북부 시민들보다 많은 실질적인 희생을 치러야 했다는 점이다.

[07-08] **Choose the one that is grammatically NOT correct.**

07 ① Some are like volcanoes in that they pose no risk to us.
② You might have heard fire safety is important.
③ The policeman saw the suspected man enter the building.
④ You ought not make a noise in the museum.

정답 ④ ought not make ⇨ ought not to make
해설 조동사 ought to + 동사원형의 부정형은 ought not to + 동사원형이기 때문에 정답은 ④이다. ②에서는 'You might have heard (that) fire safety is important.'으로 목적격 역할을 하는 명사절 접속사 that이 생략된 것으로 파악해야 한다.
해석 ① 어떤 것들은 우리에게 아무런 위험을 일으키지 않는다는 점에서 화산과도 같다.
② 화재 대비 안전이 중요하다는 얘기를 들어보았을 것이다.
③ 경찰관은 용의자가 건물 안으로 들어가는 것을 보았다.
④ 박물관에서 떠들면 안 된다.

08 ① Man is no more than a reed, the weakest in nature.
② Barbara was not so young as I expected.
③ He studied harder because his master praised him.
④ This dictionary is even more useful than that.

정답 ③ harder ⇨ the harder

해설 'the 비교급'을 쓸 경우는 문장 내에 이유를 나타내는 구와 절이 올 경우다. 'because his master praised him.' 이 쓰였기 때문에 ③의 harder 앞에 정관사 the를 써야 한다.

해석 ① 인간은 자연에서 가장 약한 존재인 갈대에 불과하다.
② Barbara는 내 예상처럼 그리 젊지 않았다.
③ 그의 선생님이 그를 칭찬해 주었기 때문에 더 열심히 공부했다.
④ 이 사전은 그 사전보다 더욱 유익하다.

[09-30] Choose the one that makes the sentence grammatically INCORRECT.

---

09 I know the subject fairly well because I ① have been studying it for long time, so far, I ② have read about three textbooks that ③ are related to. ④ No error.

정답 ③ are related to ⇨ are related to it

해설 ③ 부분에서 three textbooks가 선행사로 쓰였고 그 뒤 that은 주격 관계대명사로 쓰였다. 그래서 동사 부분부터 시작해서 완전한 문장을 이루어야 하는데 전치사 to 다음에 와야 하는 목적어가 없다. 따라서 are related to를 are related to it으로 써야 한다. 이때 it은 the subject를 지칭하는 대명사다.

해석 나는 오랫동안 공부를 해 와서 그 과목을 잘 안다. 여태까지 관련 서적을 세 권 정도 읽었다.

---

10 There are no clues ① as to who he is or what he does, but it is clear by the man's ② fixed stare ③ that he symbolizes : Self-respect ④ in the face of persecution.

정답 ③ that ⇨ what

해설 ③ 뒷부분에 he symbolizes의 목적어가 없다. it은 가주어이며 진주어가 와야 하는 부분에 완전한 문장을 이끌고 오는 that만 온다면 문법적으로 오류가 있다. 따라서 what이 와야 한다. ① as to는 '~에 관하여'라는 의미를 갖는 전치사구로 쓰였다.

해석 그가 누구이며 무엇을 하는지에 대해서는 아무런 실마리가 없지만 그의 고정된 눈빛에서 그가 무엇을 추구하는지를 알 수 있다. 그것은 박해 앞에서의 자존심이다.

11 ① <u>Speaking</u> on BBC Radio 4's Today programme, Dr James said : "We're trying to sort of mimic what normal physiology ② <u>would like</u>." "It's just connecting ③ <u>all the three</u> components together so that they can talk to each other and then work in a way that ④ <u>delivers insulin</u> in a physiological manner."

정답 ② would like ⇨ would be like

해설 would like에서 like는 동사로 쓰였다. like의 주어로 normal physiology가 되어 의미적으로 자연스럽지 않다. would be like가 되어야 '~이 어떤지, 무엇과 같은지'의 의미가 되므로 정답은 ②이다. ④에서 insulin은 불가산 명사로 문법적으로 맞게 쓰였다.

해석 BBC의 라디오 4 프로그램에서 James 박사는 말하길 "우리는 정상적인 생리학과 같이 하려 하고 있다. 이것은 단지 세 개의 부분을 이어 그들이 서로 대화할 수 있고 인슐린 생리학적 방식으로 전달할 수 있도록 하는 것이다."

12 "Children ① <u>will</u> only work if they're motivated and they'll only ② <u>motivate</u> if they're interested. They are all intelligent creatures. The experience has to be interesting and entertaining. Why on earth ③ <u>shouldn't education</u> be a pleasure?" ④ <u>No error</u>.

정답 ② motivate ⇨ be motivated

해설 의미적으로 they는 동기부여를 주는 것이 아니라 동기부여를 받는 것이므로 능동태가 아니라 수동태의 형식으로 써야 한다. 따라서 ②의 motivate를 be motivated라고 써야 한다.

해석 아이들은 그들이 동기부여가 되었을 때에만 일을 하며 흥미를 가질 때만 동기부여가 된다. 그들은 똑똑하다. 그들과의 경험은 흥미롭고 재미있다. 왜 교육이 즐겁지 않겠는가?

13 Our vision is ① <u>to create</u> a green, sustainable urban village, built ② <u>by and for ourselves</u> using ③ <u>mostly</u> donated and/or recycled materials, solar and wind power, composting toilets, and ④ <u>grow</u> our own organic food in our gardens and on our farm. To read more about our vision, please see our website.

정답 ④ grow ⇨ growing

해설 ④에서 Our vision is to create ~ and (to) grow ~로 병치되는 것으로 파악할 수 있지만 의미적으로는 'using mostly donated ~'와 연결되어야 하기 때문에 현재분사 구문의 병치로 파악해야 한다. 그러므로 ④의 grow를 growing으로 써야 한다.

해석 우리의 비전은 대부분 기부 받거나 재활용된 자재, 태양 및 풍력발전, 퇴비용 변기, 유기농산물들로 이뤄진 환경 친화적이고 지속 가능한 도시마을을 만드는 것이다. 우리의 비전에 대해 자세히 읽으려면 우리의 웹사이트를 보십시오.

14 Injury is the worst thing that can happen to a pitcher. It ① has well documented that Jackson's numbers in Triple A are partly ② due to that. Recently it was revealed that he ③ has had a little arm trouble (very minor) throughout the year that prevented him from going out and throwing at 100% ④ every start.

정답 ① has ⇨ has been

해설 ① 부분에서 It은 가주어, that 이하가 진주어로 쓰였다. 동사 document는 타동사로 '~을 기록하다'라는 의미로 뒤에 목적어를 취해야 하는데 목적어가 없다. 따라서 ①은 능동형이 아니라 수동태가 되어야 한다. has documented가 아니라 has been documented가 문법적으로 맞다.

해석 투수에게 있어 부상은 최악의 상황이다. Jackson의 최근 트리플 에이 리그에서의 성적은 이로 인한 것이었다. 최근 그가 사소하지만 팔에 문제가 있었던 것으로 나타나 이것이 1년 내내 그가 100% 실력을 발휘하지 못한 원인으로 지적되었다.

15 Orta lives alone, ① having no knowledge of who she is, where she came from, or even ② who are her real parents. But one fateful night, the Empire and the Dragonmares ③ come tearing through the valley, destroying anything – and anyone – that gets in their way. They ④ make for Orta's tower, and break through the walls.

정답 ② who are her real parents ⇨ who her real parents are

해설 'who you are'이 어순이 맞다. '의문사 + 주어 + 동사'의 어순이 원칙이기 때문이다. 그러므로 ②에서는 'who are her real parents'를 'who her real parents are'로 써야 한다. ③에서는 come 다음에 유사보어로 현재분사가 온 것이다. ④에서는 make for가 '~로 향하다'라는 의미로 쓰였다.

해석 Orta는 자신이 누구인지, 어디서 왔는지, 또는 진짜 부모가 누구인지도 모르는 채로 혼자 산다. 하지만 한 운명적인 밤에 Dragonmare와 그 황제가 계속을 거쳐 와 모든 것과 모든 사람을 파괴했다. 그들은 벽을 부수고 Orta의 탑에 들어왔다.

16 Do you ① have trouble finding enough time to study? Do you frequently find yourself rushing to places, missing deadlines, feeling you ② have insufficient time for relaxation and personal relationships, or having a general sense ③ of overwhelming? Do you realize that you probably have ④ as many as 70 hours of available time each week?

정답 ③ of overwhelming ⇨ of being overwhelmed

해설 overwhelm은 타동사로 목적어를 취해 '~을 압도하다, 당황하게 하다'라는 의미를 갖는다. 전치사 of 다음에 overwhelming으로 쓸 경우 능동의 의미로 뒤에 목적어가 있어야 하는데 없기 때문에 수동형으로 써야 한다. ③을 of being overwhelmed로 써야 한다.

해석 충분한 공부시간을 갖는 데 어려움을 겪고 있습니까? 자주 시간에 늦고 기한을 넘기며 휴식과 인간관계를 가질 시간이 부족하거나, 일에 치이는 느낌을 갖고 있습니까? 당신은 당신이 일주일에 70시간을 가질 수 있다는 사실을 알고 있습니까?

17 As well read as I am, I have only read a fraction of even ① English language literature, and ② much less other tongues, but my own inner pattern detection system is ③ as close to flawless in sniffing out clichés as ④ anything could be.

정답 ② much less other tongues ⇨ much less those of other tongues

해설 ①에서 English language literature로 쓰인 것으로 보아 ②은 다른 언어들로 쓰여진 문학책이라는 의미가 되어야 한다. 그러므로 much less 다음에는 비교대상인 literature의 복수형인 those가 와야 하므로 정답은 much less those of other tongues로 수정해야 한다.

해석 책을 많이 읽었지만 나는 영어 문학책의 일부분만을 읽었을 뿐이며 다른 언어의 책은 더욱 적다. 그러나 나의 내적인 패턴인식 시스템은 상투어구를 찾는 데 있어 거의 완벽하다.

18 The tragedy of the commons is a term ① coining to describe the way that human populations overuse and undermaintain common resources, ② leading to their destruction. The evidence of the trend is everywhere, from our over-fished oceans, polluted air and ③ spendthrift use of fossil fuels to the ④ unloved public spaces and graffiti-covered buildings in many cities.

정답 ① coining ⇨ coined

해설 coin이 동사로 쓰일 경우에는 타동사로 목적어를 취해 '~을 신조어로 만들다'라는 의미로 쓰인다. a term을 후치 수식하며 뒤에 목적어가 없기 때문에 과거분사형이 되어야 하므로 ①의 현재분사형을 과거분사형인 coined로 고쳐야 한다.

해석 공유지의 비극이란 사람들이 공유자원을 남용하고 부실하게 관리한 결과 공유자원을 파괴하는 과정을 기술하기 위해 만들어진 용어이다. 이러한 추세가 존재한다는 증거는 남획된 대양, 오염된 공기, 화석연료의 낭비에서부터 시작하여 사람들이 기피하는 공공장소 및 그라피티로 뒤덮인 도시의 건물에 이르기까지 어디에나 존재한다.

19 Both books cover topics like Participatory Design (in that instance, in quite similar ways too). But Crabtree ① essentially just sketches in the sorts of things ② you would have to do. While he ③ does discuss what each technique involves and gives some illustrations, it's doubtful ④ if a reader could then go away and try the techniques out.

정답 ④ if ⇨ whether

해설 if는 타동사의 목적어 역할을 하는 것 이외에는 주어, 보어, 전치사의 목적어로 나올 수 없다. 따라서 가주어로 쓰인 it 다음에 진주어를 쓸 경우에는 that이나 whether를 써야 한다. 의미적으로 '~인지 아닌지'에 해당하는 어휘는 whether이므로 정답은 ④이다.

해석 두 개의 책이 모두 참여적 디자인의 토픽을(매우 유사한 형태로) 다룬다. 하지만 Crabtree의 책은 기본적으로 당신이 해야 할 것에 대해 가볍게 스케치하는 형식이다. 그가 각각의 기법에 대해 다루고 일러스트레이션을 주긴 하지만 독자가 이를 실제로 현실에 적용할 수 있을지는 의문이다.

20 If you can't ① make it through a 40-minute Fringe show without snacking, ② skip the show and just go for dinner—because when you try to eat a snack with a crinkly wrapper quietly, it ends up ③ being much louder and, therefore, much more ④ annoyed to the rest of us who snacked ahead.

정답 ④ annoyed ⇨ annoying

해설 'ends up being much louder'과 병치를 이루는 부분을 찾아내는 것이 단서다. much more annoyed에서 감정 분사인 annoyed가 과거분사로 쓰일 경우에는 주로 사람을 주어로 한다. 하지만 주어진 문장에서는 it ends up과 연결되기 때문에 annoying으로 써야 하므로 정답은 ④이다.

해석 만일 40분간의 Fringe 쇼를 버틸 수 있다면 스낵을 먹지 않고 나중에 저녁을 먹는 것이 낫다. 왜냐하면 소리 나는 봉투에 싸여 있는 스낵을 먹으려고 할 때 결국 너무 큰소리가 나게 되어 먼저 스낵을 먹은 사람들을 짜증나게 하게 된다.

21 None of the men ① dared speak. They could only stare as the bubble floated a few feet off the dirty floor. After a few seconds, Rip shook off his wonder and charged her, ② having had enough and being too ignorant ③ to recognize the true danger. Kevin, ④ the smarter of the three, shouted a warning too late.

정답 ④ the smarter ⇨ the smartest

해설 'the + 비교급'을 쓸 경우에는 뒤에 'of the two'의 형식이 나올 때 가능하다. 하지만 'of the three'가 쓰일 경우에는 'the + 비교급'을 쓰지 않고 의미적으로 최상급이 와야 한다. ④의 the smarter를 the smartest로 수정해야 한다.

해석 아무도 말하려 하지 않았다. 그들은 몇 피트 앞의 더러운 바닥에서 올라오는 거품만을 쳐다보고 있었다. 몇 초가 흐른 후 진정한 위험을 알기엔 너무 어리석었던 Rip은 놀라움에서 벗어나 그녀에게 다가갔다. 셋 중 가장 똑똑한 Kevin이 경고했을 땐 이미 늦었다.

22 ① Compared with placebo, kava extract is an effective symptomatic treatment for anxiety although, ② at present, the size of the effect seems small. The effect lacks robustness and is ③ based on a relatively small sample. The data available from the reviewed studies suggest that kava ④ be relatively safe for short-term treatment (1 to 24 weeks), although more information is required.

정답 ④ be ⇨ is

해설 suggest 동사가 that절을 취할 경우에는 직설법 시제 또는 가정법 시제로 써야 한다. 주어진 문장에서는 '~을 해야 한다'라는 의미로 쓰인 것이 아니라 '~라는 사실을 시사하다'라는 의미로 쓰였기 때문에 ④의 (should) be를 is로 써야 맞다. The data는 that절의 내용을 주장하는 것이 논리적으로 자연스럽지 못하기 때문이다.

해석 비록 현재 효과가 미미해 보이기는 하지만 위약과 비교하여 kava 추출물은 노이로제에 대한 효과적인 처방이다. 효과에 대한 검증은 표본수가 상대적으로 적고 일반화하기 어려운 상태이다. 더 많은 정보가 요구되기는 하지만 검토된 연구의 자료에 따르면 단기적인 처방(1-24주)에 있어 kava는 상대적으로 안전하다.

23 Now Friedman probably knows exactly how much unemployment ① this will cause. He probably knows how many people ② will lose their homes. He probably knows how many kids won't be able to ③ go to the college. He probably knows something of the social unrest that ④ could happen if the U.S. economy is hit with $100/barrel oil.

정답 ③ go to the college ⇨ go to college

해설 '학교에 (공부를 하러) 가다'는 go to school이지 go to the school이 아니다. 주어진 문장에서 대학교 건물로 가는 것이 아니고 대학에 진학하는 것이므로 ③의 정관사 the는 생략해야 한다.

해석 이제 프리드만도 이것이 어느 정도의 실업을 야기할 것인지 알 것이다. 그는 아마도 많은 사람들이 집을 잃고 얼마나 많은 아이들이 대학에 못가는지 알 것이다. 또 만일 미국경제가 배럴당 100달러대의 유가시대를 맞게 되면 어떤 사회적 혼란에 빠질지도 알 것이다.

24 The publish/subscribe model of podcasting ① is a version of push technology, ② in that the information provider chooses ③ to offer which files in a feed and the subscriber chooses among available feed channels. While the user is not "pulling" individual files from the Web, there is a strong "pull" aspect in that the receiver is free to ④ subscribe to a vast array of channels.

정답 ③ to offer which files ⇨ which files to offer

해설 ③에서 choose 동사 다음에 부정사가 온 것이 문법적으로 맞지만, offer의 목적어로 which files가 온 것이 자연스럽지 않다. 따라서 이때 '의문사 + to 부정사'의 형식을 떠올려야 한다. to offer which files가 아니라 which files to offer의 어순이 되어야 한다. 이때 which는 명사 files을 수식하는 의문형용사로 쓰였다.

해석 Podcasting의 발간/구독 모델은 정보 제공자가 어떤 파일을 제공할지 결정하며 구독자가 제공되는 채널 중에 고른다는 점에서 "밀기 기술(push technology)"의 일종이라 할 수 있다. 사용자가 개별적인 파일을 웹상에서 끌어내는 것이 아니고 수용자가 자유롭게 다양한 채널을 구독할 수 있다는 점에서 밀어내는 경향이 있다.

25 Because the river deposits more silt closer to its banks, the riverbed ① itself has been built up ② so little that the river's surface is actually higher than the surrounding land at about 11 feet above sea level. Only the natural levee along its banks is higher than the river's surface, ③ and since the levee is only a foot or two higher than the river's surface, the river is naturally ④ prone to overflow.

정답 ② so little ⇨ so much

해설 has been built up 다음에 so ~ that 구조로 연결되는 문장이다. 이때 동사를 수식하는 부사는 의미적으로 much가 와야 하므로 ②의 so little을 so much로 고쳐야 한다. ④의 prone은 형용사로 '~하기 쉬운, ~하는 경향이 있는'이라는 의미로 'be prone to'의 형식으로 쓰인다.

해석 강물이 강둑에 보다 많은 침적토를 옮기기 때문에 강바닥이 올라가고 강물도 해수면보다 11피트 이상으로 올라갔다. 자연적인 제방만이 강표면보다 높으며 제방 역시 강표면보다 1-2피트밖에 높지 않으므로 이 강은 자연히 범람의 위험을 갖고 있다.

26 Employees quite often ① kid themselves that a job change is a logical affair. Not true, especially at middle to senior levels. While the prospective employee has made a logical choice, his heart may "still not be there". He might look for something that ② appeals to his heart. When that happens, he ③ swept away. Comfort, emotional fit, the feel good factor are ④ all very important.

정답 ③ swept away ⇨ is swept away

해설 동사 sweep은 away와 함께 쓰여 '일소하다; 털어내다, 휩쓸다; (전염병 등이 많은 사람 · 가축을) 쓰러뜨리다'라는 의미를 갖는다. ③에서는 의미적으로 수동태가 되어야 하므로 is swept away로 고쳐야 한다. ①에서는 kid가 타동사로 '농담을 하다, 조소하다'라는 의미로 쓰였다.

해석 직원들은 자주 농담으로 이직은 논리적인 것이라고 말한다. 하지만 특히 중간관리자나 임원급에서는 그렇지 않다. 만일 직원이 이직하려는 합당한 선택을 내릴지라도 그의 마음도 거기에 있지는 않을 수 있다. 그는 마음을 옮길 수 있는 것을 찾을 것이다. 이런 일이 일어나면 그는 끝이다. 편안함, 정서적 적응, 기분이 좋아지는 등의 요인이 매우 중요하다.

27 The more yellow a banana is, ① the sweet it will taste. Bananas are fully ripened when brown spots appear on the peel. These bananas have a ② softer texture and are very sweet. The next time you and your family are at the grocery store, ③ buy two bunches of bananas—a bunch of yellow bananas to eat immediately and a bunch of ④ green-tipped bananas that will be ready to eat in 2-3 days!

정답 ① the sweet ⇨ the sweeter

해설 'The more yellow a banana is,' 부분을 단서로 'the 비교, the 비교'의 형식에 맞춰서 써야 한다. 그러므로 ①의 sweet의 원급을 sweeter의 비교급으로 고쳐야 문법적으로 맞다. ③의 buy는 명령문에서 you가 생략되어 동사원형으로 쓰였다. ④에서는 tip은 동사로 '~의 끝을 이루다'라는 뜻으로 과거분사형이 되어 bananas를 수식하고 있다.

해석 바나나가 더 노랄수록 그 맛이 더 달다. 바나나는 갈색 점들이 껍질에 나타날 때 제일 잘 익은 것이다. 이런 바나나들은 부드럽고 매우 달다. 다음에 당신과 당신 가족들이 상점에 갈 때 바나나 두 뭉치를 사라, 하나는 바로 먹을 수 있는 노란 것으로 또 하나는 초록색으로 2-3일 후 먹을 수 있는 것으로.

28 The warmer air over the land expands and becomes ① lighter. This creates a low pressure situation. The air over water is cooler and denser (heavier), ② than the land air and this creates a high pressure situation. The high pressure air over the water pushes into the low pressure area on the land. The air ③ moved in from the water toward the land pushes the lighter land air up and out of its way. This movement is ④ what causes a sea breeze.

정답 ③ moved ⇨ moving

해설 The air가 주어, pushes가 동사로 쓰였기 때문에 moved는 동사가 아니라는 것을 알 수 있다. 자동사 move가 명사를 후치 수식할 경우에는 과거분사형이 아니라 현재분사형으로 수식하며 능동의 의미를 갖는다.

해석 땅 위의 따뜻한 공기는 팽창하며 가벼워진다. 이로 인해 저기압이 형성된다. 물 위의 공기는 차갑고 땅 위의 공기보다 밀집되어(무거우며) 있으며 땅 위의 저기압 지역으로 밀려간다. 물 위에서 땅으로 이동하는 공기는 가벼운 땅 위의 공기를 진행방향에서 밀어낸다. 이러한 이동이 바닷바람을 만들어 낸다.

---

29 I was surprised at how ① <u>influentially</u> George Washington has been on all the presidents after him. The language they use in inaugural addresses and State of the Union messages ② <u>still has</u> Washingtonian echoes. I was surprised at how shy ③ <u>certain of</u> our Founding Fathers were about public speaking, even though they were gifted writers : Jefferson ④ <u>in particular</u>, and Madison even more.

정답 ① influentially ⇨ influential

해설 의문사 how 다음에는 how가 부사이기 때문에 형용사나 부사가 올 수 있다. 주어진 문장에서는 'George Washington has been' 다음에 올 수 있는 품사는 부사가 아니라 형용사가 되어야 한다는 것을 알 수 있다. 따라서 ①의 부사 influentially를 influential 형용사로 수정해야 한다.

해석 나는 George Washington이 이후의 대통령들에 얼마나 영향을 미쳤는지를 보고 놀랐다. 그들이 취임사에 사용한 단어들을 보면 워싱턴의 분위기가 난다. 나는 조국의 개국공신들 중 일부가, 그들의 글은 훌륭했지만, 얼마나 대중연설에 약했는지에 놀랐다. 특히 Jefferson이 그랬고 Madison의 경우 더했다.

---

30 This much I can declare of the Persians ① <u>with entire certain</u>, from my own actual knowledge. There is another custom which is spoken ② <u>of with reserve</u>, and not openly, concerning their dead. ③ <u>It is said that</u> the body of a male Persian is never buried, until it has been torn either by a dog or a bird of prey. That the Magi have this custom ④ <u>is</u> beyond a doubt, for they practice it without any concealment.

정답 ① with entire certain ⇨ with entire certainty

해설 전치사 with 다음에는 목적어로 명사가 와야 하는데 ①에서는 certain 형용사가 와서 문법적으로 오류가 있다. 그러므로 certainty 명사형으로 수정해야 한다. ②의 전치사 of는 is spoken of의 전치사이며 with reserve는 부사구로 '삼가해서, 조건부로'라는 의미를 갖는다.

해석 이만큼은 확신을 가지고, 나의 실질적인 지식을 통해 페르시아에 대해 주장할 수 있다. 비공개적으로 언급되어 왔던 죽음과 관련된 다른 풍습이 또 있다. 죽은 페르시아 남성은 개나 새들에 의해 훼손되기 전까지는 매장되지 않는다고 한다. 그들은 이런 풍습을 공개적으로 진행하기 때문에 Magi가 이런 풍습을 가진 것은 의심할 여지가 없다.

05 실전모의고사 정답 및 해설

01	③	02	④	03	③	04	②	05	③	06	④	07	②	08	④	09	②	10	①
11	①	12	③	13	①	14	②	15	④	16	②	17	④	18	③	19	③	20	①
21	④	22	③	23	③	24	②	25	③	26	①	27	②	28	③	29	①	30	③

[01-06] **Choose the one that could best complete each of the following sentences.**

01 **Unwilling to lose his filberts, and yet unable to withdraw his hand, ____________ and bitterly lamented his disappointment.**

① tears were in his eyes ② that tears were in his eyes
③ he burst into tears ④ it burst into tears

정답 ③ he burst into tears

해설 문두에 쓰인 'Unwilling to lose his filberts, and yet unable to ~' 이 부분은 being이 생략된 분사구문이다. 이때 분사구문의 주어는 주절의 주어가 같기 때문에 생략되었다. 의미적으로 이 분사구문의 주어가 될 수 있는 것은 사람이며 보기 항에서는 ③만이 정답이 될 수밖에 없다.

해석 자신의 체면을 잃지 않으려 하면서도 손을 빼지 못했던 그는 울음을 터뜨리며 자신의 실망을 한탄했다.

02 **He offers problem-solving guidance by way of narrative biography, ____________ his extensive experience in defining and tackling tough problems.**

① he described ② described
③ being described ④ describing

정답 ④ describing

해설 첫 부분에서 이미 주어와 동사를 갖춘 주절이 나와 있어서 빈칸에는 두 문장을 연결할 수 있는 장치가 있어야 한다. 보기 항에 접속사가 없기 때문에 분사구문이 와야 한다는 것을 알 수 있다. 빈칸 뒤에 'his extensive experience'가 목적어 역할을 할 수 있어 능동의 의미를 갖고 현재분사형이 올 수 있으므로 정답은 ④이다.

해석 그는 자신의 폭넓은 어려운 문제해결 경험을 설명한 서술식의 전기를 통해 문제해결에 대한 지침을 제시한다.

03 **He only worked the harder, concentrating upon his business those extra hours ______________ instead.**

① when another sort of home-life would have claimed
② that another sort of home-life would have been claimed
③ which another sort of home-life would have claimed
④ whose another sort of home-life would have been claimed

정답 ③ which another sort of home-life would have claimed
해설 those extra hours 뒤에 연결할 수 있는 구조를 묻는 문제다. 보기 항에 공통적으로 들어간 동사 claim의 용법을 먼저 살펴보자. claim은 타동사로 뒤에 목적어를 취할 수 있다. 따라서 those extra hours를 선행사로 하는 목적격 관계대명사가 필요하기 때문에 that이나 which가 와야 한다. ②에서는 claim 동사가 수동태로 되어 있어 정답이 될 수 없다. 정답은 ③의 which와 함께 'would have claimed'의 능동태 형식으로 쓴 것이 맞는 문장이다.
해석 그는 집에서 생활할 수도 있었던 나머지 시간을 사업에만 치중하며 열심히 일하기만 했다.

04 **Perhaps no other city in the world is so misunderstood as Las Vegas. Although "Sin City," as it is commonly called, ___________ for about 50 years, it has left an indelible impression on the American consciousness.**

① was only around
② has only been around
③ had only been around
④ only has been around

정답 ② has only been around
해설 '라스베이거스' 도시의 일부의 역사를 설명하는 문장으로 'it has left an indelible impression on ~'에서 현재완료로 표현하고 있고, 빈칸 뒤에 for about 50 years와 함께 기간을 나타내는 부사구가 쓰였기 때문에 정답은 ②이 될 수밖에 없다.
해석 아마도 라스베이거스처럼 잘못 이해되는 도시는 세상에 없을 것이다. 비록 죄악의 도시로 보통 불리고, 탄생한 지 50년 정도밖에 되지 않았지만 미국인들 뇌리에 지울 수 없는 인상을 남겼다.

05 **The summit was a key step towards realizing the plans, ________________ were merely investing with a view to a rapid £60m flotation.**

① eased fears that the hedge fund owners
② it eased fears which the hedge fund owners
③ easing fears that the hedge fund owners
④ easing fears what the hedge fund owners

정답 ③ easing fears that the hedge fund owners

해설 ①과 ②은 정답이 될 수 없다. ①에서 eased 동사가 동사의 병치가 되려면 마지막 부분에 'and 과거형 동사'가 또 하나 나와야 하는데 또 다른 동사가 발견되지 않는다. ②은 접속사 없이 두 문장이 연결될 수 없어서 정답이 될 수 없다. 결국, 분사구문이 쓰인다는 것을 알 수 있고 fears 다음에 동격의 that의 쓰인 ③이 정답이다. ④에서는 fears 명사 다음에 쓰인 what의 역할을 알 수 없다.

해석 그 회담은 계획을 성사시키고 헷지펀드 소유자들이 단지 6천만 파운드의 채권 발행을 목적으로만 참여한다는 우려를 종식시키는 주요 발단이 되었다.

---

06 **If you experience the same thing as I __________ now several times, I can guarantee you that __________ the battery completely will not help.**

① have had … charging
② had … to charge
③ had had … charging
④ have … to charge

정답 ④ have … to charge

해설 첫 번째 빈칸에는 the same thing as 다음에 주어 + 동사의 형식에 맞는 동사를 선택하는 문제다. if절에 experience라는 현재 시제가 쓰인 조건절이므로 가정법 시제가 아닌 직설법의 시제가 와야 한다. 두 번째 빈칸에는 that절의 주어에 해당하는 명사구가 와야 한다. 이 모두를 충족시키는 것은 ④이다.

해석 내가 몇 번씩 겪은 것과 같은 경험을 하고 있다면 배터리를 완전히 충전시키는 것은 도움이 안 된다는 것을 보장할 수 있다.

[07–08] Choose the one that is grammatically NOT correct.

---

07 ① Our teacher taught us that water boils at 100℃.
② Statistics shows that the population of the city has increased.
③ Neither of them has succeeded in the test.
④ The school is stricter about grades than it used to be.

정답 ② shows ⇨ show

해설 'Statistics'가 통계학이 아니라 '통계자료'라는 의미로 쓰여야 자연스럽고 이렇게 의미가 달라질 경우에는 동사를 '복수 취급'해야 한다.
① 불변의 진리를 나타낸다. 따라서 that절 속에 현재 시제를 쓰는 것이 맞다.
② than의 시제가 주절과 달리 과거가 될 수 있다(비교대상의 시제가 과거일 뿐이다).
④ either와 neither가 주어로 사용될 경우에는 단수 동사로 받는 것이 맞다.

해석 ① 우리 선생님은 물이 100℃에서 끓는다고 가르쳐 주셨다.
② 통계 자료는 그 도시의 인구가 증가해 온 것을 보여 준다.
③ 그들 중 누구도 시험에 합격하지 못했다.
④ 학교는 성적에 대해 과거보다 더 엄격하다.

08 ① The DMZ extends about two hundred kilometers from east to west.
② Katherine always looks her best in a dress of that color.
③ The temperature's rising by about three degrees a week.
④ The carrots are my favorite vegetable.

정답 ④ The carrots ⇨ Carrots

해설 '특정한 당근'이 아니므로 the를 없애야 하며, 'the + 보통명사 복수형'에 한정어구가 있는 것도 아니기 때문에 Carrots라고만 써야 의미적으로 자연스러운 문장이 된다.
① from east to west : 대구로서 관용적인 용법으로 쓰인다.
② a dress : any의 뜻인 부정관사가 명사 앞에 와야 한다.
③ a week : week 앞에 one, every의 뜻이 필요하므로 부정관사가 쓰여야 한다.

해석 ① DMZ(비무장지대)는 동쪽에서 서쪽으로 약 200킬로미터 뻗어 있다.
② 캐서린은 그런 색이면 어떤 옷이든 언제나 가장 아름답게 보인다.
③ 기온은 일주일에 약 3도씩 올라가고 있다.
④ 당근은 내가 제일 좋아하는 채소다.

[09-30] Choose the one that makes the sentence grammatically INCORRECT.

09 ① Paying for primary care ② by hour would be ③ better for both doctors and patients, and it ④ would return a measure of rationality to our health care system.

정답 ② by hour ⇨ by the hour

해설 'by + the + 단위명사'의 형식을 묻는 문제다. '일당, 시간당, 매달'을 표현하는 방법에 정관사 the를 써야 하므로 정답은 ②이다.

해석 주요 진료에 대한 지불을 시간당으로 하는 것이 의사와 환자 모두에게 좋으며 이것이 우리 보건시스템에 이성적인 제도를 제공할 것이다.

10 In order that people may be happy in their work, ① three these things ② are needed : They must be ③ fit for it. They must not do too much of it. And they must have a sense of success ④ in it. — John Ruskin

정답 ① three these things ⇨ these three things

해설 형용사의 어순으로 '지시형용사 + 수량형용사'가 되어야 하므로 ①에서는 three these things가 these three things로 수정해야 한다. ③과 ④에 공통으로 쓰인 it은 문맥적으로 their work를 지칭하므로 단수형의 지시대명사가 문법적으로 맞게 쓰였다.

해석 사람들이 직장에서 행복하기 위해서는 다음 세 가지가 필요하다. 적성에 맞아야 한다. 적정선 이상 일해서는 안 된다. 그리고 일에서 성공의 느낌을 받아야 한다. — John Ruskin

11 I am sure everybody is ① aware that the government's tough regulations to ban driving while you are ② on the phone, but ③ to my surprise, yesterday as I was coming back from post office, guess ④ what I saw?

정답 ① aware that ⇨ aware of

해설 ① 뒤의 that 뒤에는 '주어와 동사'의 형식이 와야 하는데 'the government's tough regulations'의 명사구가 왔기 때문에 aware that이 아니라 'be aware of'으로 써야 한다. ③은 'to one's 감정명사'는 '~하게도'라는 의미다.

해석 나는 모든 사람들이 운전 중 전화통화를 금지하는 정부의 강력한 규제에 대해 알고 있을 것이라고 확신했지만 놀랍게도, 어제 내가 우체국에서 돌아오던 중 무엇을 보았을지 맞춰 보아라.

05

12 "The total cost of manufacturing in China is not ① as cheap as it might appear to be", says Mr Howard. Shipping costs ② have been rising, containers are expensive and ③ staffs have to be maintained in ④ both countries to manage the operation. It is also difficult to react quickly if the market changes.

정답 ③ staffs ⇨ staff

해설 명사 staff는 'the people who work for an organization'의 의미로 그 자체에 구성원을 내포하기 때문에 '150 staff'이라고 표현하지 '150 staffs'라고 하지 않는다. 따라서 ③의 staffs를 staff로 수정해야 한다. 또한 뒤에 복수동사가 쓰인다.

해석 중국에서의 전체적인 생산비용은 생각만큼 그리 저렴하지는 않다고 하워드는 말한다. 선적비용은 오르고, 컨테이너는 비싸고, 이러한 작업을 관리하기 위해서는 양국에 직원들이 상주해야 한다. 더불어 만약 시장이 변하면 빠르게 대응하기도 어렵다.

13 She tapped him ① on his shoulder and asked ② if he remembered her ③ from previous brief ④ encounters when she'd told him about the photo project.

정답 ① on his shoulder ⇨ on the shoulder

해설 신체 부위를 나타낼 경우에는 '전치사 + 정관사 + 신체의 일부분'의 형식으로 쓴다. ①의 his 소유격을 정관사 the로 고쳐야 문법적으로 옳다. ④의 encounter는 명사로 쓰였고 복수 형태로 쓰일 수 있다.

해석 그녀는 그의 어깨를 툭 치고는 예전에 사진 프로젝트에 관해 그녀가 말했었던 때 만났던 것을 기억하느냐고 물었다.

14 He was also struck by ① a lack of awareness among clients about the extent ② at which in-house lawyers offer ③ advice on business matters, as well ④ as on legal issues.

정답 ② at which ⇨ to which

해설 the extent를 선행사로 할 경우에는 'to the extent : 어느 정도까지'의 표현을 쓰기 때문에 the extent at which가 아니라 'the extent to which'로 써야 맞다. 물론 to which절 이하는 완전한 절이 와야 한다. 정답은 ②이다.

해석 그는 사내 변호사들이 법적인 이슈뿐 아니라 비즈니스 관련 조언도 한다는 사실을 대부분의 고객들이 모르고 있다는 사실에 충격을 받았다.

15 For decades it was ① no more than a whispered rumour in the corridors of Soviet medicine but now ② a team of doctors claim to have proved ③ that Lenin, communism's greatest icon, ④ dying of syphilis.

정답 ④ dying ⇨ died

해설 to have proved that 이하에는 주어와 동사가 완전하게 갖춘 문장이 와야 한다. Lenin이 주어이고 communism's greatest icon은 동격 부분이다. 그러므로 ④의 dying은 동사의 형태가 되어야 하므로 died가 문법적으로 맞다.

해석 수십 년간 그것은 소련 의약계의 공공연한 루머일 뿐이었지만 이제 의료진들이 사회주의의 우상인 레닌이 매독으로 죽었다는 증거를 가졌다고 밝히고 있다.

16 A body ② pulled from Stockton Deep Water Channel late Thursday was believed to be ② those of an elderly longshoreman who appeared ③ to have been driving a truck that plunged into ④ the water.

정답 ② those ⇨ that

해설 ②에서는 문맥적으로 the body를 지칭해야 하므로 단수형의 that을 써야 한다. 비교대상을 나타낼 경우에는 this, these를 쓰지 않고 that, those를 쓴다. 단수 명사를 지칭하는지 복수 명사를 지칭하는지 주의해야 한다. ③의 완료부정사를 써야 appeared보다 한 시제 과거인 이전의 시제를 나타낼 수 있다.

해석 목요일 Stockton 해저채널에서 끌어올려진 사체는 트럭을 몰고 물로 뛰어든 것으로 보이는 나이 든 하역인부로 추정되고 있다.

17 ① All other holidays are in a more or less degree ② connected with conflicts and battles of man's prowess over man, of strife and ③ discord for greed and power, of glories ④ are achieved by one nation over another.

정답 ④ are achieved ⇨ achieved

해설 전체 문장의 주어는 'All other holidays'이고 본동사는 'are'로 이미 주어진 문제는 한 문장이다. 'of glories'에서 of는 'of man's prowess ~, of strife and discord, of glories'와 연결된 구조로 파악해야 한다. 명사 glories를 후치 수식할 경우 의미적으로 과거분사구 'achieved by ~'가 되어야 하기 때문에 ④의 are를 삭제해야 한다.

해석 모든 다른 공휴일들은 대개 일정 부분 인간 간의 분쟁이나 전쟁, 탐욕과 권력에 관련된 분쟁과 부조화, 국가들 사이에 일어난 영광과 관련되어 있다.

18 ① Considering that the ② existing international conventions, recommendations and resolutions ③ concerned cultural and natural property demonstrate the importance, for all the peoples of the world, of ④ safeguarding this unique and irreplaceable property.

정답 ③ concerned ⇨ concerning

해설 'cultural and natural property' 부분이 전치사 concerning의 목적어 역할을 해야 하기 때문에 ③의 concerned를 concerning으로 고쳐야 한다.

해석 국제적인 관습을 고려할 때 문화와 자연적 재산에 대한 제안과 해결책은 세계인들에게 이 독특하고 대체될 수 없는 재산의 보존에 대한 중요성을 알려준다.

19 The collection is ① made from 100% organic cotton ② grown in Paraguay and is the brainchild of two sisters ③ risen in South America. The natural color of the cotton that enhances the handmade quality of all their knits is a bit of a quiet respite from all the colors.

정답 ③ risen ⇨ raised

해설 'the brainchild of two sisters'를 수식하는 과거분사는 risen이 아니라 raised가 되어야 한다. 타동사 raise가 '기르다, 성장시키다'의 목적어를 후치 수식하기 때문에 자동사의 과거분사형 risen이 잘못 쓰였다. 이와 같은 원리로 ②에서도 과거분사 grown이 organic cotton을 수식하고 있다.

해석 이번 작품은 100% 파라과이산 유기농 면화로 만들어졌으며 남미에서 자라난 2명의 자매들이 만들어낸 작품이다. 수제품 니트의 품질을 보다 높여주는 면의 자연색은 다른 색깔들로부터 조금 떨어져 있는 듯한 느낌을 준다.

20 This minor point is important since it ① demonstrated to me that you miss small but significant facts and ② read into things that are not there, things that you want to see. Since you ③ have done this here and in other places in our discussion, I suspect that you have also done it in ④ determining to believe there is no God.

정답 ① demonstrated ⇨ demonstrates

해설 보통 '주어 + 현재완료 ~ since + 주어 + 과거동사'의 형식으로 쓰는 것이 일반적이다. 이때 since는 시간을 나타내는 접속사로 '~이래로'라는 의미를 갖는다. 하지만, 주어진 문장에서는 since가 이유를 나타내는 접속사로 쓰였고, 과거사건을 의미하지 않기 때문에 ①의 demonstrated를 demonstrates로 쓰는 것이 자연스럽다. ②에 쓰인 read 동사는 자동사로 into와 함께 '~의 뜻으로 해석하다'라는 의미로 쓰였다.

해석 이 사소한 점이 중요하다, 왜냐면 이것이 나에게 당신이 작지만 중요한 사실을 간과하여 없는 것을 보게 되고 당신이 원하는 것만을 보게 되었다는 점을 보여주기 때문이다. 당신이 여기저기서 있었던 토론에서 그렇게 한 만큼, 나는 당신이 신이 없다는 결정을 내릴 때에도 그렇게 했을 것이라고 의심하고 있다.

21 One attempt at a solution has already ① been hinted at in the process of defining the paradox. The notion that the linguistic term 'heap' is vague ② begs the question of whether or not further elaboration of our ③ existing language, or the inclusion of a meta-language, ④ removing the vagueness.

정답 ④ removing ⇨ could remove

해설 'whether or not' 이하의 부분을 분석해 보자. whether절 이하의 주어는 further elaboration이 주어로 쓰였다. 그 다음에 동사가 나와야 하는데 removing의 형태로 나와 있어 문법적으로 오류가 있다. 따라서 removing을 'could remove'로 고쳐야 한다. could까지는 정확하게 떠올릴 수 없다 하더라도 틀린 부분을 찾아내기만 하면 된다.

해석 해결을 위한 한 가지 시도는 이미 모순을 정의하는 과정에서 힌트가 주어졌다. heap이라는 언어적 용어가 모호하다는 점은 기존 언어의 확장 또는 메타언어의 포함이 모호성을 없앨 수 있는지 여부에 대한 질문을 유발한다.

22 Just a quick tip for ① those of you who might unexpectedly encounter the danger fruit this weekend : if the peach tastes funny, ② stop eating it right away – even if the odd smell you think you smell ③ go away each time to attempt to confirm it. Not at all. ④ No error.

정답 ③ go away ⇨ goes away

해설 even if 다음에 주어는 'the odd smell'이고 'the odd smell that you think you smell'로 목적격 관계대명사로 길어졌고, 그 다음에 동사가 와야 한다. 동사는 go away가 아니라 주어가 단수 명사이므로 goes away가 와야 하므로 정답은 ③이다. ①은 those가 단독으로 쓰일 수도 있고, those of us, those of you라는 표현도 가능하다. ②은 if절에 연결된 주절로 명령문의 형식이다. stop 다음에 동명사를 목적어로 취할 경우에는 '~을 그만두다'라는 뜻인데, 문맥적으로 맞게 쓰였다.

해석 이번 주말 위험한 과일을 먹게 될지도 모르는 사람들에 대해 조언하겠습니다. 만일 복숭아 맛이 이상하면 당장 그만 먹도록 하세요, 만일 이상한 냄새가 다시 확인해 보면 사라진다고 해도, 절대로 먹이지 마세요.

---

23 The arrest was made Wednesday evening when a detective located Derrick Larue White ① walking near the Cabell County Courthouse. The man was ordered ② to stop, but did not comply. A foot chase then ③ was ensued, and he was arrested. He ④ was charged with felony first-degree robbery and misdemeanor fleeing on foot.

정답 ③ was ensued ⇨ ensued

해설 동사 ensue는 자동사로 쓰인다. 타동사 용법으로 쓰이는 경우가 현대 영어에서는 드물다. 그러므로 단정적으로 'be + p.p'가 없다고 암기해도 지장이 없을 정도다. 그러므로 ③의 was ensued를 ensued로 수정해야 한다. ④은 '기소하다'라는 의미로 뒤에 전치사 with가 온다는 것에 주의해서 암기하자.

해석 지난 수요일 형사들이 Derrick Larue White가 Cabell 카운티 법정에서 나오는 것을 포착했을 때 체포가 이뤄졌다. 그는 멈추도록 명령받았지만 응하지 않았다. 곧 추격이 벌어졌으며 그는 체포되었다. 그는 1급 강도의 중죄와 도주에 따른 경범죄로 기소되었다.

---

24 Like his father, Bell was a ① noted speaker and involved in numerous scientific and philanthropic ② association. He was ③ founder of the American Association to promote the Teaching of Speech to the Deaf, and for a time he served as ④ president of the National Geographic Society. He was appointed a Regent of the Smithsonian Institution in 1898.

정답 ② association ⇨ associations

해설 형용사와 명사에 관한 수 일치 문제다. numerous 다음에는 복수 가산명사가 와야 한다. 따라서 ②의 association을 associations로 바꿔야 한다. 'scientific and philanthropic' 모두 형용사로 명사를 수식하는 어휘이므로 그 앞에 쓰인 numerous에 주의해야 한다. ③과 ④에서는 관사가 생략될 수 있는 문장이므로 문법적 오류가 없다.

해설 자신의 아버지처럼 벨은 유명한 연설가였고 많은 과학 협회 및 자선 단체에 관여했다. 그는 농아들의 언어 지도 프로그램을 활성화시키기 위한 미국 협회의 창립자였으며, 한동안 미국 지리학회 회장직을 지냈다. 1898년 스미스소니언 연구소의 평의원에 임명되었다.

25 The transfer of heat and water vapor from the ocean to the air above it ① depends on a disequilibrium at the interface of the water and the air. Within about ② a millimeter of the water, air temperature ③ is close to the surface water, and the air is nearly ④ saturated with water vapor.

정답 ③ is close to ⇨ is close to that of

해설 'air temperature'가 'the surface water'와 가깝다는 말이 논리적이지 않다. 'be close to'에서도 비교대상을 일치시키면서 진술해야 한다. 비교대상은 the temperature가 되기 때문에 'is close to'를 'is close to that of'로 수정해야 한다. 이때 that은 지시대명사로 the temperature를 지칭한다.

해석 대양으로부터 그 상층부 공기까지 열과 수증기가 전달되는 것은 해수면과 공기의 접촉면의 불균형 여부에 따라 달라진다. 수증기 약 1밀리미터 이내에서는 기온이 해수면 표면의 온도에 가깝고, 공기는 수증기로 거의 포화되어 있다.

26 The twentieth century has produced books of power not only in science and in politics ① but also philosophy and literature. However, ② this being an age of specialization, we often find that the influential ideas contained in these books have first been propounded or ③ mentioned in theses and papers for experts before reaching the layman. The popular magazine articles and the ④ works of interpretation come last.

정답 ① but also ⇨ but also in

해설 not only A but also B의 구조에서 A와 B의 형식은 같아야 한다. 주어진 문장에서 not only 다음에 in science ~가 온 것으로 보아 ①의 but also 뒤에도 전치사 in이 쓰여야 한다는 것을 알 수 있다.

해석 20세기에는 과학, 정치는 물론 철학과 문학에서도 강력한 서적들이 출판되었다. 하지만, 이 시대는 전문분야의 시대이므로 이 서적에 담긴 영향력 있는 사상들이 보통 사람들이 접하기 전에 전문가들을 위한 논문이나 문헌에서 먼저 주창되거나 언급된다는 사실을 종종 알 수 있다. 그러고 나서 대중잡지의 기사나 번역 작품으로 만나볼 수 있다.

27 Education if it is ① to be adapted to our modern needs must fit young people ② to understanding the problems raised by the situation. The ③ imparting of knowledge in education has always had two objects : on the one hand, to give skill ; and on the other, to give a vaguer thing which we may call ④ wisdom.

정답 ② to understanding ⇨ to understand

해설 'fit + 목적어 + to ⓥ'의 형식에 맞게 써야 한다. 다음과 같은 문장에서 살펴보자. 'The training fitted us to swim across the river.(그 훈련의 덕분으로 강을 헤엄쳐 건너갈 수 있게 되었다.)'에서 to swimming이 아니라 to swim으로 쓰는 것이 맞기 때문에 ②의 동명사형을 부정사로 고쳐야 한다.

해석 교육은 현대의 필요에 맞게 적응되려면 젊은이들이 상황에 의해 야기된 문제들을 이해할 수 있게 해주어야 한다. 교육에서 지식을 전달하는 것은 항상 두 가지 목적을 지녀왔다. 한편으로는 기술을 전해주는 것이고, 다른 한편으로는 우리가 지혜라고 부르는 어떤 더 막연한 무엇인지를 전달해 주는 일이다.

28 How ① much of the observed difference in contraceptive use between the two countries can be explained by differences in the quality of the national programs? Although we can not directly answer this question ② with these data, we argue that extra-programmatic factors must also be significant because the improvements in the Kenyan program, dated around the mid-1980's, ③ could have had enough time to be exclusively responsible for the sharp use differences observed by 1988-1989, when ④ the data were gathered.

정답 ③ could have had ⇨ could hardly have had

해설 전체적으로 문맥을 잘 살펴봐야 하는 건국대 또는 이화여대형 문법 문제다. 국가 가족계획의 질적 차이점을 피임약 사용으로 설명할 것인가, 아니면 그 외적인 문제로 설명할 것인가에 관한 주장이 이 글의 핵심이다. '외적인 요인이 중요하다'라고 설명하고 그 뒤에 피임약이 사용된 연도가 2년 정도에 지나지 않는다는 점을 설명하기 때문에 ③의 조동사 다음에는 문맥적으로 부정적 의미가 들어가야 한다.

해석 두 국가 사이의 관찰된 피임약 사용 차이가 국가 가족계획의 질적 차이점을 얼마나 설명해 줄 수 있을까? 비록 우리가 이 자료로 직접적인 설명을 할 수는 없지만, 프로그램의 외적 요인들 또한 중요하다고 생각한다. 왜냐하면 1980년대 중반부터 시작된 케냐의 프로그램 개선으로 인해 데이터가 수집된 1988~1989년 사이에 피임약 사용에 현저한 차이가 있다는 것만을 유일한 요인으로 추정할 수 있어 충분한 시간이 있었다고 보기 어렵기 때문이다.

29 In a recent study on family and family values, Americans ① <u>were asked of</u> their definition of the family. ② <u>Only 22 percent</u> thought a family was "a group of people related by blood, marriage or adoption." The definition ③ <u>preferred</u> by 74 percent was much broader. A family, ④ <u>the majority</u> felt, was "a group of people who love and care for one another."

정답 ① were asked of ⇨ were asked for

해설 동사 ask는 'ask me a question = ask a question of me'의 형식으로 쓴다. 하지만 'ask me for help'에서처럼 전치사 for를 쓸 경우도 있다. 주어진 문장에서는 '미국인들이 가족의 정의를 요청 받았기' 때문에 'asked Americans for their definition of the family'의 수동태 형식이 와야 한다. 수동태 형식에서도 전치사 for가 와서 'be asked for'로 써야 하므로 정답은 ①이다.

해석 가족과 가족의 가치에 관한 최근의 한 연구에서, 미국인들은 가족에 대한 그들의 정의를 묻는 질문을 받았다. 단지 22%만이 가족을 "혈연, 결혼, 혹은 입양에 의해 맺어진 사람의 집단"이라고 생각하고 있었다. 74%의 사람들이 선호하는 정의는 훨씬 더 광범위했다. 대다수의 사람들은 가족을 "서로 사랑하고 돌보는 사람들의 집단"이라고 생각하고 있었다.

30 Despite all the controversy, GM crops ① <u>are spreading</u> rapidly : in 2004 the area sown with them increased by 20%. Even though it faces considerable pressure from European customers, Brazil has lifted ② <u>its ban on</u> GM soy, and is getting ready to ③ <u>dispense</u> its other restrictions ; European customers are now free to choose whether to eat GM foods, or pay more for the old-fashioned kind. In Britain, at least, it seems inevitable that ④ <u>bio-engineered</u> crops will become commonplace.

정답 ③ dispense ⇨ dispense with

해설 동사 dispense는 전치사 with와 함께 '~없이 지내다, ~의 수고를 덜다, ~의 필요를 없애다'라는 의미로 쓰인다. ③의 타동사로 쓰인 dispense를 '자동사 + 전치사'의 형식으로 수정해야 한다. ②에서는 ban이 명사로 쓰였고 뒤에 전치사 on이 올바르게 쓰였다.

해석 모든 논란에도 불구하고, 유전자 변형 농산물은 빠르게 확산하고 있다. 2004년에 이런 작물이 재배된 지역은 20% 증가했다. 유전자 변형 농산물이 유럽의 소비자들로부터 상당한 압박을 받고 있음에도, 브라질은 유전자 변형 콩 작물 생산 금지를 해제했고, 다른 제한요소들을 없애고 있다. 유럽의 소비자들은 지금 그들이 유전자 변형 농산물을 먹는 것을 선택하든지, 아니면 재래식 재배법으로 생산된 농산물에 더 많은 가격을 지불할지를 자유롭게 선택하고 있다. 영국에서 적어도 생명공학의 농작물들이 보편화되는 것 역시 불가피해 보인다.

06 실전모의고사 정답 및 해설

01	①	02	④	03	④	04	④	05	④	06	②	07	①	08	④	09	①	10	③
11	③	12	③	13	③	14	④	15	①	16	③	17	①	18	②	19	③	20	④
21	①	22	③	23	①	24	②	25	②	26	③	27	②	28	③	29	①	30	①

[01-06] **Choose the one that could best complete each of the following sentences.**

01 **A licensee who changes the place __________ shall notify the Council of such change of address within 7 days.**

① which he lives in
② in that he lives
③ where he lives at
④ that he lives

정답 ① which he lives in

해설 the place를 선행사로 하는 관계부사는 where다. 이때 where는 in which로 바꾸어 쓸 수 있다. 전치사 in은 which절 안에 쓰일 수 있으므로 정답은 ①이다. ② 전치사 다음에 관계대명사 that을 쓸 수 없다. ③에는 at이 없어야 한다. ④에는 that he lives in으로 써야 문법적으로 맞다.

해석 그가 사는 곳을 변경한 허가대상자는 7일 이내에 그러한 주소의 변화를 알려야 한다.

02 **I studied in a private university with the help of a 50% scholarship and now I am willing to continue my studies but I __________ enough money to do so.**

① did not have
② will not have
③ had not had
④ do not have

정답 ④ do not have

해설 문맥적으로 but 앞에는 now I am ~으로 현재 시제로 진술하고 있기 때문에 빈칸에는 현재 상황에 대한 진술이 나와야 하기 때문에 정답은 ④이다.

해석 나는 50% 학자금을 지원받으며 사립대학에서 공부를 했고 지금도 계속 공부를 하고 싶지만 학업을 이어갈 충분한 돈이 없다.

03 **Substantial numbers of drivers say that it is completely unacceptable to drive 15 mph over the speed limit on freeways, yet admit ＿＿＿＿＿ that in the past month.**

① had done
② to have done
③ doing
④ having done

정답 ④ having done

해설 동사 admit은 동명사를 목적어로 취한다. 뒤에 in the past month로 보아 과거 사실에 대한 일을 인정하고 있는 진술이고, admit이 현재 시제로 쓰였기 때문에 목적어로는 '완료형 동명사'가 와야 하기 때문에 'having p.p'의 형식으로 쓴 ④이 정답이다.

해석 상당한 수의 운전자들은 고속도로에서 시속 15마일로 운전한다는 것은 절대 받아들일 수 없다고 말하지만, 지난달에는 그렇게 했다는 것은 인정했다.

04 **The most daring thing about the room is the pricing, but a lot of people don't mind paying ＿＿＿＿＿＿＿ to taste something truly outstanding.**

① double the price usual
② the usual double price
③ usual double the price
④ double the usual price

정답 ④ double the usual price

해설 double은 전치한정사로 쓰였기 때문에 정관사 앞에 와야 한다. 'double the price'의 어순에서 형용사 usual은 the usual price로 써야 문법적으로 맞기 때문에 정답은 ④이다.

해석 이 방과 관련해서 가장 충격적인 것은 가격이었지만 많은 사람들이 진정으로 뛰어난 것을 맛보기 위해 평소 가격의 두 배를 내는 것을 개의치 않았다.

05 **It is the same with design ; it's ＿＿＿＿＿ to have a hint unobtrusively available ＿＿＿＿＿ to ask your audience to memorize and track everything on the site.**

① prefer … rather
② more … than
③ just as … so
④ better … than

정답 ④ better … than

해설 it is 다음에 빈칸에는 it is good to V ~의 기본구조에 해당하는 문장이 올 수 있다. 이때 good의 비교급은 better이므로 정답은 ④이다. ③은 정답이 될 수 없는 이유가 it은 가주어이고 'to V ~' 이하가 진주어이기 때문에 as 뒤 이하가 문장으로 성립될 수 없다.

해석 디자인과 마찬가지로 사용자에게 사이트의 모든 내용을 외우고 따라오게 하는 것보다는 정도 내에서 힌트를 주는 것이 좋다.

06 **Botanists are not sure where the fist plant was grown or even ______________.**

① what plant was ② what plant it was
③ it was what plant ④ what plant was it

정답 ② what plant it was
해설 접속사 or로 연결되는 명사절의 병치문제로, 의문사가 명사절을 이끌 때 '의문사 + 주어 + 동사'의 형태가 되어야 한다. 보기 항에 쓰인 what은 의문형용사로 명사 plant를 수식해야 하며 주어는 it, 동사는 was이므로 정답은 ②이다.
해석 식물학자들은 어디에서 최초의 식물이 자랐는지 그것이 어떤 식물이었는지 확신을 갖지 못했다.

[07-08] Choose the one that is grammatically NOT correct.

07 ① The soldier entered into the building occupied by the enemy.
② The children who attend that school receive a good education,
③ Several years ago, he was badly off, but he is now better off than he used to be.
④ By our next anniversary, we will have been married for 5 years.

정답 ① entered into ⇨ entered
해설 enter가 '~에 들어가다'라는 의미로 쓰일 경우에는 타동사라서 뒤에 전치사 into를 쓰지 않는다.
해석 ① 그 병사는 적군이 점령한 그 건물에 들어갔다.
② 그 학교를 다니는 아이들은 좋은 교육을 받는다.
③ 몇 년 전, 그는 궁핍하게 살았지만 지금은 과거보다 잘살고 있다.
④ 다음 기념일까지는 우리가 결혼한 지 5년이 될 것이다.

08 ① You had better be on time, or we will leave without you.
② I overslept this morning because I didn't set my alarm clock.
③ I'm disappointed not to have been invited to the party last night.
④ I don't like the movies, most of them are imported from America.

정답 ④ them ⇨ whom
해설 I don't like the movies 다음에 most of them are가 연결되기 위해서는 접속사가 있어야 하거나 most of them에서 them이 whom이 되어야 한다.
해석 ① 당신은 정각에 와야 한다. 그렇지 않으면 우리는 당신 없이 떠날 것이다.
② 알람을 맞추지 않았기 때문에 나는 오늘 아침에 늦잠을 잤다.
③ 나는 지난 밤 파티에 초대받지 않았기 때문에 실망스럽다.
④ 나는 그 영화들이 싫다. 왜냐하면 대부분이 미국에서 수입되었기 때문이다.

[09-30] **Choose the one that makes the sentence grammatically INCORRECT.**

09 In closing let me say that I trust you may learn to love all the young folks in the story, ① as deep as I have, in introducing them ② to you. Like ③ many a book, it grows more and more interesting as the reader becomes well ④ acquainted with the characters.

정답 ① as deep as ⇨ as deeply as

해설 문맥적으로 as deep as 부분은 'learn to love'에서 love를 수식하게 된다. 그러므로 동사를 수식하는 품사는 부사가 와야 하므로 deeply를 써야 문법적으로 옳다.

해석 끝을 맺으며 이 이야기에 나오는 젊은이들을 나처럼 당신도 좋아하게 될 것이라고 믿고 있으며 그렇기에 소개하게 되었다는 말을 하겠다. 다른 많은 책들처럼 독자들이 등장인물에 대해 더 잘 알게 될수록 더욱 흥미진진해진다.

10 This information ① described below is designed as ② a guide only. It does not take the place of ③ immediately emergency medical attention. If you have ④ any doubts, call your doctor or 911 for emergency medical services right away.

정답 ③ immediately ⇨ immediate

해설 'emergency medical attention'어구는 명사구에 해당한다. 이를 수식하는 품사는 형용사가 되어야 하기 때문에 ③의 부사인 immediately는 immediate가 되어야 한다. ④의 any는 if절에 쓰일 수 있고 명사 doubt을 수식할 수 있으며 명사 doubt은 가산명사, 불가산명사 모두 쓰일 수 있다.

해석 아래에 제공된 이 정보는 가이드로서의 역할만을 하는 것으로 응급의료지원을 대체할 수 있는 것이 아닙니다. 만일 의문이 드는 상황이라면 의사를 부르거나 911 응급의료서비스를 즉시 부르십시오.

11 ① Although the combination of formal learning and informal learning already ② takes place at MIT, the relationship between them is sometimes undervalued in the way we think about education. The two ③ often treated as separate, perhaps because they ④ tend to take place in different physical spaces and times, and they often involve different groups of people.

정답 ③ often treated as ⇨ are often treated as

해설 treat는 타동사로 목적어를 취해야 하는데 밑줄에서는 목적어가 없기 때문에 수동태 형식으로 써야 한다. treat A as B의 형식에서 수동태로 쓰일 경우에는 'A be treated as B'가 되기 때문에 'are often treated as'로 써야 한다.

해석 이미 형식적인 학습과 비형식적인 학습이 MIT에서 이뤄지지만 둘 간의 관계는 우리가 교육을 생각할 때 과소평가되는 경향이 있다. 이 둘은 자주 독립된 것으로 생각되는데 아마도 서로 다른 물리적 공간과 시간에 의해 이뤄지고, 또 다른 그룹의 사람들에 의해 이뤄지기 때문에 그런 듯하다.

12 Man must find peace, tranquility, happiness, unity, love, and ① every good quality within his own life, within his own innermost heart. Only a person who does ② that can understand the difficulties, the pain, and the misery of others. ③ A man of wise will know this, understand this, and rectify ④ his own mistakes. Then he can help others.

정답 ③ A man of wise ⇨ A man of wisdom

해설 전치사 of 다음에 나와야 하는 품사는 명사라야 하기 때문에 ③의 형용사 wise는 명사형 wisdom으로 써야 한다. ②의 that은 does의 목적어이고 'Only a person can understand ~'로 연결되기 때문에 문법적으로 맞다.

해석 인간은 평화, 고요함, 행복, 일체감, 사랑, 그리고 그의 인생과 가슴속의 모든 좋은 것들을 찾아야 한다. 이를 할 수 있는 사람만이 고난, 고통, 그리고 다른 사람들의 불행을 이해할 수 있다. 지혜로운 인간은 이를 알고, 이해하고, 자신의 실수를 통해 강화할 것이다. 그리고 그때 비로소 남을 도울 수 있다.

13 As a post-script, I do wish someone ① would have the kindness to stretch-print those ② speeded-up action scenes, which only look ludicrous to modern eyes. If these films can be "colourised," they can be ③ restored to a more naturalistic speed. ④ No Error.

정답 ③ restored to ⇨ restored at

해설 a more naturalistic speed 부분이 전치사 to 이하와 연결되어 있다. speed는 전치사 at과 함께 쓰이기 때문에 ③의 전치사 to를 at으로 바꿔야 한다.

해석 추신으로, 현대인의 눈에는 이상하기만 한 속도가 너무 빠른 영화 장면들을 누군가 늘여서 프린트해 주었으면 좋겠다. 만일 이들 필름들에 색상이 넣어진다면 이것들은 보다 자연스러운 속도로 저장될 수 있을 것이다.

14 ① Once you have the basics (i. e. – how to construct a simple sentence), try to use them ② as much as possible. Instead of just saying "two" and pointing at the bananas, ③ learn to say "I'd like to buy two bunches of bananas," and then practice ④ to say it.

정답 ④ to say it ⇨ saying it

해설 동사 practice는 동명사를 목적어로 취하는 동사이므로 ④의 to say it을 'saying it'으로 바꿔야 한다. ①의 once는 접속사로 쓰였고 ②에서 much는 동사를 수식하므로 오히려 many로 쓰지 않는 것이 문법적으로 맞는 표현이다. ③은 Instead of ~, 다음에 you가 생략된 명령문이므로 맞게 쓰였다.

해석 당신이 기초를 닦은 후에(예를 들어 문장 구성)는 이를 최대한 사용하려고 노력하라. 바나나를 가리키며 두 개라고 하는 것보다는 "나는 두 뭉치의 바나나를 사고 싶다"라는 말을 배우고 말하도록 해라.

15 It is said that "Necessity is the Mother of Invention." If we need something, there is always a creative person around ① to invent. Where would our world be today without ② all of the millions of inventions that people use everyday? Quite often they ③ are put to use without a thought about their history, creation, or the imagination of the person who first had ④ the initiative to invent.

정답 ① to invent ⇨ to invent it

해석 'a creative person around'에서 around는 부사적 용법으로 쓰였다. 명사구를 수식하는 to 부정사구에 타동사가 쓰일 경우에는 바로 앞에 수식하는 명사가 부정사의 목적어 역할을 할 수 있다. to invent라고 쓸 경우 invent의 목적어가 a creative person이 되어야 하는데 문맥적으로 성립할 수 없다. 따라서 문맥적으로 need something에서 something을 받는 대명사가 필요하기 때문에 'to invent it'이라고 써야 논리적으로 맞는 표현이다.

해석 필요성이 바로 발명의 어머니라는 말이 있다. 우리가 무언가가 필요하다면 그곳에는 항상 창의적인 사람이 있어 그것을 발명한다. 우리가 매일 사용하고 있는 수백만 개의 발명품이 없다면 우리 세상은 어떨 것인가? 많은 경우 이러한 것들은 역사, 발명, 그리고 그것을 발명한 사람의 상상력에 대한 생각 없이 그냥 사용되곤 한다.

16 I saw Scott in concert on a Yoga Cruise and was just ① stunned by his playing. He is ② an Einstein on the guitar. At first his concert was ③ very unusual that I was disoriented and later I realized that it was because I had become so disconnected with nature and the inner music of the earth ④ that resides all around us.

정답 ③ very unusual ⇨ so unusual

해설 very unusual 다음에 that 이하를 분석해 보면 완전한 문장이 나와 부사절로 쓰인 것을 알 수 있다. 따라서 so ~ that 용법으로 써야 한다. ②은 고유명사가 부정관사와 함께 쓰여 '~와 같은 사람'이라는 의미로 쓰였다. ④의 reside는 자동사로 맞게 쓰였다.

해석 나는 요가 크루즈의 콘서트에서 Scott을 보았으며 그의 연주에 놀랐다. 그는 기타계의 아인스타인이었다. 처음엔 그의 콘서트가 너무 이상해서 헷갈렸으나 나중에 나는 내가 그동안 자연과 우리주변에 있는 대지의 음악에서 동떨어져 있어 그러했던 것을 알았다.

17 ① For the time of the Chou Dynasty (11th-3rd Century BCE), there was a man named Lao Lai-tzu, who was ② by nature extremely filial. He took care of both his parents and ③ provided for them with the choicest delicacies. After he himself ④ turned seventy, he never spoke about his age.

정답 ① For ⇨ During

해설 특정기간을 나타내며 'when ~?'에 대한 정보의 답은 during이 아니라 전치사 for를 쓴다. 따라서 정답은 ①이다. ②은 '천성적으로'라는 의미의 부사구이며 ③에서 provide는 provide for로 '부양하다'라는 의미로 쓰였기 때문에 4형식으로 쓰이는 공급동사의 의미를 갖는 provide의 형식과는 혼동해서는 안 된다.

해석 주나라때 Lao Lai-tzu라는 효자가 살고 있었다. 그는 부모님들을 모시고 있었으며 가장 맛있는 음식을 대접해드렸다. 그의 나이가 70이 넘게 되자 그는 자신의 나이에 대해 절대로 말하지 않았다.

18 The orbit of ① <u>the new dwarf planet</u> is even more eccentric than ② <u>Pluto</u>. Pluto moves from 30 to 50 times the sun-earth distance over its 250 year orbit, ③ <u>while</u> the new planet ④ <u>moves</u> from 38 to 97 times the sun-earth distance over its 560 year orbit.

정답 ② Pluto ⇨ that of Pluto 또는 Pluto's

해설 The orbit of the new dwarf planet과 Pluto와 비교하는 내용이다. 행성 자체를 비교하는 것이 아니고 the orbit of Pluto와 비교하는 것이므로 ②은 that of ~의 형식이나 's를 사용해서 표현해야 한다.

해석 새로운 난쟁이 행성의 궤도는 명왕성의 그것보다 더 특이하다. 명왕성은 지구와 태양 간 거리의 30 ~ 50배의 거리를 250년에 걸쳐 이동하는 데 반해 이 새로운 행성은 38 ~ 97배 거리를 560년에 걸쳐 이동한다.

19 When someone uses ① <u>a stolen card</u> and gets away with it, the bank refuses the charges, and so it is the store that ② <u>gets ripped off</u>. The store then finds ways to make up that loss – adding a bit of extra profit to all of their merchandise that we all ③ <u>end up to pay</u>. The same applies ④ <u>to shoplifting</u>, etc. All retails stores have built-in charges into their prices to cover for these kinds of losses.

정답 ③ end up to pay ⇨ end up paying

해설 '~로 끝내다'라는 의미는 end up ~ing로 표현한다. 따라서 ③의 to pay를 paying으로 써야 맞다. ①에 stolen은 '도난당한'이라는 의미로 명사 card를 수식하고 있다. ②은 get + p.p의 표현으로 rip off가 '(돈 · 재물을) 사취하다, 속이다'라는 의미로 문맥상 수동태 형식으로 쓰는 것이 맞다.

해석 누군가가 도난당한 카드를 사용하고 발각되지 않으면 은행은 비용을 부담하지 않고 그래서 결국 사기를 당하는 것은 바로 가게이다. 그래서 가게는 결국 우리 모두가 사는 제품에 추가적으로 이윤을 내면서 손실을 보충할 방법을 찾는다. 똑같은 것이 상품 절도 등에도 적용된다. 모든 소매점들은 이런 모든 손실들을 떠맡을 수 있는 내재되어 있는 비용부담분이 있는 것이다.

20 Why ① <u>was it that</u> the most talented women at the firm I worked for seemed to disappear shortly after the birth of their first or ② <u>second child</u>? And how was it that ③ <u>all the rising stars</u> at that firm were men, and ④ <u>those who</u> were dads, nearly all had stay-at-home wives?

정답 ④ those who ⇨ of those who

해설 ④ 뒤 부분에 나와 있는 nearly all이 주어이고, had가 동사이며 stay-at-home wives가 목적어다. 그렇다면 those who가 전체 문장에서는 부사구로 쓰여야 맞기 때문에 문법적으로나 의미적으로 전치사 of가 필요하다는 것을 알 수 있다.

해석 왜 회사에서 가장 재능 있는 여자들이 첫째 또는 둘째 아이를 낳은 후 사라지는가? 그리고 회사의 떠오르는 스타들은 남자들이며, 아이가 있는 경우 대부분이 아내가 전업주부인가?

21 Charlie Chaplin is extremely amorous and ① <u>he is difficult</u> to go without romantic relationships for very long. When he ② <u>is attracted to</u> someone, Charlie Chaplin pursues them very ardently and sometimes ③ <u>comes on</u> too strong. Doing creative work or artistic work can also satisfy ④ <u>the very strong desire</u> for love and beauty that Charlie feels.

정답 ① he is difficult ⇨ it is difficult for him

해설 ①에서 난이형용사 difficult의 주어는 사람으로 쓸 수 없다. 따라서 'it is difficult for him'으로 써야 맞다. ②은 타동사 attract의 수동태 표현이다. ③의 come on은 '~라는 인상을 주다'라는 의미로 쓰였다. ④에서는 정관사 이하의 어순이 문법적으로 오류가 없다.

해석 찰리 채플린은 극도로 연애를 즐겼으며 그에게 장기간 연애를 하지 않는 것은 불가능했다. 그가 누군가에게 끌릴 때에 그는 정열적으로 이를 좇았으며 어떤 경우 너무 강하게 나가기도 했다. 창의적인 작업이나 예술 활동 역시 찰리 채플린이 느낀 사랑과 아름다움에 대한 욕구를 충족시켜 줬다.

22 The city of Montreal ① <u>lies</u> in the east of Canada, just 50 miles ② <u>north</u> of the border with the USA. It has a total population of 3.3 million and ③ <u>situated</u> on an island in the Saint Lawrence River and ④ <u>on</u> its adjacent shores.

정답 ③ situated ⇨ is situated

해설 situate는 타동사로 '~에 위치해 있다'는 'be situated'라고 써야 한다. 앞에 and의 구조로 이어지고 있어 앞문장의 구조를 살펴보아야 한다. 'It is ~ and ~'의 구조라면 is가 공통이라서 ③의 과거분사 형태로만 써도 병치의 원칙에 맞지만 'It has ~ and ~'의 구조라서 has가 공통으로 쓰일 수가 없기 때문에 'is situated'가 되어야 한다.

해석 몬트리올은 캐나다 동부에 있으며 미국과의 국경에서 50마일 떨어져 있다. 인구는 330만명이며 세인트로렌스강의 섬과 그 근접한 연안에 위치해 있다.

23 Moreover, of the various efforts ① <u>made on</u> the improvement of university education, ② <u>those which</u> are unique and superior have been selected and broadly <u>publicized</u>. This way, universities are able to use the efforts of other universities as ③ <u>a reference to</u> promote the revitalization of ④ <u>higher education</u>.

정답 ① made on ⇨ made toward

해설 made 과거분사는 앞의 명사구인 the various efforts를 후치 수식하고 있다. 기본 구조는 'make the various efforts ________ the improvement'가 되어야 한다. 의미적으로 '~을 위한, 향한 노력'이라는 해석이 완성되어야 하므로 전치사 on을 for 또는 toward로 고쳐야 한다.

해석 게다가 대학의 교육개선을 위한 다양한 노력 중에서 독창적이고 우월한 것들은 선택되어 널리 알려졌다. 이런 방식을 통해 대학들은 다른 대학들의 노력을 참고로 삼아 고등교육을 새롭게 발전시킬 수 있다.

24 Up the hill from this location ① was a village built by the North British Railway for the railway employees. Employees had to travel by train to go shopping and ② attended church as there ③ were no roads to the location. In the 'v' of the junction at the south end of the station was a signalbox ④ lying between the lines to Carlisle and Hexham.

정답 ② attended ⇨ (to) attend

해설 의미적으로 ②의 attended는 had to의 had와 연결되어 과거형으로 쓰였다는 것을 알 수 있다. 그러나 문맥적으로 '쇼핑을 하고, 교회에 가고 ~'라고 해야 '기차를 타는 목적'을 나타낼 수 있다. 따라서 'to go shopping and (to) attend ~'가 되어야 맞다.

해석 여기서 언덕을 올라가면 노스 브리티쉬 철도공사(North British Railway)에서 직원들을 위해 지은 마을이 나온다. 길이 없었으며 직원들은 기차를 타고 쇼핑을 하고 교회에 가야 했었다. 남쪽 끝의 v자의 교차로에는 캐리슬(Carlisle)선과 핵스햄(Hexham)선 간의 신호탑이 있었다.

25 Ziegler looks at the ① increasing corporate conflicts and legal restrictions ② to be imposed ③ on free speech, particularly when it comes ④ to political speech.

정답 ② to be ⇨ being

해설 look at은 지각동사로 쓰였고 목적어 다음에는 동사원형이나 현재분사가 와야 한다. 수동태가 올 경우에는 적어도 (being) p.p의 형태가 와야 하므로 정답은 ②이다.

해석 지글러는 점점 커져가는 조직의 갈등과 특히 정치적인 강연에 대해 언론 자유에 부과된 법적인 제한을 보았다.

26 An ear is the organ used by a human or an animal ① to detect sound waves. The term may refer to the entire system responsible for collection and ② early processing of sound, or merely the ③ external-visibly part. Not all animals have ears in the same part of the body. Audition is the scientific name ④ for the sense of hearing.

정답 ③ external-visibly ⇨ externally-visible

해설 어순에 관한 문제다. '관사 + 부사 + 형용사 + 명사'의 어순이 기본적 구조다. 따라서 ③의 명사 part를 수식하려면 '부사 + 형용사'의 형태가 되어야 하므로 각 어휘의 품사를 수정해야 한다.

해석 귀는 인간이나 동물들이 음파를 탐지하는 데 사용되는 기관이다. 이 용어는 소리를 수집하고 초기 처리하는 것 또는 외부에 보이는 부분을 의미한다. 모든 동물이 모두 같은 부위에 귀를 가지고 있지는 않다. 청각은 들을 수 있는 감각의 과학적인 용어이다.

27 Her husband, Frank Foster, who ① died in June 1996, left ② little her money, and he had no life insurance. But in April 1999, Mrs. Foster said, she ③ received more than $200,000 in the settlement of a lawsuit ④ brought when her mother died in "horrible conditions" in a Wylie nursing home.

정답 ② little her ⇨ her little

해설 먼저 수량형용사에 속하는 little이 명사를 수식해서 little money가 되고 소유격을 나타내는 형용사 her가 그 앞에 와서 'her little money'가 되어야 형용사의 어순에 맞게 쓴 것이다.

해석 1996년 6월에 사망한 그녀의 남편, Frank Foster, 그녀에게 얼마 안 되는 돈을 물려줬으며 생명보험에 들지 않았었다. 하지만 1999년 4월 Foster 부인은 말하길 그녀는 그녀의 어머니가 와일리(Wylie)의 양로원에서 최악의 상태에서 죽은 것에 대한 소송의 합의금으로 20만불 이상을 받았다고 말했다.

28 She remembered her mother ① mainlining with a dirty needle injecting its discolored point into a dirtier thigh. She remembered her mother as ② a drunken lady who refused to cook a meal ③ to her children or wash either their clothes or ④ them or herself.

정답 ③ to her children ⇨ for her children

해설 4형식 동사를 3형식으로 전환할 때 간접목적어가 뒤로 가면 전치사 for를 쓰는 동사에 관한 문제다. cook, order, choose, call 동사가 이런 형태를 쓴다. 따라서 ③의 전치사 to를 for로 써야 한다.

해석 그녀는 그녀의 엄마가 더러운 주사기의 색깔이 더러워진 끝을 더 더러운 허벅지의 정맥에 주사하던 일들을 기억하고 있다. 그녀는 그녀의 엄마를 아이들이나 자신을 위해서 밥을 하지도 않고 옷도 빨지 않는 술 취한 여인으로 기억하고 있었다.

29 Of the 19 ① alleging hijackers identified by the FBI, at least six turned up ② alive after the attack. The FBI's identifications included names, photographs, and, in several cases, other personal details – ③ all of which matched the six persons who ④ surfaced after the attack to proclaim their innocence.

정답 ① alleging ⇨ alleged

해설 동사 allege는 타동사로 뒤에 목적어를 취해 '증거 없이 주장하다'라는 의미로 쓰인다. 주로 '추정되는, 의심받는' 의미로는 alleged 과거분사형을 쓰지 능동형의 alleging를 쓰지는 않는다. 따라서 정답은 ①이다.

해석 FBI에 의해 공중납치 혐의를 받고 있는 19명 중 적어도 6명은 공격 이후 살아남았다. FBI의 신원파악 내용에는 이름, 사진, 그리고 많은 경우 신상명세가 있었다. 이들은 모두 공격 이후 나타나서 결백을 주장하고 있는 이들 6명에 대한 사실과 일치했다.

30 Next week, the incredible heat across the Southwest, especially Southern California, ① <u>ease</u> just a bit Monday and ② <u>into</u> Tuesday. A strengthening, onshore flow ③ <u>will begin</u> to cool the immediate coast. Thunderstorms will also retreat ④ <u>back toward</u> the east as more stable air pushes in from the west.

정답 ① ease ⇨ eases

해설 문장의 주어와 동사 일치에 관한 문제다. 주어는 the incredible heat이 되고 동사는 ease가 되어야 하는데, 주어는 단수이므로 ease가 아니라 eases가 되어야 한다. 미래를 나타내는 현재 시제는 흔히 미래를 나타내는 부사(tomorrow, next week 등)와 함께 쓰일 수 있기 때문에 will ease라고 써도 맞고 현재형으로 써도 문법적으로 맞다.

해석 다음 주 월요일에서 화요일 사이 남서부 특히 남부 캘리포니아에 걸쳐 있는 뜨거운 바람이 약세를 보인다. 바다에서 불어오는 차가운 공기가 연안지역 온도를 낮출 것으로 보이며 안정적인 대기가 서쪽으로부터 밀려나옴에 따라 천둥번개는 동쪽으로 물러날 것으로 보인다.

06

07 실전모의고사 정답 및 해설

01	②	02	③	03	①	04	③	05	③	06	①	07	③	08	③	09	③	10	④
11	④	12	③	13	③	14	③	15	③	16	①	17	③	18	②	19	②	20	③
21	④	22	①	23	④	24	②	25	②	26	③	27	③	28	③	29	①	30	④

[01-06] Choose the one that could best complete each of the following sentences.

01 **He did not know who was saying these things to him nor did he know what it meant _________ back home.**

① him coming ② for him to come
③ for his coming ④ he would come

정답 ② for him to come
해설 what it meant에서 it은 가주어로 쓰였기 때문에 빈칸에는 진주어에 해당하는 to 부정사가 와야 한다. 부정사의 의미상 주어는 'for + 목적격'으로 나타내기 때문에 정답은 ②이 된다.
해석 그는 이런 것을 누가 그에게 얘기했는지 잘 몰랐고, 그가 집으로 돌아오는 게 무엇을 의미하는지 잘 몰랐다.

02 **Upon arriving in Tucson one could hardly miss how _________, sort of in perpetual drought.**

① a desert city may be dry ② may a desert city be dry
③ dry a desert city can be ④ a desert city dry may be

정답 ③ dry a desert city can be
해설 의문사 how절이 miss 동사의 목적어에 해당한다. 의문부사 how는 형용사를 수식하므로 제일 먼저 how dry의 어순을 갖추어야 한다. 그리고 나서 how + 형용사 + 주어 + 동사의 순서로 나와야 하기 때문에 정답은 ③이다.
해석 투손(미국 애리조나 주의 도시)에 도착하자마자, 누구라도 사막이 얼마나 메마를 수 있는지에 대해 그냥 지나칠 수는 없다. 일종의 끊임없이 계속되는 가뭄과 같이.

03 **However, if Shawn _________ to Alabama, he would owe the company an extra 50 percent to buy the contract out.**

① were to return ② was to return
③ is to return ④ were returned

정답 ① were to return

해설 주절에 '주어 + would 동사원형'이 나왔기 때문에 주어진 빈칸에는 가정법 과거에 해당하는 'if + 주어 + were / 과거동사'의 형식이 쓰여야 한다. 따라서 정답은 ①이 된다. ④이 정답이 될 수 없는 이유는 return은 자동사로 '~로 돌아오다'라는 의미를 갖고 수동태로 쓸 수 없기 때문이다.

해석 그렇지만, 숀이 앨라배마로 돌아온다면 그는 주식을 사들이기 위하여 회사에게 추가적인 50% 빚을 더 져야 한다.

---

04 **He doesn't believe in God, but ____________ occasionally because he believes everyone should grapple with key moral questions in life.**

① go to church ② went to church
③ goes to church ④ goes to the church

정답 ③ goes to church

해설 but 다음에 주어는 he가 생략될 수 있다. '교회에 가다'는 문맥적으로 '예배드리러 가는' 것이기 때문에 정관사 the를 쓰지 않아야 한다. 시제는 현재 시제로 써야 하므로 정답은 ③이다.

해석 그는 신을 믿지 않지만 모든 사람들이 인생에 있어 중요한 도덕적인 질문에 대해 생각해 봐야 한다고 믿기 때문에 가끔 교회에 간다.

---

05 **Such is life in an Internet age ; an age that __________ the way the reporters had approached the Watergate investigation had it occurred today.**

① would be greatly changed ② would greatly change
③ would have greatly changed ④ would have been greatly changed

정답 ③ would have greatly changed

해설 'had it occurred today.' 부분이 가정법 과거완료에서 if절이 생략된 형태이기 때문에 빈칸에는 '주어 + would have p.p'의 형태가 와야 한다. change 동사는 자동사와 타동사의 용법으로 모두 쓰일 수 있지만, 주어진 문장에서는 굳이 수동태로 쓸 이유가 없어서 ③이 정답이 된다.

해석 인터넷 시대에는 인생이란 그런 것이다. 만약 오늘날 그런 일이 일어났다면 워터게이트 사건에 접근했던 보도의 방식이 엄청나게 바뀌었을 그런 시대이다.

---

06 **Any student may enter college provided that the _________ requirements have been met : The student must have a 2.00 cumulative ___________ average and must demonstrate the ability to complete total requirements within nine semesters.**

① following — grade-point ② following — grade-pointed
③ followed — grade-point ④ followed — grade-pointed

정답 ① following … grade-point

해설 첫 번째 빈칸에는 '다음에 뒤따르는, 이어지는'이라는 의미로 쓰여야 하므로 following이 와야 하고, 두 번째 빈칸에는 '평균점수'를 의미하는 grade-point가 와야 하니까 정답은 ①이 된다.

해석 어떤 학생이라도 다음 요건사항들을 충족시킬 경우 입학이 가능하다. 2.0의 누적된 평균점수가 있어야 하며 반드시 9학기 이내에 전체 요건 사항들을 이수할 수 있다는 자질을 증명해야 한다.

[07-08] Choose the one that is grammatically NOT correct.

---

07 ① Kevin delivered a speech and was asked many questions afterwards.

② The doctor who examined the patient was very gentle.

③ The news that the candidate was elected president was shocked.

④ When will the media and other powerful elements in our society stop insisting that thinness is the ideal?

정답 ③ shocked ⇨ shocking

해설 감정분사는 기본적으로 사람을 주어로 쓸 경우 과거분사를 쓰며, 사물을 주어로 쓸 경우에는 현재분사형을 쓰기 때문에 ③의 'The news was shocking.'으로 써야 한다. ④에서 insist는 '~해야 한다'라는 주장의 의미로 쓰인 것이 아니라 직설법의 '~라는 사실을 단언하다, 역설하다'라는 의미로 쓰였기 때문에 thinness should be ~가 아니라 thinness is ~가 온 것이므로 문법적으로 오류가 없다.

해석 ① 캘빈은 연설을 하고 나서 많은 질문을 받았다.

② 그 환자를 진료했던 의사는 매우 친절했다.

③ 그 후보자가 대통령으로 선출되었다는 소식은 매우 충격적이었다.

④ 우리 사회의 언론과 다른 강력한 기관들은 언제 약한 것이 이상적이라고 주장하는 것을 멈출 것인가?

---

08 ① The students learned that the French Revolution broke out in 1789.

② Cities themselves generate heat from a lot of sources, including motor vehicles.

③ Helen was most intelligent of all the students.

④ If there is a fire in your home, you must stay close to the floor and leave the building immediately.

정답 ③ most intelligent ⇨ the most intelligent

해설 최상급을 나타낼 경우에는 정관사 the를 써야 한다. ①에서는 '과거의 역사적 사실'을 나타내므로 broke out이 과거형으로 맞게 쓰였다.

해석 ① 학생들은 프랑스 혁명이 1789년에 일어났다고 배웠다.

② 도시 자체가 자동차를 포함해 많은 원천에서 열기를 내뿜는다.

③ 헬렌은 모든 학생 중에서 가장 영리했다.

④ 만약 당신의 집에서 화재가 발생한다면, 반드시 아래층과 가까운 곳에 있다가 즉시 건물 밖으로 나와야 한다.

[09-30] **Choose the one that makes the sentence grammatically INCORRECT.**

09 The fabricated document is ① all the more extraordinary because it suggests that local Christian, Muslim and Sikh leaders ② are in support of the casino. In fact, all three faiths ③ explicitly oppose to gambling. ④ No Error.

정답 ③ explicitly oppose to ⇨ explicitly oppose
해설 oppose는 타동사로 전치사 to 없이 목적어를 취하기 때문에 ③의 전치사 to를 삭제해야 한다. ①은 'all the 비교급 + 이유를 나타내는 어구'의 형식대로 맞게 쓰였다.
해석 조작된 서류는 더욱더 가관이다. 왜냐하면 이것은 이 지역의 기독교, 무슬림, 시크교 지도자들이 모두 카지노를 지원한다고 했기 때문이다. 사실 세 개의 종교모두 도박을 반대하고 있음을 천명하고 있다.

10 Chomsky's work in the field of linguistics thirty years ago revolutionized the science and in the process ① transformed the field of psychology as well. He argued persuasively that language is an innate ability, ② unique to the human species, ③ that behaviorist learning principles cannot account for. For his work in the field, Chomsky has been called ④ Einstein of linguistics.

정답 ④ Einstein of linguistics ⇨ the Einstein of linguistics
해설 고유명사에 부정관사 또는 정관사를 써서 '~와 같은 사람'의 의미를 나타낼 수 있기 때문에 ④의 Einstein 앞에는 정관사 the를 써야 한다. ③의 that은 cannot account for 다음에 나와야 하는 목적어를 선행사로 하는 목적격 관계대명사로 쓰였다. 선행사는 an innate ability다.
해석 30년 전 언어학에서 Chomsky의 연구는 이 분야에 혁명을 일으키고 그 과정에서 심리학마저 변화시켰다. 그는 설득력 있게 언어는 행동과학자가 원칙을 연구한다고 알 수 없는 인간만이 타고난 능력이라고 주장했다. 그의 업적으로 인해 그는 언어학의 아인슈타인이라고 불렸다.

11 "You shut the door, then," said the goblin, ① pointing to the door that ② had never been closed, "and I'll wash the pearl." So the little girl ran to close the door, and the goblin began to rub the pearl ; but it only seemed to grow darker. Now the door had been open so long that ③ it was hard to move, and it creaked on its hinges as the little girl ④ trying to close it.

정답 ④ trying to ⇨ tried to
해설 as the little girl에서 as는 전치사가 아니라 접속사로 쓰였기 때문에 the little girl을 주어로 하는 동사의 형태가 필요하다. 따라서 trying을 전체 문장의 시제에 맞게 과거동사 tried로 써야 한다.
해석 한 번도 닫혀본 적이 없는 듯한 문을 가리키며 "일단 문을 닫으면 진주를 씻겠다고" 요정은 말했다. 작은 소녀는 문을 닫기 위해 달려갔고 요정은 진주를 문지르기 시작했다. 그러나 진주는 오히려 더 더러워지는 듯 했다. 문은 너무 오랫동안 열려져 있어 닫기가 힘들었으며 소녀가 문을 닫으려 하자 옆 부분에서 소리를 냈다.

12 I ① remembering sitting next to this guy—in his mid-30s—and ② insisting to him that he looked like a Kennedy. He ③ dressed in a suit and I remarked ④ at how uncomfortable he must be.

정답 ③ dressed ⇨ was dressed

해설 동사 dress는 재귀대명사를 목적어로 'I dressed myself.'와 같이 쓰며 수동태로 'I was dressed.'로 나타내기 때문에 ③의 dressed를 was dressed로 써야 한다. ④의 at 다음에는 의문사절이 목적어로 올 수 있기 때문에 문법적으로 오류가 없다. 어순 또한 how 다음에 형용사가 오고 주어, 동사의 어순대로 썼기 때문에 맞게 쓰인 문장이다.

해석 나는 30대 중반 정도로 보이는 남자의 옆에 앉아 그가 케네디와 비슷하게 생겼다고 말했던 기억이 있다. 그는 정장을 입고 있었으며 그가 얼마나 불편했을 것인지에 대해 언급했다.

13 It's clever and does require ① some form of concentration behind it as you need to really pick up clues and what not, especially the really cool English ② they speak throughout the movie. Such as : "Yesterday you were better off than you are today, ③ but this took today for you to realize it. But today ④ has arrived and it's too late."

정답 ③ but this ⇨ but it

해설 'took a day for you to realize that.'에서 'for + 목적격 + to 부정사'가 진주어 역할을 하기 때문에 주어는 this가 아니라 가주어인 it이 필요한 문장이다. 따라서 정답은 ③이다. ②의 they speak는 앞의 명사 the really cool English를 목적격 관계대명사 that안에 있는 주어, 동사에 해당한다.

해석 이 얘기는 멋지며, (이를 이해하기 위해서는) 단서를 찾고 아닌 것을 걸러내기 위해서는 약간의 집중력이 필요하다. 특히 영화 내내 그들이 구사하는 세련된 영어의 경우 더욱 그러하다. 예컨대 "과거의 자신이 현재의 나보다 더 멋지지만, 이를 알아차리는 데 하루가 꼬박 걸렸다. 그런데 오늘이 돼서 보니 너무 늦었네."라는 얘기를 들으면.

14 The simplest explanation said that the Earth is round, not flat. Pythagoras noted that the shadow of the Earth ① falling on the Moon during a lunar eclipse was always curved and the amount of the curvature ② was always the same. The only object that always ③ cast a circular shadow regardless of ④ its orientation is a sphere.

정답 ③ cast ⇨ casts

해설 ③에서 always 다음에 쓰인 cast는 과거 형태다. 불변의 진리를 진술하는 부분이므로 현재 시제로 써야 한다. 따라서 cast가 아니라 casts가 되어야 한다. ②의 was는 and 앞 문장에서 쓰인 'was always curved ~' 부분과 병치를 이루고 있기 때문에 문법적으로 오류가 없다.

해석 가장 간단한 설명은 지구가 평평하지 않고 둥글다고 말했다. 피타고라스는 월식 동안 달에 지는 지구의 그림자는 곡선을 이루며 그 각도는 언제나 같다고 했다. 방향에 상관없이 항상 원형의 그림자를 만드는 것은 구형뿐이다.

15 A revolutionary cancer treatment available and which ① was hailed a "wonder drug" can damage the heart, scientists have warned. Glivec, which is used ② to treat leukaemia and a rare type of ③ the tumour, was the first of a new generation of so-called "magic bullet" cancer drugs. But now the researchers will have it ④ scrutinized for its side effects.

정답 ③ the tumor ⇨ tumor

해설 질병을 나타내는 어휘는 불가산명사로 써야 하며, a type of, a kind of, a sort of다음에는 무관사 명사를 써야 한다. 따라서 ③의 정관사 the를 삭제해야 한다. ①에서는 be hailed (as)의 형식에서 as가 생략된 형태이므로 문법적으로 오류가 없다.

해석 혁신적이며 기적의 약이라고 평가받던 암 치료제에 대해 이것이 심장을 해칠 수 있다고 과학자들이 밝혔다. 글리벡이라는 이 약은 백혈병과 특이종양의 치료에 쓰여 왔으며 "마법의 총알"이라고 불려왔으나 과학자들은 이제 이 약의 부작용에 대해 세밀히 조사할 것이다.

16 He requires that animals ① demonstrated human-like mental abilities in situations ② contrived, or ③ at least observed, by professional researchers. ④ No Error.

정답 ① demonstrated ⇨ (should) demonstrate

해설 require 동사는 that절 안에 should 또는 동사원형이 와야 하기 때문에 ①의 demonstrated는 (should) demonstrate로 써야 한다. ②에서는 situations (contrived or observed by ~)의 분석으로 과거분사형이 후치 수식하고 있기 때문에 문법적으로 오류가 없다.

해석 그는 전문연구직들이 설정한 또는 최소한 관찰하는 실험상황에서 동물들이 인간과 같은 정신적 능력을 보여주기를 요구하고 있다.

17 As Aristotle humorously puts it, "he is ① not the man to bolt and run away, ② swinging his arms." He harbors in his heart a certain noble scorn for the impertinence of aggressive wickedness and ③ in the pomp and pride of evil powers. He is not easily excited. He will meddle only with big things, and with ④ little things as they bear on big things.

정답 ③ in the pomp and pride ⇨ the pomp and pride

해설 He harbors의 목적어는 'a certain noble scorn'이다. 그 사이에 in his heart의 부사구가 온 구조다. 그러므로 ③의 and 다음에 전치사 in을 쓸 경우, 이 부사구가 in his heart와 병치를 이루는 부분이 될 수 없다. 문맥적으로 'aggressive wickedness'와 병치를 이루어야 하기 때문에 전치사 in이 없어야 한다.

해석 아리스토텔레스가 익살스럽게 표현한 대로, "그는 팔을 휘두르며 달려갈 사람이 아니다." 그는 주제 넘는 부도덕성과 악한 자들의 허례허식을 근본적으로 경멸하는 성격을 지녔다. 그는 쉽게 흥분하지 않는다. 그는 큰 문제를 가지고 씨름하거나 또는 작은 것이라도 큰 문제와 관련된 것만을 다룬다.

18 ① Whoever should imagine that I have intended to write a panegyric would be strangely mistaken, and on reading this book he will perceive that such was not my design ; nor ② it has been my object to advocate any form of government in particular, for I am ③ of the opinion that absolute perfection ④ is rarely to be found in any system of laws.

정답 ② it has been ⇨ has it been

해설 nor는 접속사로 '~도 역시 아니다'라는 의미로 뒤에는 'nor + 조동사 + 주어 + 동사원형'의 어순을 취한다. 따라서 정답은 ②이다. has it been으로 고쳐야 한다.

해석 누구든 내가 찬사문을 쓰려고 했다고 생각하는 사람들은 잘못 생각하는 것이며 이 책을 읽어보면 그것이 내 의도가 아니며, 내가 특정 정부를 홍보하려는 것이 아님을 알 수 있을 것이다. 왜냐면 나는 법 체계하에서 완벽한 것은 거의 찾을 수 없다는 의견을 갖고 있기 때문이다.

19 In high school, students may not have received comments on language problems, or they may have received only ① global remarks such as "you ② need keep working on your grammar." In order to help students ③ continue to acquire academic English and to correct patterns of error that may persist in their writing, they need ④ structured help.

정답 ② need keep ⇨ need to keep

해설 ②에 쓰인 need는 부정문에서 조동사 용법으로 쓰여 'need not + 동사원형'으로 쓰지만 주어진 문장에서는 일반동사로 쓰였기 때문에 to 부정사를 목적어로 취해야 한다. 따라서 need keep이 아니라 need to keep으로 바꿔야 한다.

해석 고등학교에서 학생들은 언어 문제에 대한 견해를 받지 못하거나 그냥 일반적인 "문법에 신경을 써라"라는 언급만 받을 것이다. 학생들이 학문적인 영어를 습득하고 오류를 고치기 위해서는 구조적인 도움이 필요하다.

20 Justified force, ① if used, should directly and intentionally target only the guilty, and the means ② used should be such as to avoid harm to others so far as possible. Michael Walzer has it right, I believe, in arguing that the moral principles governing the use of ③ force implication a special care to protect innocent parties from "collateral damage" due to force ④ aimed at the guilty.

정답 ③ force implication ⇨ force imply

해설 'in arguing that' 부분을 분석해보자. that절의 주어가 the moral principles이며 governing은 현재분사로 명사를 후치 수식하고 있다. governing의 목적어로 명사구가 와야 한다. the use of force가 바로 목적어에 해당한다. 그리고 a special care의 명사구가 어떤 기능을 하는지 따져 보어야 한다. 또한 that절의 동사가 없다는 것을 알 수 있다. 그러므로 implication은 that절의 동사 역할을 하면서 a special care를 목적어로 취해야 한다.

해석 정당한 힘은, 만일 사용된다면, 직접적으로 그리고 의도적으로 죄를 지은 자에게만 향해야 하며 사용되는 방식은 다른 쪽의 피해를 최대한 줄이는 방식으로 행해져야 한다. 나는 그런 면에서 힘의 사용에 대한 도덕적 원칙이 부수적 피해를 최소화해야 한다는 Michael Walzer의 주장이 옳다고 본다.

21 Global Dimming is a phenomenon ① that's been on the increase over the past 100 years. Basically, particles of pollution ② are thrown up into the atmosphere and block the sun. But that's not all — they also collect water molecules ③ around them in clouds, causing clouds to mirror-back the sunlight out into space. ④ No Error.

정답 ④ No Error

해설 ①은 주격 관계대명사 that과 over the past 100 years라는 부사구와 함께 현재완료형이 올바르게 쓰였다. ②에서 주어가 사물이기 때문에 의미적으로 수동태가 쓰였다. ③에서 around는 전치사이며 them은 molecules를 지칭하고 있다. 따라서 정답은 ④이다.

해석 지구가 흐릿해지는 현상은 지난 100년간 증가해왔다. 기본적으로 이것은 공해로 인한 입자들이 대기 중에 증가하며 태양을 가리는 것이다. 하지만 그것이 다가 아니다, 이들은 구름 주위의 수분을 끌어들여, 태양광선을 우주로 반사시키고 있다.

22 OSU has received ① $1.5 million grant from the prestigious Howard Hughes Medical Institute ② to bolster science education at all grade levels throughout the state. This grant will provide many young Oregonians with ③ experiences that will propel them into careers as scientists, which ④ is good for Oregon and the nation.

정답 ① $1.5 million ⇨ a $1.5 million

해설 grant가 '보조금, 조성금, 장학금'이라는 의미로 쓰일 경우 가산명사로 쓰이기 때문에 부정관사가 필요하다. ④의 is가 맞는 이유는 which의 선행사가 앞 문장의 내용을 받기 때문이다.

해석 OSU는 오레곤 주내 전체 학년들의 과학교육을 증진하기 위해 150만 달러의 기부금을 하워드 휴즈 의료기관으로부터 받았다. 이 기부금은 많은 젊은 오레곤 학생들에게 과학자로서 성장할 수 있는 경험을 제공하게 되어 오레곤 주와 국가 전체에도 좋을 일이다.

23 Jack Hubbard ① has been involved in print and broadcast journalism for more than four decades. He has been ② associate director at the Stanford News Service since 1992, and oversees news issues for broadcasters, ③ including live television and radio feeds, ④ coordinated live events and news conferences, and daily coverage of the university.

정답 ④ coordinated ⇨ coordinating

해설 ④은 'and oversees news issues'의 문장에 연결되는 현재분사 구문으로 써야 맞다. including의 목적어로 계속 연결되는 부분으로 분석하는 것이 아니라 '~을 감독 또는 조직하면서'라는 의미로 'S + V ~, coordinating + 목적어 ~.'의 구조가 되야 한다.

해석 잭 허바드는 그동안 인쇄 및 방송 저널리즘에 40년간 관여해왔다. 그는 1992년부터 스탠포드 뉴스서비스의 부국장으로 근무하며 실황중계, 뉴스 컨퍼러스, 일간뉴스 등 TV, 라디오 등의 뉴스를 감독해왔다.

24 The administration has been hiding ① <u>to the extent that</u> most Americans are not aware of just how dire it is and how ② <u>many progresses</u> has been made. They keep talking about how the Iraqi army ③ <u>is doing</u> much better and taking over responsibilities, but for the most part ④ <u>that's</u> not true.

정답 ② many progresses ⇨ little progress

해설 명사 progress는 불가산명사로 쓰인다. 따라서 much progress 또는 little progress로 써야 한다. 주어진 문맥에 따라 '진전이 얼마나 더딘지'라는 말이 자연스럽기 때문에 little progress가 와야 한다.

해설 정부는 그동안 미국인들이 얼마나 상황이 심각한지, 그리고 진전이 얼마나 더딘지를 모르도록 숨겨왔다. 정부는 이라크 군대가 얼마나 개선되었으며 책임을 떠맡고 있다고 말해왔지만 대부분 이것은 거짓이다.

25 So far scientists have not found a way ① <u>to determine</u> the exact age of the Earth directly from Earth rocks because Earth's oldest rocks have ② <u>recycled and destroyed</u> by the process of plate tectonics. If there ③ <u>are</u> any of Earth's primordial rocks left in their original state, they have ④ <u>not yet</u> been found.

정답 ② recycled and destroyed ⇨ been recycled and destroyed

해설 because 이하의 주어가 'Earth's oldest rocks'이며 동사가 recycled인데 have와 함께 능동형으로 쓰였다. 뒤에 by the process로 연결되는 것으로 보아 의미적으로나 형식적으로나 수동태가 와야 함을 알 수 있다. 따라서 have been recycled and (have been) destroyed의 구조가 완성되어야 한다.

해석 지구의 돌들은 그동안 지구판의 구축과정에서 재활용되었거나 파괴되어 아직까지 과학자들은 돌을 통해서 지구의 연령이 얼마나 되는지 결정하는 방법을 찾지 못했다. 만일 태초의 돌들이 원형대로 남아 있다면 그것은 아직 발견되지 않았다.

26 After dealing with far ① <u>too much water</u>, southern Louisianans must now cope with far too little : In the century that records ② <u>have been</u> kept, the region has never been so dry. The drought started in April of last year, and since then only hurricanes Katrina and Rita ③ <u>overfilled</u> rain gauges. Despite devastating flooding, climatologists worry Louisiana ④ <u>is</u> on the verge of exceptional drought conditions.

정답 ③ overfilled ⇨ have overfilled

해설 'since then'의 구조로 보아 주절에는 현재완료형이 와야 문법적으로 옳다. since 다음에는 과거 시점을 나타내는 어구가 와야 하는데 then이 이를 충족시키고 있다.

해석 그동안 물이 너무 많아 문제였던 남부 루이지애나주가 이제는 물이 너무 없어 고심하고 있다. 기록이 남아 있는 100년 동안 이 지역이 요즘처럼 가뭄이 심했던 적은 없었다. 지난해 4월 시작된 가뭄 기간 동안 태풍 카트리나와 리타를 제외하고는 강우량을 채워준 적이 없었다. 파괴적이었던 홍수에도 불구하고 기상학자들은 루이지애나주가 극심한 가뭄에 시달리고 있다고 우려하고 있다.

27 We ① stayed at the Atlantis and everything there was very expensive. The water activities were fun though. The island was absolutely ② breathtaking and was the most relaxing place that I ③ have ever been. A little tip is that there ④ is a strip of shops right of the grounds of the Atlantis with an excellent pizza place, and it is cheap!

정답 ③ have ever been ⇨ had ever been

해설 주어진 문장의 기준 시제는 '과거'다. the most relaxing place를 의미적으로 강조하기 위해 관계사절이 쓰였는데, 이때 시제는 현재완료가 아니라 대과거가 쓰여야 '그 이전에 이미 내가 가 보았던 곳'으로 연결되어 논리적이다.

해석 우리는 아틀란티스에 있었는데 그곳의 모든 것이 매우 비쌌다. 수상스포츠는 즐겁기는 했지만. 이 섬은 경관이 매우 좋았으며 내가 가본 곳 중 가장 편안한 곳이었다. 귀뜸하자면 아틀란티스 섬의 오른쪽으로 가게들이 늘어서 있는데 이 중 아주 훌륭한 피자 가게가 있고 가격도 아주 싸다.

28 When Boulanger's daughter crashed his car, ① an initial police report determined that she was at fault. In his capacity as ② police chief, Boulanger ordered ③ the second investigation, which determined that his daughter was not at fault in ④ the crash.

정답 ③ the second ⇨ a second

해설 일반적으로 서수사는 정관사 the와 함께 쓰는 것이 맞다. 그러나 second가 '2등, 2위'의 의미가 아니라 '또 한 차례의'의 의미로 쓰일 경우에는 부정관사와 쓰일 수 있다. 주어진 문장에서는 '재수사'라는 의미로 쓰였기 때문에 부정관사가 오는 것이 자연스럽다.

해석 블랑저의 딸이 그의 차로 사고를 냈을 때 첫 경찰보고서는 그녀의 잘못으로 판단하였다. 그러나 블랑저는 경찰서장의 권한으로 재수사를 명령하여 그의 딸의 잘못이 아니라는 결과를 얻어냈다.

29 Attacking Iran would ① height the risks to American and coalition forces inside Iraq. ② What if one hundred thousand Iranian volunteers ③ came across the border? They were going to come to Iraq before, but ④ didn't.

정답 ① height ⇨ heighten

해설 would 다음에 쓰인 height의 품사는 명사다. 올바른 동사의 형태는 heighten이므로 정답은 ①이다. ②의 what if는 '만약 ~라면 어떨까?'라는 의미로 쓰였고 ③의 동사구는 '건너다, 횡단하다'라는 뜻으로 뒤에 명사를 목적어를 받을 수 있다. ④의 didn't는 didn't come to Iraq의 구를 생략해서 쓰였다.

해석 이란을 공격하는 것은 이라크 내의 미국과 연합군의 위험을 증가시킬 것이다. 만일 수천만의 이란 자원군이 국경을 넘어오면 어떻게 될 것인가? 그들은 예전에도 이라크에 오려고 했지만 안 왔다.

30 This was striking, the researchers added, especially ① given that past research has shown aggression, misfortune and other negative thoughts tend ③ to weigh prominently even in healthy people's dreams. Yet the sleep disorder patients were no more violent in real life than ③ ordinary, the researchers wrote, and some past reports have suggested they may be even ④ little so.

정답 ④ little ⇨ less

해석 주어진 문장에서 no more ~ than의 비교급이 쓰이고 있고, 뒤에 연결되는 문장에서는 '오히려 덜 공격적인'이라는 문맥으로 완성되고 있다. even은 비교급을 강조하는 부사로 쓰이고 있기 때문에 ④의 원급 little은 비교급 less라고 써야 맞다.

해설 특히 과거 연구 결과가 공격성, 불행 등 부정적인 생각이 건강한 사람의 꿈에서조차 상당한 영향을 준다는 점에서 연구자들은 그것이 충격적이었다고 덧붙였다. 그러나 수면장애환자들이 현실사회에서 정상인보다 공격적인 것은 아니라고 연구자들은 밝히고 있다. 그리고 기존 연구에 따르면 수면장애환자들이 오히려 덜 공격적인 경우도 있다.

08 실전모의고사 정답 및 해설

01	④	02	②	03	④	04	③	05	④	06	②	07	③	08	①	09	①	10	④
11	③	12	③	13	②	14	②	15	④	16	③	17	②	18	④	19	③	20	①
21	②	22	③	23	②	24	④	25	④	26	①	27	②	28	①	29	②	30	①

[01-06] Choose the one that could best complete each of the following sentences.

01 **Man cannot live alone, ________ he live confined within the four walls of his close-knit family.**

① or can
② nor
③ and
④ nor can

정답 ④ nor can
해설 빈칸에는 he live가 들어갈 수 있는 어휘를 찾아야 한다. live가 동사원형으로 쓰인 것으로 보아 도치가 발생했고 이를 충족시키는 것은 nor밖에 없다. 따라서 정답은 ④이다.
해석 인간은 홀로 살아갈 수 없으며, 가족에게만 둘러싸여 살아갈 수도 없다.

08

02 **No High Fructose Corn Syrup : If you prefer your coffee ________, our white chocolate powder and natural caramel are a great option.**

① to be sweetened
② sweetened
③ being sweetened
④ that is sweetened

정답 ② sweetened
해설 prefer 동사가 5형식으로 쓰일 경우에는 'prefer + 목적어 + 과거분사'를 쓰기 때문에 정답은 to be가 들어간 ①이 아니고 ②이다.
해석 더 이상의 액상과당은 없다. 만약 당신이 커피를 달게 마시고 싶다면 우리가 제공하는 화이트 초코릿 파우더와 천연 캐러멜을 넣어라.

03 **For the first thing which a scholar should bear in mind is that a book ________ for mere amusement.**

① ought to not be read
② not ought to be read
③ ought to be not read
④ ought not to be read

정답 ④ ought not to be read
해설 조동사 'ought to + 동사원형'의 부정형은 'ought not to + 동사원형'이다. 따라서 정답은 ④이다.
해석 맨 처음 학자가 마음에 새겨야 할 것은 책은 단지 즐거움을 위해 읽혀서는 안 된다는 것이다.

04 **There was a man who checked out of a hotel, and after he went out, he realized that he ________ his umbrella so he went back inside.**

① had been forgotten
② forgot
③ had forgotten
④ has forgotten

정답 ③ had forgotten
해설 시제에 관한 문제다. he realized that ~으로 보아 동사 forget은 문맥적으로 had p.p가 되어야 하므로 정답은 ③이다.
해석 그곳에는 호텔에서 체크아웃을 하고 나오는 남자가 있었으며 그는 나온 후 그가 우산을 잊었다는 것을 알고 다시 안으로 들어갔다.

05 **As you walk toward the maintenance shop, you will ____________ and see light gray smoke coming from the window.**

① something burning smell
② smell burning something
③ burning smell something
④ smell something burning

정답 ④ smell something burning
해설 빈칸에는 조동사 will 다음에 동사가 먼저 와야 한다. '~thing, ~body'로 끝나는 어휘는 형용사가 후치 수식을 하게 되므로 정답은 ④이다.
해석 정비소를 향해 걸어가면서 무언가 타는 냄새와 창문에서 나오는 연한 회색의 연기를 볼 수 있을 것이다.

06 **Most causes of infection (bacteria and viruses) are quite fragile and only able to survive in ______________.**

① a temperature range very narrowly
② a very narrow temperature range
③ a range very narrowly temperature
④ a very narrow range temperature

정답 ② a very narrow temperature range
해설 survive in 다음에는 결국 명사를 만나야 한다. 보기 항에서 명사로 끝나는 것은 ②와 ④밖에 없다. range temperature와 temperature range 중에서 복합명사의 어순을 잘 따르고 있는 것은 ②이다. '온도 범위'의 의미를 지니고 있기 때문이다.
해석 감염(박테리아, 바이러스)의 대부분의 경우가 매우 취약한 정도이며 단지 극히 제한된 범위의 온도 내에서만 생존할 수 있다.

[07-08] **Choose the one that is grammatically NOT correct.**

08

07 ① When I opened the window, a bird flew into the room.
② Everyone was amazed at the change in his appearance.
③ We will reach for the top of the mountain in five minutes.
④ Light from the nearest star has been traveling for 4 years.

정답 ③ reach for ⇨ reach
해설 reach는 '~에 도달하다'라는 의미로 타동사 용법으로 쓰기 때문에 뒤에 전치사 for를 삭제해야 한다.
① flew는 fly의 과거동사로, 이 문장에서는 자동사로 맞게 쓰였다.
② 사람을 주어로 쓸 경우 감정분사인 amazed가 과거분사형으로 맞게 쓰였다.
④ 형용사 near가 최상급을 쓸 경우에는 전치수식이 가능하다. 시제 또한 맞게 쓰였다.
해석 ① 내가 창문을 열었을 때, 새 한 마리가 방으로 날아들어 왔다.
② 그의 외모 변화에 모든 사람이 놀랐다.
③ 우리는 5분 후에 그 산 정상에 올라갈 것이다.
④ 가장 근접한 별에서 오는 빛은 4년 동안 이동해왔다.

08 ① Tom wondered where Jane was. He had not seen her from their quarrel.
② I had intended to leave the party before midnight.
③ Whether he graduated from a college or not doesn't matter.
④ If we are willing to open our minds and listen and learn, we may be able to overcome our ignorance.

정답 ① from ⇨ since
해설 완료 시제와 함께 쓰이는 전치사는 since가 오기 때문에 전치사 from을 since로 써야 한다.
② 'had + 소망동사의 과거분사형 + to 부정사'는 이루지 못한 소망을 나타낸다.
③ Whether 명사절이 주어로 쓰였고 graduate 다음에 from 역시 맞고, matter는 '중요하다'라는 의미로 자동사로 쓰였다.
④ if절이 단순조건절로 쓰여서, 주절에 현재형 조동사가 쓰였다.
해석 ① Tom은 Jane의 어디에 있었는지 궁금해 했다. 그들이 싸운 이래로 Tom은 Jane을 보지 못했다.
② 나는 자정 전에 파티에서 떠나려고 했으나 그러지 못했다.
③ 그가 대학을 졸업했는지 안 했는지는 중요하지 않다.
④ 만약 우리가 마음을 열고 듣고 배우려고 한다면, 우리의 무지를 극복해 낼지도 모른다.

[09-30] Choose the one that makes the sentence grammatically INCORRECT.

09 My weekly workout ① consists in jogging ② two to four kilometers two to three times a week. During summer, I run on the beach and swim. In the winter months, my jog ③ takes me around Sydney's Centennial Park. I also change my routine and run on the weekends during summer. ④ No Error.

정답 ① consists in ⇨ consists of
해설 consist in은 lie in의 의미로 '~에 있다, 존재하다'라는 의미다. 주어진 문장에서는 '~로 구성되다'라는 의미가 논리적으로 맞게 때문에 ①의 전치사 in은 of로 고쳐야 한다.
해석 나의 주간 운동계획은 일주일 동안 2-3회의 2-4킬로미터 조깅을 하는 것이다. 여름에는 해변가를 뛰거나 수영을 한다. 겨울에는 조깅으로 시드니의 센트럴파크를 돈다. 여름에는 일정을 바꿔서 주말에 뛰기도 한다.

10 ① The reason why difference in profession ② makes one feel worlds apart and two of a trade can ③ never agree ④ due to a lack of mutual understanding.

정답 ④ due to ⇨ is due to
해설 전체 문장의 주어는 The reason이다. 이를 관계부사인 why가 수식하고 있다. why절안의 주어는 difference와 two of a trade가 된다. 따라서 전체 문장의 주어인 The reason의 본동사가 없다는 것을 알 수 있다. 그러므로 ④의 due to는 is due to 로 써야 한다.
해석 직업의 차이로 인해 서로 다른 세계에 사는 느낌이 들고, 합의를 이루지 못하는 이유는 상호 이해가 부족하기 때문이다.

11 We walked out and ① checked everything out, but I'm not going to write about ② all that right now ③ because of I want to do a photo diary ④ in a day or two.

정답 ③ because of ⇨ because

해설 because of 다음에는 명사구가 목적어로 나오고 because 뒤에는 주어, 동사가 나와야 하기 때문에 ③의 전치사 of를 삭제해야 한다.

해석 우리는 모든 것을 훑어보고 검토했지만 그것에 대해 지금 글을 쓰지는 않을 것이다. 왜냐하면 하루나 이틀 후에 포토다이어리를 만들 것이기 때문이다.

12 Neither of the books ① is laden with heavy technical or academic jargon, and the essays flow together ② quite smoothly. Going Green may appeal to ③ wider audience, with lots of photographs, uncrowded pages, and large print captions in the wide margins — ④ somewhat of a coffee table book for activists.

정답 ③ wider audience ⇨ a wider audience

해설 ③에 쓰인 audience는 집합명사로 '많은 관객'을 'a large audience'라고 하기 때문에 부정관사가 없다는 것을 알 수 있다. 물론 정관사 the를 못쓰는 것은 아니다. ④의 somewhat of는 '다소간, 얼마'라는 의미를 갖는다.

해석 두 책 모두 기술적이거나 학술적인 용어를 가지지 않았으며 에세이들은 자연스럽게 연결되었다. Going Green은 많은 그림과 넉넉한 페이지, 큰 활자와 여백으로 인해 아마도 많은 사람들에게 읽힐 것으로 보인다.

13 If it ① is to the user that I address my anger, as he as well as I ② am motivated by anger. It is ③ all the fault of anger — I should ④ be angry at that.

정답 ② am motivated ⇨ is motivated

해설 A as well as B에서 동사의 수 일치는 A에 맞추는 것이라서 am을 he is에 맞게 써야 하므로 정답은 ②이다. ③에 쓰인 fault는 가산명사, 불가산명사로 모두 쓰인다.

해석 내가 만일 사용자들에게 내가 화난 것을 보인다면, 그 역시 나와 마찬가지로 내가 화를 내는 것에 동요할 것이다. 이는 모두 화 때문이며 나는 그것에 대해 화를 내야 한다.

08

14 As a conclusion, I ① would say that this camp have brought me to further steps ② to understanding more about people and culture in Korea. The Korean are very ③ warm hospitable people. I enjoyed very much and ④ wish to have more opportunities to visit Korea again in the near future.

정답 ② to understanding ⇨ to understand

해설 'the step to ~'는 '~하는 단계'라는 의미로 이때 to는 전치사의 to가 아니라 부정사 to이기 때문에 ②의 to understanding을 to understand로 고쳐야 한다. ③에서는 warm과 hospitable 형용사가 나열되어 명사 people를 수식하고 있으므로 문법적으로 오류가 없다.

해석 결론적으로 이번 캠프가 한국의 사람들과 문화에 대해 더 깊이 이해할 수 있도록 해주었다. 한국인들은 따뜻하고 개방적인 사람들이었다. 나는 즐거운 시간을 보냈으며 나중에 한국을 다시 방문할 기회가 있었으면 한다.

15 It ① is aimed to create no useless or expensive tastes. Plain living and high thinking ② is the right formula for educational work. In all the work and living at Hampton, the idea is to surround the students with influences that shall stimulate self-respect, and that shall develop the higher and better nature by a practical ④ recognition for it.

정답 ④ recognition for it ⇨ recognition of it

해설 타동사인 recognize가 명사로 쓰일 경우에는 뒤에 전치사 of를 수반하지 for를 쓰지 않는다. 그래서 다음과 같은 숙어도 있다. 'in recognition of : ~을 인정하여, ~의 답례로'라고 쓰인다. ④의 전치사 for를 of로 바꾼다.

해석 이것은 불필요하거나 비싼 취향을 만들지 않기 위한 목적을 갖고 있다. 단순한 생활과 고차원의 사고가 바로 교육 활동의 적절한 공식이다. Hampton의 모든 일에서 목적은 자아존중 의식에 영향을 주는 환경에 둘러싸이게 하는 것이다.

16 The only major conflict that ① existed was the rivalry of the Hellenes and Iranians over economic and strategic advantage. There was no feeling of intense cultural rivalry ② at all, and no ③ resort in religious propaganda. Each had ④ its own unique cultural tradition.

정답 ③ resort in ⇨ resort to

해설 명사 resort는 '도움, 의지, 호소, 수단'이라는 의미로 뒤에 '~에 대한'이라는 의미를 갖게 될 경우 목적어 앞에 전치사 to를 써야 한다. ③의 전치사 in을 쓰지 않는다. ④의 its는 주어인 Each에 맞게 단수형으로 쓴 것이 맞다.

해석 헬레니즘 국가와 이란 간의 주요 분쟁은 경제 또는 전략적 우위를 위한 것이었다. 문화적인 라이벌 관계는 당시 존재하지 않았으며 종교적인 선동도 없었다. (그들은) 각각 서로 다른 독특한 문화적 전통을 가지고 있었다.

17 "My children, this is ① the last lesson I shall give you. The order has come from Berlin to ② teach only Germans in the schools of Alsace and Lorraine. The new master ③ comes tomorrow. This is your last French lesson. I want you to ④ be very attentive."

정답 ② teach only Germans ⇨ teach only German

해설 언어를 지칭할 경우에는 English, French, Korean과 같이 부정관사나 복수형으로 쓰지 않는다. 주어진 문장에서는 '독일어'를 지창하기 때문에 ②의 Germans를 German으로 고쳐야 한다.

해석 "얘들아, 오늘이 내가 하는 마지막 수업이란다. 베를린에서 지침이 내려와서, (이제부터는) 알자스와 로렌 지방에서는 독일어로만 가르쳐야 한단다. 내일 새로운 선생님이 오실 거야. 오늘이 마지막 프랑스어로 하는 수업이니, 너희들이 집중하길 바란다."

18 If ① you've read the bargain notebook Labs over the previous ② few pages and decided to buy one, you'll no doubt be thinking of extras ③ to add to the order. But before you simply put the suggested accessories in your basket on the supplier's website, ④ take while to browse our own recommendations.

정답 ④ take while to ⇨ take a while to

해설 while은 명사로 '시간, 동안'이라는 의미로 쓰인다. 'for a while'처럼 부정관사가 있어야 하므로 정답은 ④이다. ③에 쓰인 add는 자동사 용법으로 뒤에 전치사 to를 수반하고 있다.

해석 만일 바겐세일 중인 노트북에 관한 내용을 읽었고 구매할 생각을 하고 있다면 당연히 조금 더 지불하고 몇 가지를 더할 생각이 있을 것이다. 하지만 제안된 기타 주변기기를 구입항목에 넣기 전에 우리의 사이트의 추천내용을 검토하라.

19 Tea becomes a meditation for the senses. ① Listen for the gentle sounds of the ② water boiling in the kettle and observe the graceful dance of rising steam. Admire the beauty of the ③ teawares and the wonder of the leaves as they slowly unfurl to release their green, golden, or amber liquor. Delight in the ④ comforting warmth and texture of the cup in your hands, as you inhale the fragrant aroma and savor the delicate flavors.

정답 ③ teawares ⇨ teaware

해설 ware는 집합적 명사로 '도기, 도자기'를 의미한다. hardware(철물), silverware(은제품), earthenware(도자기) 등은 부정관사나 복수형으로 쓸 수 없다. 따라서 ③의 teaware(차 그릇, 도구)도 문법적 성격이 같기 때문에 복수형인 teawares를 tearware로 고쳐야 한다.

해석 차는 명상의 도구가 되고 있다. 주전자에 물이 끓는 소리를 듣고 증기가 춤추듯 피어오르는 것을 감상하라. 다구의 아름다움을 감상하고 찻잎이 천천히 초록, 황금색 또는 살굿빛 액체를 뿜어내는 것을 보라. 향기를 들여 마시고 섬세한 맛을 느낄 때 당신 손에 들린 찻잔의 따뜻함과 촉감을 느껴라.

20 There's four different ① kind of fundamental forces, ② but as we will see later some of them have been unified and it's thought that they are ③ all the same force only in different "modes", but for the sake ④ of simplicity we will first talk about them as different forces.

정답 ① kind of ⇨ kinds of

해설 four different에서 수식을 받는 명사는 복수형이 되어야 한다는 것을 알 수 있다. ①의 kind of를 kinds of로 써야 한다. ②에서 as는 as we will see later까지 부사절을 이룬다. but 뒤에 주절의 주어는 some of them이며 have been 이하가 동사가 되므로 맞는 표현이다. ④의 for the sake of는 '~을 위해'라는 의미로 of 전치사가 맞게 쓰였다.

해석 여기에는 네 가지 근원적인 힘이 있다. 나중에 보게 되지만 일부는 통합되고 단지 방식이 다른 같은 힘이라고 간주되고 있다. 우선 단순성을 위해 우리는 이들을 서로 다른 힘이라고 볼 것이다.

21 A significant number ① go into computer science ; but other philosophy students pursue careers in a great range of fields, ② business and medicine to writing, arts administration, publishing, and so on. Experience shows that students who choose to study philosophy do not, in any way, jeopardize ③ their chances for success after college, however success ④ might be defined.

정답 ② business and medicine ⇨ from business and medicine

해설 'in a great range of'의 표현에서 힌트를 찾아야 한다. range의 범위가 from A ~ to B로 문맥적으로 연결되어야 하고 'to writing, arts administration, publishing, and so on.'에서 전치사가 to가 쓰인 것으로 보아 ② 명사구 앞에 전치사 from이 필요하다.

해석 꽤 많은 학생들의 컴퓨터 과학을 택한다. 하지만 다른 철학과 학생들은 비즈니스, 의약, 작문, 예술경영, 출판 등 다양한 분야로 간다. 성공을 어떻게 정의하든 간에 내 경험상 철학을 선택한 학생들은 졸업 후 성공하지 못할 위험이 없다.

22 A new study helps to explain why smokers tend to have ① boozier nights out than non-smokers. The work, done in rats, shows that a heavy dose of nicotine can cut blood-alcohol levels ② in half. If cigarettes similarly ③ lowers intoxication in people, it could mean that smokers need to drink more than non-smokers ④ to get the same buzz.

정답 ③ lowers ⇨ lower

해설 if절에 쓰인 주어는 cigarettes이므로 동사는 lowers가 아니라 lower의 형태를 써야 한다. ①은 뒤에 비교급 than과 호응을 이루고 있고, ②에 쓰인 half는 명사로 썼다. ④의 부정사는 부사적 용법으로 쓰였고 same 형용사는 정관사 the와 함께 쓰인 것이 문법적으로 옳다.

해석 최근 연구는 왜 흡연자들이 비흡연자들에 비해 술을 더 마시는지를 밝혀줬다. 쥐들을 통한 연구는 니코틴의 흡수가 혈중 알콜 농도를 반으로 낮춘다고 밝혔다. 만일 담배가 유사하게 인간의 혈중 알콜 농도를 낮춘다면 이것은 곧 흡연자들은 같은 수준으로 취하기 위해 비흡연자들보다 술을 더 많이 마셔야 한다는 의미가 된다.

23 It seems plausible, then, given the knowledge at hand and a chain of inference ① which in retrospect at least appears ② straightforward Archimedes could have suspected the universality of gravitation. But could he have demonstrated it? I think he ③ could, with the help of some ④ tools and reasoning.

정답 ② straightforward ⇨ straightforward that

해설 전체 문장 구조를 잘 분석해야 한다. 첫 문장의 It seems에서 it은 가주어로 쓰였다. ①에 쓰인 which는 a chain of inference를 선행사로 하는 주격 관계대명사로 쓰였다. 그렇다면 진주어를 나타내는 that이 없다는 것을 알 수 있다. 따라서 that이 들어가야 할 적절한 자리는 ② 단어의 뒤다.

해석 당시의 지식수준과, 적어도 되돌아봤을 때, 간단한 추론구조를 보았을 때 아르키메데스가 중력의 보편성을 생각했다는 의견은 적절한 것 같다. 그렇지만 그가 이를 보여줄 수 있었을까? 나는 몇 가지 도구와 사고과정을 통해 가능했다고 생각한다.

24 Students are encouraged to refer ① back to these guidelines while they are running their experiments to understand how to deal with any difficulties they might encounter and ② how to interpret their results. We have also included some hints on ③ how to present these results in a competition once the projects ④ complete.

08

정답 ④ complete ⇨ are completed 또는 are complete

해설 once는 '일단 ~하면'이라는 뜻의 접속사이고 주어는 the projects이다. 따라서 동사가 ④ 부분에 쓰여야 하는데 complete은 여러 가지 품사로 쓰인다. 동사로 쓰인다면 형태적으로 수동태가 되어야 하고 형용사로 쓰인다면 be 동사 are가 필요하다는 것을 알 수 있다. 따라서 the projects are completed 또는 are complete가 되어야 문법적으로 맞다.

해석 실험을 직접 수행하여 결과를 해석할 때 부딪히게 될 어려움을 이해하기 위해 학생들이 이와 같은 지침을 검토할 것을 권장한다. 우리는 또 프로젝트가 완성되었을 때 경쟁상황에서 결과를 발표할 때 필요한 힌트를 포함시켰다.

25 We might hypothetically possess ourselves of every technological ① resource on the North American continent, but ② as long as our language is inadequate, our vision remains formless, our thinking and feeling ③ are still running in the old cycles, our process may be revolutionary but not ④ transformation.

정답 ④ transformation ⇨ transformative

해설 'our process may be revolutionary but (our process may) not (be) transformative'의 구조로 분석해야 한다. 따라서 revolutionary와 병치를 이루어야 하므로 명사형인 transformation이 아니라 형용사형이 와야 한다.

해석 우리는, 가정적으로, 북미대륙의 모든 기술적 자원을 가지고 있을 수 있다. 하지만 우리의 언어가 적절하지 못하다면 우리의 목표는 형태를 가지지 못한다. 우리의 사고와 느낌은 기존의 사이클에 의존할 것이며 그 과정이 혁신적일지라도 변화를 이루지는 못할 것이다.

26 We ought to show gratitude to others and ① held accountable for our conduct. We should seek justice, equity. We should manifest tolerance, ② be cooperative, seek to negotiate any differences ③ peacefully, and work out compromises whenever ④ possible.

정답 ① held ⇨ be held

해설 '~에 대해 책임지다'라는 표현은 'hold + 목적어 + accountable'이다. 따라서 held 다음에 목적어가 없으므로 수동태로 써야 한다. 그런데 and 앞에 'ought to 동사원형'의 형태만 있지 be 동사가 없으므로 수동형태를 완전하게 써주어야 한다. 그러므로 ①은 'and (ought to) be held'로 써야 한다.

해석 우리는 남들에게 감사해야 하며 자신의 행동에 책임질 수 있어야 한다. 우리는 정의와 평등을 추구해야 한다. 우리는 관용, 협력을 중시하고 서로의 다른 점을 평화적으로 해결하도록 노력해야 하며 가능한 한 양보하도록 노력해야 한다.

27 If ① for any reason you must limit your visit to a very short time, call your host in advance to explain. That might sound like, "② I'd loved to be there for the entire party, but I ③ promised to pick my brother up at the airport. Would you mind if I stop ④ by for a few minutes?" Generally, a stay should be at least 30 minutes.

정답 ② I'd loved to ⇨ I'd love to

해설 '~하고 싶다'라는 의미의 표현은 'would like to + 동사원형' 또는 'would love to + 동사원형'이므로 ②의 loved는 like 또는 love로 써야 문법적으로 맞다.

해석 만일 어떤 이유에서 당신이 단기간 방문을 제한하여야 한다면 호스트를 미리 접촉하여 이유를 설명하시오. 이는 마치 "나는 파티에 계속 있고 싶지만 공항에서 동생을 데려와야 한다, 나중에 잠깐만 와 있어도 될까?"라는 말과 같다. 일반적으로 방문기간은 최소 30분이 되어야 한다.

28 Does this suggest that we ① do no longer prepare clinical specialists or ② advanced practice nurses in master's programs? No. It ③ does suggest that there be increased opportunities for nurses to pursue ④ preparation as educators.

정답 ① do ⇨ (should)

해설 첫 문장에 쓰인 suggest는 that절을 목적어로 받아 '~해야 한다'라는 의미로 쓰인 것을 알 수 있다. 따라서 '주장, 제안, 요구, 명령' 따위의 동사가 쓰일 경우 that절에는 'S + (should) 동사원형'의 형식을 써야 하므로 ①의 강조로 쓰인 do는 should로 쓰거나 should가 생략된 구조로 나타내야 한다.

해석 이것은 우리가 더 이상 임상 전문가나 고급 간호사 양성을 우리의 석사과정에서 제외하자는 의미입니까? 아닙니다. 간호사들이 교육자로서의 준비가 되도록 기회를 늘려야 하는 것을 제안하고 있습니다.

29 We agree that we ① should find diplomatic solutions to the problem as far as Iran is concerned. I strongly encourage the Iranian government ② respond positively and constructively to the proposal ③ presented by the international community. We also discussed the situation in Iraq. We would ④ very much like to see a strong role for the UN in Iraq.

정답 ② respond ⇨ to respond

해설 동사 encourage는 'encourage + 목적어 + to 부정사'의 형태를 취한다. 따라서 ②의 respond는 to respond가 되어야 한다.

해석 이란과 관련하여 나는 우리가 외교적 해법을 찾아야 한다는 점에 동의한다. 나는 이란정부가 긍정적이고 건설적으로 국제사회의 제안에 응답할 것을 희망한다. 우리는 이라크 문제에 대해서도 논의를 한바 UN의 보다 강력한 역할을 기대하고 있다.

30 It's been 11 months ① that Hurricane Katrina devastated the Gulf States. Students at Nazareth College ② didn't need to go very far to help families ③ devastated by Hurricane Katrina. For months, they ④ have been building a home for one lucky family in Mississippi, right here on campus.

정답 ① that ⇨ since

해설 앞 문장에 쓰인 'It's been ~'에서 It은 '비인칭주어'로 쓰였다. 따라서 주절에 쓰인 현재완료와 함께 ①은 '~이래로'를 나타내는 since가 쓰여야 한다. it ~ that 강조구문이나 가주어, 진주어로 쓰인 구문이 아니기 때문에 혼동하지 말아야 한다.

해석 태풍 카트리나가 걸프지역을 강타한 지 11개월이 지났다. Nazareth 대학의 학생들은 태풍으로 파괴된 가구들을 돕기 위해 그리 멀리 갈 필요는 없었다. 수개월 동안 그들은 미시시피의 운 좋은 한 가족을 위해 캠퍼스 내에서 집을 짓고 있다.

09 실전모의고사 정답 및 해설

01	④	02	②	03	③	04	②	05	②	06	①	07	④	08	②	09	④	10	③
11	③	12	②	13	④	14	②	15	①	16	④	17	④	18	③	19	④	20	④
21	①	22	①	23	②	24	③	25	①	26	④	27	②	28	①	29	④	30	①

[01-06] Choose the one that could best complete each of the following sentences.

01 **________ a week off, I'd go back to the Two Bunch Palms Resort and Spa in the desert.**

① If I have
② If I have had
③ What I would have
④ If I had

정답 ④ If I had

해설 주절에 'I'd go back'의 표현으로 보아 빈칸에는 가정법 과거의 시제가 와야 한다는 것을 알 수 있다. 따라서 have 동사가 과거 동사로 쓰인 ④이 정답이다.

해석 만약 내가 일주일만 쉴 수 있다면, 나는 사막에 있는 Two Bunch Palms Resort and Spa로 다시 돌아갈 텐데.

02 **Ever ________ nationalized in 1969, banks have been playing a major role in the socio-economic life of the country.**

① because they were
② since they were
③ after they were
④ when they were

정답 ② since they were

해설 주절에 쓰인 'have been playing'의 시제로 보아 빈칸에는 접속사가로 since가 와야 한다는 것을 알 수 있다.

해석 1969년 국유화된 이래로 은행들은 국가의 사회·경제적인 삶 속에서 주요한 역할을 해왔다.

03 **Jeremy Clarkson's popularity is hardly surprising, ________ that he transformed Top Gear from a traditional information programme to one filled with supercars, stunts and humour.**

① being considered
② considered
③ considering
④ our considering

정답 ③ considering

해설 빈칸 뒤에는 that절을 목적어로 취할 수 있는 형태가 와야 한다. 능동형으로 써야 하기 때문에 ①과 ②은 정답이 될 수 없다. ④처럼 일반일 주어를 의미상 주어로 나타내지 않고 생략하기 때문에 정답은 ③이다.

해석 Jeremy Clarkson이 Top Gear를 전통적인 정보 제공 프로그램에서 초고성능 자동차, 묘기, 유머가 있는 프로그램으로 바꿔놓은 것을 고려하면, 그의 인기는 놀랍지 않다.

04 **Who is the cause of this fear and this feeling of insecurity? It is certain ________ everyone would announce, "Not I, but he is the cause." A very interesting position indeed! And this is the culture ________ we have attained in the sunlit midday of this century.**

① what … to which
② that … to which
③ what … of which
④ which … which

정답 ② that … to which

해설 It is certain에서 it은 가주어이고 빈칸 뒤에 완전한 문장이 오기 때문에 진주어 역할을 하는 that이 와야 한다. 동사 attain은 자동사, 타동사 용법으로 모두 쓰인다. 자동사일 경우에는 '(노력이나 자연적인 경과로) (도)달하다, 이르다'로 쓰기 때문에 to which가 들어갈 수 있다. 따라서 정답은 ②이다.

해석 누가 두려움과 불안감을 제공하는 근원인가? 모두들 나는 아니고 그가 바로 원인이라고 말할 것이 분명하다. 참으로 흥미롭다. 그리고 이것이 바로 우리가 이 세기의 정오에 얻은 문화이다.

05 **Generally speaking, video download sites ________ themselves with respect to image quality — although things are clearly improving in that area.**

① had to prove
② have yet to prove
③ have been proved
④ have to prove

정답 ② have yet to prove

해설 'although ~'이하의 내용으로 보아 빈칸에는 '아직 영상 품질에 대해 더 입증이 되어야 한다.'는 의미가 와야 한다. '아직까지 ~하지 못했다'라는 표현은 'have yet to ⓥ'이므로 정답은 ②이다.

해석 일반적으로 말할 때, 비디오 다운로드 사이트들은 비록 요즘 발전이 이뤄지고 있지만 영상 품질에 있어 더 발전해야 한다.

06 **Not only ________ too small to be seen with a light microscope, they also cannot be detected through ______ biological activity, except ________ it occurs in conjunction with other organisms.**

① are viruses – their – as
② are viruses – its – that
③ is virus – their – that
④ virus is – its – as

정답 ① are viruses – their – as

해설 'they also cannot be detected'에서 주어는 복수 명사이며 Not only가 문두에 나와 도치가 되어야 하므로 첫 번째 빈칸에는 'are viruses'가 와야 한다. 두 번째 빈칸에는 앞의 명사 bacteria를 지칭하므로 their를 써야 한다. 마지막으로는 접속사 역할을 할 수 있는 as가 올 수 있으므로 정답은 ①이다.

해석 바이러스는 너무 작아서 가벼운 현미경으로도 발견되지 않을 뿐만 아니라, 생물학적 활동이 다른 유기체들과 함께 일어나는 경우를 제외하고, 바이러스의 생물학적 활동을 통해서도 발견하기란 불가능하다.

[07-08] **Choose the one that is grammatically NOT correct.**

07 ① I closed the door quietly because she was still sleeping.
② The form has to be signed in the presence of a witness.
③ People were waiting at the airport, hoping to see the politician arriving.
④ It will not be long till mother comes back from America

정답 ④ till ⇨ before

해설 '머지않아 ~ 할 것이다.'라는 표현은 'It will not be long before + S + 현재동사'의 형식대로 써야 한다. ④의 till을 before로 고친다.

해석 ① 그녀가 여전히 잠을 자고 있었기 때문에 조용히 문을 닫았다.
② 증인이 출석한 채 그 양식은 서명이 되어야 한다.
③ 사람들은 그 정치가가 도착하기를 바라면서 공항에서 기다리고 있었다.
④ 머지않아 어머니가 미국에서 돌아오실 것이다.

08 ① We postponed our trip because the weather was bad.
② More often words add to help make the meaning of a sentence clear.
③ He is a man of few words, but when he does speak, he is very eloquent.
④ We have been playing soccer since early this morning.

정답 ② add ⇨ are added

해설 add to는 자동사 용법으로 쓰여 increase와 같은 의미를 갖는다. 그러나 주어진 문장에서는 수동태로 'be added to~ (~에 추가되다)'로 써야 문맥적으로 자연스럽다.

해석 ① 우리는 악천후 때문에 여행을 연기했다.
② 종종 어휘들이 추가되어 한 문장의 의미를 명료하게 도와준다.
③ 그는 말 수가 적은 사람이지만 그가 말을 할 경우에 매우 설득력이 있다.
④ 우리는 오늘 아침 일찍부터 축구를 계속하고 있다.

[09-30] **Choose the one that makes the sentence grammatically INCORRECT.**

---

09 John Keats's mother, brother, and good friend Richard Woodhouse all ① died of tuberculosis, ② which was then termed "consumption." He long suspected that he had ③ the disease himself, and when on February 3, 1820, he had a severe hemorrhage of the lungs, he knew that he ④ could not survive from another English winter.

정답 ④ could not survive from ⇨ could not survive

해설 동사 survive는 타동사이므로 뒤에 전치사 from을 쓸 필요가 없다. 따라서 정답은 ④이다. ①에서는 '질병으로 죽다'의 뜻일 경우에는 die of를 쓰고, ③에서 the disease라고 한 이유는 폐결핵을 나타내기 때문이다. himself는 강조 용법으로 쓰였다.

해석 John Keats의 어머니, 형제, 그리고 친구인 Richard Woodhouse는 모두, 당시에는 노환으로 알려졌던, 폐결핵으로 사망했다. 그는 오랫동안 자신도 그 병에 걸린 것으로 짐작했으며 폐의 출혈을 보인 1820년 2월 3일 그가 긴 영국의 겨울을 버티지 못할 것임을 알았다.

---

10 If you ① currently have a pair of glasses that ② is a comfortable fit, then read the numbers from the arm and choose a frame from our selection with the dimensions that closely ③ match to the ones that you have. You can then be confident ④ that the glasses that you order will fit nicely!

정답 ③ match to ⇨ match

해설 동사 match는 자동사 용법도 있지만 주로 '~에 적합하다, 맞추다'라는 의미로는 목적어를 취해 타동사 용법으로 쓰기 때문에 ③의 전치사 to가 어색하다. ④에서 첫 번째 that은 confident의 목적어 역할을 하고 있고, 두 번째 that은 you order의 목적어로 선행사 the glasses를 선행사로 하는 목적격 관계대명사로 쓰였다.

해석 만일 잘 맞는 안경을 가지고 있다면 안경걸이에 쓰인 숫자를 읽고 우리 안경테 제품목록 중 당신이 가진 것과 가장 비슷한 것을 고르십시오. 그렇다면 당신은 당신이 고른 안경이 잘 맞을 것이라고 확신할 수 있습니다.

11 One person who boarded the train in New York ① refused to accept his seat assignment, as he was not facing in the direction that the train ② was going in. I offered to ③ exchange a seat with him, but he wouldn't have ④ any of that. He was eventually put in a forward-facing seat by himself in the last row of seats at the end of the car.

정답 ③ exchange a seat ⇨ exchange seats

해설 상호복수에 관한 문제다. '~와 자리를 바꾸다'라는 표현은 'exchange seats with'라고 쓰기 때문에 ③의 a seat을 seats로 바꾼다.

해석 뉴욕에서 탄 한 승객이 자신이 기차가 향하는 방향을 바라보지 않는다며 좌석배정을 거부했다. 나는 그와 좌석을 교환할 것을 제안했지만 그는 이를 거부했다. 그는 결국 마지막 칸 마지막 줄에 앞쪽을 향한 좌석에 혼자 앉게 되었다.

12 'Romeo and Juliet' is thought to ① have been written in 1595 or 1596. The story was adapted by Shakespeare but it is his version that ② was known by old and young the world over. It is a tragic story of ③ forbidden love. The whole episode of Romeo and Juliet's meeting, falling in love, marriage, and tragic end, ④ takes place within five days.

정답 ② was known by ⇨ is known to

해설 'be known by'는 by가 판단의 기준이나 근거를 나타낼 때 쓰인다. 문맥적으로 '~에게 알려지다'가 와야 하기 때문에 ②의 전치사 by를 to 로 고친다. ①은 is thought보다 먼저 일어난 일이라서 완료부정사를 쓴 것이므로 문법적으로 오류가 없다.

해석 로미오와 줄리엣은 1595년 또는 1596년에 쓰인 것으로 추정되고 있다. 이야기는 셰익스피어에 의해 옮겨졌으나 그의 버전만이 세상에 알려져 있다. 이것은 금지된 사랑에 대한 비극으로 로미오와 줄리엣이 만나 사랑하고 결혼하고 비극으로 끝나는 것이 5일 내에 이루어진다.

13 We asked Barbara for her suggestions a year ① before putting our house on the market. This gave us adequate time to have the house painted and the landscaping ② perfected. We followed her suggestions in every detail. We accepted ③ a good, strong offer six days after the house was on the market. Barbara and her assistant David are extremely efficient and ④ calmly under pressure. Barbara knows the market and knows how to sell.

정답 ④ calmly ⇨ calm

해설 ④ 앞에 'efficient and ~' 다음에 연결되어야 하기 때문에 형용사형이 와야 한다. 부사형인 calmy를 calm으로 고친다.

해석 우리는 집을 내놓기 1년 전에 Barbara에게 조언을 구했었다. 그래서 우리는 집을 칠하고 조경을 완벽히 꾸밀 시간을 벌었다. 우리는 그녀의 조언을 세심히 따랐다. 우리는 집을 시장에 내놓은 지 6일 후 나온 좋고 강력한 제안을 받아들였다. Barbara와 그녀의 비서 David는 매우 효율적으로 일하며 스트레스가 있는 상황에서도 침착하게 일한다. Barbara는 시장을 이해하고 있으며 매매하는 방법을 알고 있다.

14 The eagle ① represents freedom. Living ② as it is on the tops of lofty mountains, amid the solitary grandeur of Nature, it has unlimited freedom, whether with strong pinions ③ it sweeps into the valleys below, or ④ upward into the boundless spaces beyond.

정답 ② as it is ⇨ as it does
해설 분사구문의 강조를 나타내는 형식을 묻는 문제다. 현재분사를 강조할 경우에는 'as + 주어 + do'를 써야 한다. 주어는 The eagle이며 시제는 현재이므로 does 동사가 와야 하므로 정답은 ②이다.
해석 독수리는 자유를 의미한다. 높은 산위와 장엄한 자연 속에 사는 독수리는 계곡 밑으로건 아니면 무한한 창공으로건 날아가며 제한 없는 자유를 가지고 있다.

15 ① Briefly spoken, this formation has a dual dimension : of course we have to learn, and to acquire knowledge, ability, ② know-how, as they say. In this sense Europe, and in the last decades America, ③ have done a lot, and that's important for the advancement of strategy in this game. ④ No Error.

정답 ① Briefly spoken ⇨ Briefly speaking
해설 '간단히 말해'라는 무인칭 독립분사구문에서 정확한 표현은 'briefly speaking'이므로 정답은 ①이다. 단순히 this formation이 사물이라 과거분사를 써야 한다고 실수하면 안 된다.
해석 간단히 말해 이러한 구성은 이중적인 차원을 갖는다. 물론 우리는 배우고, 지식, 능력, 경험을 그들이 말하는 것처럼 습득해야 한다. 그런 의미에서 유럽과 지난 수십 년간의 미주는 이를 실천해왔다. 그리고 이 게임의 전략이 발전하기 위해 이것은 중요하다.

09

16 ① Talking of music, I recently ② read that you tend to ③ listen to your favorite record of the moment over and over again ④ on weeks or even months.

정답 ④ on ⇨ for
해설 '기간'을 나타내는 전치사가 필요하기 때문에 ④은 on이 아니라 for를 써야 한다. ②의 read 동사가 목적어로 that을 취할 수 있다.
해석 음악 얘기인데, 최근에 읽은 기사에 따르면 사람들은 자신이 좋아하는 음반을 몇 주나 몇 달간 계속 듣는다고 한다.

17 ① Until about 60 years ago, most New Zealand stamps still had a picture of ② the King's or Queen's head. Except for the colour and price of the stamp, they all looked the same. Today, New Zealand stamps are all very different – ③ showing animals, cars, ships, flowers, birds, pretty scenes, famous people, and more. ④ No Error.

정답 ④ No Error

해설 ① until은 전치사이며 about은 대략을 의미하는 부사로 쓰였다. ② 정관사 the를 하나만 쓴 것은 상식적으로 (the) Queen's이 생략되었다는 것을 알고 있기 때문에 쓰지 않은 것이다. ③ 현재분사구문으로 뒤에 'animals, cars, ships, flowers, birds, pretty scenes, famous people, and more.'를 목적어로 취하고 있다.

해석 한 60년 전쯤까지 뉴질랜드의 모든 우표는 왕이나 여왕의 초상을 담고 있었다. 색깔이나 가격을 제외하고 모든 우표는 같아 보였다. 요즘엔 뉴질랜드의 우표는 동물, 자동차, 배, 꽃, 아름다운 풍경, 유명인 등을 담아 매우 다양하다.

18 I myself am an Indian, but I ① have never lived in India. I do have the utmost respect for my fellow Indians, but I am an American first and foremost. This is my home, I ② was raised here all my life. There is ③ not more annoying than getting on a call and talking with someone who cannot communicate clearly. I have family members with the accent, but ④ nothing compared to this. I can't even understand them!

정답 ③ not more annoying ⇨ nothing more annoying

해설 There is 다음에는 주어가 와야 한다. 주어 역할을 할 수 있는 것은 (not more) annoying이 아니라 nothing이 되어야 하고 more annoying은 후치 수식을 해야 하기 때문에 정답은 ③이다.

해석 나 자신도 인도인이지만 인도에서 살았던 적은 없었다. 나는 나의 조국의 인도인들을 존경하지만 나는 우선 미국인이다. 여기가 나의 집이고 나는 여기서 자라났다. 전화를 받았는데 상대방과 의사소통이 안 되는 것만큼 짜증나는 것은 없다. 나의 가족들은 (인도) 억양을 가지고 있지만 이것과는 비교도 안 된다. 나는 그들의 말을 이해할 수조차 없다.

19 ① Any child can do a puzzle, ② given the right support. Puzzles build spatial awareness and logical thinking, and reinforce concepts ③ such as letters, numbers, shapes and themes. ④ No Error.

정답 ④ No Error

해설 ① 긍정문에 쓰인 any는 양보의 의미를 갖고 있다. ② given은 과거분사로 '~을 받을 경우'라는 의미로 쓰일 수 있고 뒤에 목적어를 한 개 취할 수 있다. ③ concepts를 부연 설명해 주는 어휘로 such as가 쓰였고 뒤에는 명사들이 나열되어 있다. 따라서 정답은 ④이다.

해석 적절한 지원이 있다면 모든 아이들이 퍼즐을 할 수 있다. 퍼즐은 공간 지각력과 논리적 사고를 키우고 철자, 숫자, 모양, 주제에 관한 개념을 강화시킨다.

20 But back ① <u>in early 1930</u>, Walt had another matter to ② <u>attend to</u> : the creation of the comic strip after Iwerks' departure. At first Walt was content to ③ <u>continue scripting</u> it and assigning the art to Win Smith. However, Walt's focus ④ <u>has always been</u> in animation and Smith was soon assigned with the scripting as well.

정답 ④ has always been ⇨ had always been

해설 전체 문장의 시제는 '과거'의 일을 진술하고 있다. 따라서 과거를 기준으로 이미 발생한 사건은 had p.p의 형태로 써야 하므로 정답은 ④이다.

해석 1930년대 초반 Walt는 다른 것을 염두에 두고 있었다. 그것은 Iwerk가 떠난 후 새로운 만화를 만드는 것이었다. 처음 Walt는 미술을 Win Smith에 맡기고 대본을 맡는 것에 만족했지만 Walt는 항상 애니메이션을 생각하고 있었으며 Smith는 곧 대본까지 맡게 되었다.

21 I ① <u>think generally</u> that it's good for the country when at least one house ② <u>majority is</u> opposite the president because it provides a check on ③ <u>the more extreme</u> decisions. Your example of the Supreme Court is ④ <u>a good one</u>. It's one thing to appoint a moderate justice, even one who leans conservative. It's a completely different thing to appoint an ultra-conservative justice.

정답 ① think generally ⇨ generally think

해설 often, frequently, usually, regularly, rarely, almost, hardly, deeply, generally 등의 빈도부사와 정도부사의 위치는 '일반 동사 앞, be 동사 뒤, 조동사와 본동사 사이, be[have] + p.p. 사이'이다. 그러므로 generally가 think 앞에 나와야 한다.

해석 극단적인 결정에 있어 견제가 되기 때문에 나는 일반적으로 여당이 대통령의 당과 다른 경우가 국가들 위해 좋다고 생각한다. 당신의 대법원 사례는 적절한 것이었다. 보수적인 인사라도 온건한 대법관을 갖는 것과 초보수적 대법관을 갖는 것은 전혀 다르다.

22 Unlike most domestic-abuse incidents, this one ① <u>wasn't taken</u> place in the home. It's sad to say, but if a guy ② <u>beats</u> his wife within the confines of his home, it ③ <u>is up to</u> the wife to press charges — and that ④ <u>rarely</u> occurs.

정답 ① wasn't taken ⇨ didn't take

해설 '발생하다'를 의미하는 take place는 자동사 용법으로 쓰기 때문에 be p.p의 형태가 없다. ②은 조건을 나타내는 if절이므로 동사가 현재형으로 쓰였다. ③ 또한 조건절의 주절에 해당하며 현재 시제를 써도 무방하다. 'be up to ~'는 '~에 달려 있다, 책임이다'라는 의미다. ④의 rarely는 빈도부사로 일반동사 앞에 위치하는 것이 문법적으로 맞다.

해석 다른 가내폭력과 달리 이것은 집에서 행하여진 것이 아니다. 슬프지만 만일 남편이 아내에게 집안에서 폭행을 했다면 고소 여부는 아내가 결정한다, 그리고 이런 경우는 매우 적다.

23 Why don't we fix our textbooks? In case you haven't noticed, this is the year we are finally going to start ① <u>improving</u> American high schools, where progress in ② <u>rising</u> achievement has been as slow as a teenager's response to a request that he ③ <u>clean</u> his room. The government has put ④ <u>fixing</u> high schools at the top of their to-do lists, but it never happened so far.

정답 ② rising ⇨ raising

해설 rising achievement가 문법적으로 잘못된 것은 아니다. 자동사로 '상승하는'이라는 의미로 문맥적으로 자연스럽다면 상관없지만, 이 문장에는 '성적을 높이는 데 진전'이라는 말이 필요하기 때문에 타동사 'raising'이 와야 한다.

해석 교과서를 통일시키는 것이 어떨까? 아직 모르신다면 올해는 그동안 성과를 높이는 것이 청소년들에게 자기 방 청소를 시킨 것만큼이나 더뎠던 미국의 고등학교 교육에 진전이 보였던 해입니다. 정부는 고교 교과서를 통일시키는 것을 최고목표로 하고 있지만 아직까지는 이뤄지지 못하고 있습니다.

24 Let's key both the minimum wage and Congressional and other Federal ① <u>salaries</u> to per-capital gross domestic product. ② <u>Otherwise</u> the sheer competence of the federal government will continue ③ <u>to be diminished</u> over time as the talent ④ <u>drains out to</u> the private sector.

정답 ③ to be diminished ⇨ to diminish 또는 diminishing

해설 '감소하다'를 의미하는 diminish는 자동사이기 때문에 be p.p의 수동태 형식으로 쓰지 않는다. 따라서 ③의 형태를 to diminish 또는 continue 다음에 동명사도 목적어로 나올 수 있기 때문에 diminishing을 쓸 수도 있다.

해석 최저임금과 의회 및 연방정부의 임금을 GDP에 연동시킵시다. 그렇지 않으면 인재들이 민간부문으로 나가게 됨에 따라 연방정부의 경쟁력은 지속적으로 약해질 것입니다.

25 What problems are caused by thumb-sucking? ① <u>Prolonging</u> thumb-sucking can lead to dental, speech, and self-image problems. In rare cases, thumb-sucking after age 5 is ② <u>a response</u> to an emotional problem or ③ <u>other disorder</u>, such as anxiety. Children with this type of problem need ④ <u>to be evaluated</u> by a health professional.

정답 ① Prolonging ⇨ Prolonged

해설 동사 prolong은 '(시간적으로) ~을 지연시키다, ~을 오래 가게 하다, 연장하다'라는 의미로 목적어를 취해 타동사로 쓰인다. 주어진 문장에서 '엄지손가락을 오래 빨게 하는 것은'이라는 의미가 자연스럽지 않다. 쉽게 말해 '연장된, 오래 가게 된' 의미로 과거분사 prolonged가 thumb-sucking 명사를 수식해야 문법적으로 옳다.

해석 엄지손가락을 빨 경우 어떤 문제가 생기는가? 지속적으로 엄지손가락을 빨게 되면 치아, 발성, 그리고 자신의 이미지와 관련된 문제가 생길 수 있다. 희귀한 경우이지만 5세 이후의 엄지손가락 빨기가 감정적인 문제나 그 외의 문제 예를 들면 불안증에 의해 생긴다. 이러한 문제를 가진 아이들은 전문 의료인들의 검사를 받아야 한다.

26 As many as 80 Tibetans have been reported ① wounded in a clash with the Chinese authorities over China's anti-Dalai Lama campaign. Witnesses reported ② seeing two trucks of ③ badly beaten Tibetans, ④ main monks and nuns, arriving at a hospital in Lhasa, the Tibetan capital.

정답 ④ main ⇨ mainly

해설 ④의 main은 형용사로 뒤에 monks and nuns를 수식해서 '주요, 주요한, 주된'이라는 의미로 쓰여 Tibetans, main monks and nuns로 연결되어 자연스럽지 못하다. mainly를 쓸 경우에는 앞에 언급한 명사가 '주로' 누구인지를 밝혀줄 때 쓰인다. 따라서 정답은 ④이다.

해석 최소 80명의 티벳인들이 중국의 반 달라이라마 캠페인에 대한 반발에 따른 충돌로 부상당했다고 보도되었다. 목격자들에 따르면 주로 종교인들인 심각하게 구타당한 티벳인들이 2대의 트럭에 실려 티벳의 수도인 라사의 병원으로 실려왔다고 한다.

27 While it is impossible to ① objectively determine the greatest film of all time, it is possible to discuss the films that have been regarded ② the greatest ever. The important criterion for ③ inclusion in this article is that the film is the "greatest" by some specific ④ criterion or indicator

정답 ② the greatest ever ⇨ as the greatest ever

해설 regard는 5형식으로 쓸 경우에는 'regard A as B'의 형식을 쓰며 수동태는 'A be regarded as B'이다. 주어진 문장에서 'have been regarded'가 쓰여 뒤에 as가 반드시 와야 한다. as가 올 자리로 적합한 곳은 ②이다.

해석 최고의 영화에 대해 객관적으로 결정할 수는 없지만 최고의 영화들로 불리는 영화들에 대해서는 논의가 가능하다. 최고의 영화들에 포함되려면 이를 결정하는 중요한 기준은 구체적인 기준이나 근거로 판단되어야 한다.

09

28 ① The third of the lessons in England's secondary schools ② are being taught by people who do not have degrees in the subject they ③ are teaching, an official survey indicates. And ④ almost a fifth of lessons are taught by people with no qualification in the subject.

정답 ① The third ⇨ A third

해설 ①의 the third는 '3번째, 3등'을 나타내어 문맥적으로 적절하지 않다. '1/3'의 분수 표현은 a third라고 해야 한다. ②은 현재진행 수동태로 문법적으로 오류가 없다. ③의 are teaching의 목적어는 the subject로 뒤에 목적격 관계대명사가 생략되었다. ④은 '거의'라는 의미로 부사로 쓰였다. 뒤에 a fifth of의 어구를 수식한다.

해석 조사결과에 따르면 영국 중고등학교 교육의 1/3은 해당 분야에 대한 학위가 없는 사람들에 의해 가르쳐진다. 그리고 거의 1/5은 해당 분야에 대한 자격이 없는 사람들에 의해 가르쳐진다.

29 We may, in future, use an outside advertising company ① to display ads on our site. These ads may contain cookies. While we use cookies in ② other parts of our Web site, cookies received with banner ads ③ will be collected by our ad company, and we do not ④ have access in this information.

정답 ④ have access in ⇨ have access to

해설 '접근'을 나타내는 명사 access 다음에는 전치사 to를 쓴다. ①의 부정사는 본동사 use와 연결되어 '~하기 위해'라는 의미로 쓰였다. ② other 다음에 복수 가산명사가 올 수 있다. ③은 미래 수동태로 문맥적으로 시제와 태가 맞게 쓰였다.

해석 우리는 향후 외부 광고회사를 통해 광고를 웹사이트에 실을 것이다. 이들 광고는 쿠키를 가지고 있을 것이며 우리가 이 쿠키를 웹사이트의 다른 부분에서 이용하는 가운데 배너광고와 함께 나오는 쿠키는 우리의 광고회사에 의해 수집되어 우리는 이 정보에 대해 접근할 수 없게 된다.

30 What crops ① are seen from Kansas highways 50 years from now may still be in doubt. Global warming is shifting some species permanently ② north and changing migration patterns for ③ others, altering Kansas' ④ wildlife.

정답 ① are seen ⇨ will be seen

해설 '50 years from now'로 보아 미래의 일을 진술하고 있으며, 작물은 발견되는 것이므로 ①의 현재 수동태는 미래 수동형으로 써야 한다. 따라서 are seen은 will be seen으로 고쳐야 한다.

해석 캔사스 50번 고속도로 주변에서 발견될 작물이 몇 년 후 무엇일지에 대해서는 아직 알 수 없다. 지구온난화는 일부 종들을 영구적으로 북쪽으로 이동시키고 있으며 다른 종들의 이동패턴을 바꾸며 캔사스의 야생환경을 변화시키고 있다.

10 실전모의고사 정답 및 해설

01	③	02	③	03	②	04	③	05	③	06	①	07	②	08	③	09	③	10	②
11	③	12	③	13	④	14	③	15	②	16	①	17	③	18	③	19	②	20	④
21	④	22	①	23	①	24	①	25	④	26	①	27	③	28	④	29	②	30	①

[01-06] **Choose the one that could best complete each of the following sentences.**

---

01 **In Gurgaon, for instance, transformers routinely blow out because of heavy loads. Voltage fluctuations damage electrical appliances of all sorts. ______________________, many take for themselves.**

① That the state cannot provide efficiently
② The state cannot provide efficiently and
③ What the state cannot provide efficiently
④ The state cannot provide them efficiently and

정답 ③ What the state cannot provide efficiently

해설 many (people) : 주어, take : 동사 + 목적어가 일단 없고, for themselves는 부사구로 처리를 한다. 그러면 목적어에 해당하는 명사구나 명사절이 앞으로 나갔다고 판단한다. 그 목적어 기능에 알맞은 것은 ③이 된다.

해석 Gurgaon지역에는, 예를 들어, 변압기가 종종 많은 전하량 때문에 (퓨즈 따위가 끊어져) 작동이 안 된다. 전압의 변동으로 모든 종류의 전기제품들이 망가진다. 많은 사람들은 그들 스스로 국가가 효율적으로 제공하지 못하는 부분을 충당한다.

10

---

02 **After rocking or feeding baby to sleep in your arms, lie down with your sleeping baby next to you and nestle close to her _________ she is sound asleep.**

① unless ② as long as
③ until ④ otherwise

정답 ③ until

해설 문맥적으로 알맞은 접속사를 선택하는 문제다. 의미적으로 '아기가 잠들 때까지'가 가장 적합하기 때문에 정답은 ③이다.

해석 아기를 어르고 음식을 준 후 당신 품에서 잠이 들었을 때 자는 아이 옆에 같이 붙어 깊이 잠들 때까지 곁에 있으라.

03 **It depicts several New York police officers ________ on the front steps of the main Pace building and a ________ student being aided by two other people.**

① stood … wounded
② standing … wounded
③ stood … wounding
④ standing … wounding

정답 ② standing … wounded

해설 depict 동사는 5형식으로 'depict + 목적어 + 목적격 보어'를 쓸 수 있다. 이때 목적어와 빈칸에는 stand 동사가 준동사 형태로 들어가야 하고 의미적으로 능동이기 때문에 현재분사형을 써야 하므로 첫 번째 빈칸에는 standing이 들어가야 한다. 두 번째는 '부상당한'이라는 의미가 와야 하기 때문에 wounded가 적합하다. 따라서 정답은 ②이다.

해석 그것은 Pace 대학본부 건물 앞에 늘어선 뉴욕 경찰과 부상당한 학생이 두 명의 사람들에게 부축 받는 모습을 그리고 있다.

04 **Probably one of the best overall forms of exercise is swimming, ________ it does not stress the joints as much as running does.**

① while
② likewise
③ because
④ unless

정답 ③ because

해설 문맥적으로 알맞은 접속사를 선택하는 문제로 빈칸 앞뒤로 의미적으로 '인과' 관계를 이루어야 자연스럽기 때문에 정답은 ③이다.

해석 아마도 가장 좋은 형태의 운동 중 하나는 수영이다, 왜냐면 이것은 달리기만큼 관절에 무리를 주지 않기 때문이다.

05 **I ________ see relationships among variables such as ethnicity, poverty, special education, time of day, and the location of the offense.**

① am anxious about
② was anxious to
③ am anxious to
④ am anxiety to

정답 ③ am anxious to

해설 먼저 형용사 anxious about 다음에는 see 동사원형이 쓰일 수 없기 때문에 be anxious to V의 형태를 선택할 수 있다. 정답은 ③이다.

해석 나는 인종, 빈곤, 특수교육, 시간대, 위법행위의 장소와 같은 변수들 간의 관계를 너무나도 알아보고 싶다.

06 **Some of the questions that scholars ask seem to the world to be scarcely worth asking, let alone answering. They ask questions __________ for you and me to understand without years of explanation.**

① too minute and specialized ② so minute and specializing
③ so minute and specialized ④ too minute and specializing

정답 ① too minute and specialized
해설 빈칸 뒤에는 'for you and me'가 의미상 주어이고 to understand의 부정사로 연결되기 때문에 'too ~ to' 용법에 해당한다. 두 번째 빈칸에는 '전문화시키는'의 의미가 아니라 '전문화된 질문'이므로 specialized 과거분사형이 와야 한다.
해석 학자들의 질문은 대중에게는 대답하는 것은 물론이고 거의 질문할 가치가 없는 것처럼 보인다. 그들은 우리가 몇 년 동안 설명을 듣지 않고 이해하기에는 너무 상세하고 전문화된 질문을 한다.

[07-08] **Choose the one that is grammatically NOT correct.**

07 ① They believe Pat to win.
② John regrets Bacon to be real author.
③ They want Pat to win.
④ I hope for your having a happy summer.

정답 ② John regrets Bacon to be real author.
해설 believe와 want, know는 5형식 구문으로 목적어 + 목적격 보어로 부정사가 오는 구문을 쓸 수 있다. 그래서 ①, ③은 문법적으로 옳다. 그러나 ②의 regret 동사는 3형식으로만 쓸 수 있다. 'regret + ~ ing / regret + to R / regret that ~' 구문을 구성한다. ④의 hope동사는 hope for one's ~ ing 구문으로 쓸 수 있다.
해석 ① 그들은 Pat이 이길 것이라고 믿는다.
② John은 Bacon이 실제 저자라는 것을 유감으로 생각한다.
③ 그들은 Pat이 승리하기를 원한다.
④ 나는 당신이 행복한 여름을 보내기를 바랍니다.

08 ① It is not necessary to bring a lunch for hiking tomorrow.
② It is necessary that the patient exercise more regularly.
③ She is necessary to come to school earlier than others.
④ Money is absolutely necessary to carry out this plan.
⑤ Is it necessary for me to go?

정답 ③ She is necessary to come to school earlier than others.

해설 necessary의 용법을 묻는 문제다. necessary 형용사는 사람을 주어로 하여 쓰지 않기 때문에 이런 구문은 허용하지 않는다. 한국식 해석으로 문법의 정오를 판단하지 않도록 한다. ④은 사물을 주어로 'necessary to 또는 for ~'의 구문을 쓸 수 있다.

해석 ① 내일 하이킹에 먹을 점심을 가져올 필요가 없다.
② 환자는 더 규칙적으로 운동할 필요가 있다.
③ 그녀는 다른 학생들보다 더 일찍 학교에 올 필요가 있다.
④ 이 계획을 실행하기 위해 돈은 절대적으로 필요하다.
⑤ 내가 갈 필요가 있습니까?

[09-30] **Choose the one that makes the sentence grammatically INCORRECT.**

09 It is natural ① for children to first show some sort of denial that the situation really ② happened. Fears, worries or nightmares are ③ commonly following a trauma. Sleep disturbances or eating difficulties may happen. ④ No Error.

정답 ③ commonly ⇨ common

해설 ③의 문장을 분석하면 다음과 같다. '주어 are common + (following + 목적어)'. commonly가 부사형이 되어 뒤에 following을 수식하는 것으로 분석할 경우 의미적으로 현재진행형으로 써서 부자연스럽고, 의미적으로도 적합하지 않다. 따라서 정답은 ③이다.

해석 아이들은 자연스럽게 현실로 나타나기 전에 이를 부정하곤 한다. 두려움, 걱정, 그리고 악몽은 충격이후 공통적인 반응이다. 수면장애나 식이장애도 발생할 수 있다.

10 ① Nothing worthwhile is achieved through absent effort, which is why I ② emphasize on mental preparation for the task at hand. I provide ③ merely the roadmap ; it's your obligation to initiate, continue, and ④ complete the journey. Destiny is yours ; seize the moment, and GOD BLESS!

정답 ② emphasize on ⇨ emphasize

해설 동사 emphasize는 '강조하다, 역설하다'라는 의미로 타동사 용법으로 써야 한다. ②의 전치사 on을 삭제해야 한다. ③의 merely는 only와 마찬가지로 강조하고 싶은 어구에 가깝게 놓을 수 있기 때문에 문법적으로 오류가 없다. ④의 complete은 '끝내다, 완성하다'로 동사로 쓰여 뒤에 the journey를 목적어로 취한다.

해석 노력 없이 의미 있는 것이 달성되지는 않는다. 그래서 내가 주어진 일에 대한 정신적 준비를 강조하는 것이다. 나는 단지 길잡이만 제시할 뿐이다. 여행을 시작하고 지속하며 끝내는 것은 당신의 의무이다. 운명은 당신 것이다. 현재를 잡아라, 그리고 신의 축복이 있기를!

11 She thought of her life ① <u>being shaken</u> by a man – ② <u>comparable to</u> a small rain drop – who she ③ <u>had never spoken</u>. She laughed at herself thinking how silly she was to still hope that she will meet him. She decided she would put him out of her mind and life. She decided she ④ <u>wouldn't let</u> him affect her life so much.

정답 ③ had never spoken ⇨ had never spoken to

해설 ③ 'who she had never spoken.'에서 who는 she가 바로 뒤에 나오기 때문에 주격 관계대명사가 아니라 목적격인 whom이 who로 쓰였다는 것을 알 수 있다. 따라서 ③에서는 동사 had never spoken 다음에 전치사 to가 있어야 한다.

해석 그녀는 그녀의 인생이 말도 해보지 않은, 마치 빗방울과 같은 남자로 인해 흔들린다고 생각했다. 그를 만나길 희망하는 것이 바보 같다며 자신을 향해 웃었다. 그녀는 그를 자신의 생각과 인생에서 지우기로 결정했다. 그녀는 그가 그녀의 인생에 큰 영향을 주지 않도록 하기로 결정했다.

12 "In Europe," said Thomas Jefferson, "the object is to make the most of their land, labor ① <u>being abundant</u> ; here it is to ② <u>make the most of</u> our labor, land being abundant." These contrasting models of economic growth ③ <u>resulted in</u> various cultural and industrial differences at this time. It was in America, therefore, that the great advances in nineteenth-century agricultural machinery ④ <u>first came</u>.

정답 ③ resulted in ⇨ resulted from

해설 ③에서 의미적 관계를 잘 따져봐야 한다. result from 다음에는 '원인'에 해당하는 어휘가 나와야 하고, result in 다음에는 '결과'를 나타내는 어휘가 나와야 한다. 문맥적으로 '경제성장 모델은 문화와 산업 간의 차이에서 비롯되기 때문에' 전치사 in이 아니라 from이 와야 문맥적으로 논리적이다. 따라서 정답은 ③이다.

해석 토마스 제퍼슨은 "유럽에서는 노동이 풍부하기 때문에 땅으로부터 최대한 많은 것을 얻는 것이 목적이다. 여기에서는 땅이 풍부하기 때문에 노동으로부터 최대한 많은 것을 얻는 것이 목적이다"라고 말했다. 이러한 상반되는 경제성장 모델은 문화 및 산업 간 차이를 만들었다. 그러므로 19세기 농업기계가 처음 급성장한 것은 미국에서였다.

13 ① Besides giving a general information on ② what is forensic science and why one should study forensic science, this website also talks about the further course of study ③ for those of you still at school or college and ④ is interested in taking up forensics as a career. And, for this purpose the site provides a list of universities that offer courses in forensic science and specialization in various branches.

정답 ④ is interested in ⇨ (who are) interested in

해설 ③에서 for those를 수식하는 어구는 of you와 still at school or college가 된다. 그 뒤에 and로 연결되고 의미적으로 다시 for those를 수식하고 있으므로 적어도 동사형태 없이 과거분사인 'interested in ~'만으로 수식해야 한다. 따라서 정답은 ④에 is를 생략하고 'who are interested in ~' 또는 'interested in ~'으로 고쳐야 한다.

해석 이 웹사이트는 범죄의학이 무엇인지에 대해 일반적인 정보를 주고, 왜 범죄의학을 공부해야 하는지에 대해 설명할 뿐 아니라 아직 학교에 있는 사람들이나 범죄의학을 직업으로 하고 있는 사람들을 위해 졸업 후의 교육과정에 대해 설명해 준다. 그리고 그러한 목적을 위해 이 사이트는 범죄의학 및 관련 전문분야의 수업을 제공하는 대학 명단을 준비하고 있다.

14 Italian ① has always had a distinctive dialect for each city, since the cities were up until recently ② city-states. A well-known Italian dictum has it that the best spoken Italian is lingua toscana in bocca romana. The Romans are known ③ by speaking clearly and distinctly, while the Tuscan dialect is the closest existing dialect to Dante's ④ now-standard Italian.

정답 ③ by speaking ⇨ for speaking

해설 '~로 유명해지다'는 'be known for'를 써야 한다. for 이하가 이유를 나타내는 전치사이다. '판단의 기준'을 나타내는 전치사 by는 적합하지 않다.

해석 각 도시는 최근까지도 도시국가였기 때문에 이태리인들은 각 도시마다 다른 사투리를 가지고 있다. 잘 알려진 이태리 명언은 가장 좋은 이태리어는 토스카나 사투리가 로마의 목소리로 나오는 것이라고 한다. 로마인들은 명확하고 분명히 발음하는 것으로 유명하며 토스카나 사투리는 단테의 표준 이태리어와 가장 유사하다.

15 Don't let the dogs and cats ① impacted by Hurricane Katrina ② forgotten. You can read more about the rescue efforts, ③ donate money and learn how you ④ can help out at The Humane Society of the United States website.

정답 ② forgotten ⇨ be forgotten

해설 부정명령문의 수동태는 'Don't let + 목적어 + be p.p.'로 써야 한다. 따라서 ②의 과거분사 앞에 be 동사를 써야 문법적으로 맞다.

해석 고통 받는 개와 고양이를 잊지 맙시다. The Humane Society of the United States의 웹사이트에서 구호노력과 기부금, 그리고 어떻게 도울 수 있는지에 대해 자세히 알 수 있습니다.

16 I wish I ① had a toy guide like this to browse through when my daughter was younger. The trouble with a lot of toys is that some are fads and ② some are genuinely great for little people development. We've tried to steer ③ clear of the fad toys and recommend ones that we really think are fun to play ④ with and educational too.

정답 ① had ⇨ had had

해설 I wish 가정법에 관한 문제다. 주어진 문장의 내용에 따르면 'when my daughter was younger'가 기준시제가 되는 것을 알 수 있다. 즉, 현재의 반대되는 상황을 가정하는 것이 아니라 '과거'의 사실에 대한 반대되는 가정을 나타내기 때문에 가정법 과거완료를 써야 한다. 따라서 'I wish + S + had p.p~'의 형태가 와야 맞다.

해석 내 딸이 더 어렸을 때 이런 장난감 가이드가 있어서 장난감을 검색할 수 있었으면 좋았었을 것이다. 많은 장난감들의 문제는 어떤 것은 단지 유행을 타는 것이고 어떤 것은 정말로 어린이들의 성장에 도움이 된다는 점이다. 우리도 유행품에서 멀리하고 방향을 잡아, 놀면서 교육이 되는 장난감을 추천하려고 했었다.

17 All you need ① to make is a so-called argument by analogy, he says. If X has these 10 characteristics and Y has nine of them, chances ② are Y also has the tenth. From a philosophical perspective, you end up ③ to treat farmed fish as if you knew for certain they experienced pain, despite the lack of ④ scientific proof.

정답 ③ to treat ⇨ treating

해설 end up 다음에는 목적어로 부정사를 쓰는 것이 아니라 동명사형을 써야 한다. ①은 need to 동사원형에 해당하며 ②은 chances are that + S + V ~의 구조로 파악해야 한다. ④의 proof 명사는 불가산명사로 쓰였다.

해석 당신이 해야 할 것은 소위 유추에 의한 주장이라고 불리는 그것이라고 그는 말했다. 만일 X가 10가지 성질을 가지고 있고 Y가 9가지 성질을 가지고 있다면 Y가 10개째 것을 가지고 있을 가능성이 크다. 철학적 관점에서 볼 때, 과학적 증명이 없더라도 당신은 양식되는 물고기가 마치 고통을 느끼고 있다고 생각하게 될 것이다.

10

18 I know that he and the whole House will want Ministers to give ① top priority to dealing with the practical day-to-day issues, which may help us ② in bringing the epidemic to an end. I regret that he ③ repeated what has occasionally been heard from Opposition Members about the bad ④ handling of the outbreak.

정답 ③ repeated what ⇨ should repeat what

해설 동사 regret 다음에 that절에는 감정적 판단을 나타내는 조동사 should가 와야 자연스럽다. 따라서 ③의 과거형으로 쓰인 repeated를 should repeat으로 써야 한다.

해석 나는 그와 의회 모두가 장관들이 전염병을 끝낼 수도 있는 일상적인 이슈들을 일순위로 다룰 것을 원한다. 나는 초기발병에 대한 미숙한 처리에 대해 여당에서 주로 주장하는 그 과정을 그가 다시 재연하고 있다는 점에 대해 후회하고 있다.

19 Young people, particularly the 49 percent of ① 18-to-29-year-olds who live in rural and inner city communities and have no college experience, ② and don't suffer from lack of interest in politics. It's because there is lack of access. We try not to push positions. But we build an infrastructure that allows people, who ④ would not otherwise have the opportunity, ④ to engage in genuine, active dialogue with civic leaders.

정답 ② and don't suffer ⇨ don't suffer

해설 전체 문장구조를 분석해야 한다. 주어는 Young people이며 이에 해당하는 본동사를 찾아야 한다. who live in ~ and have no college experience까지가 관계사절이다. 따라서 동사는 ② 부분이 되어야 한다. and가 있으면 관계사절로 계속 연결되는 부분이 되므로 and를 삭제해야 한다.

해석 젊은이들 특히 교외와 시내에 살고 있으며 대학 경험이 없는 18세와 29세 사이 젊은이들의 49%가 정치에 대해 관심이 없다. 그것은 접근방법이 없기 때문이다. 우리는 우리의 입장을 강요하지는 않지만 기회가 없을 수도 있는 사람들이 정치지도자들과 대화를 할 수 있는 인프라를 마련하고 있다.

20 We have ① much in common. We share a history ② as nations of the New World. We ③ were founded by empires but grew up as free democracies. We are united by geography. And we ④ share common vision for our hemisphere in the 21st century.

정답 ④ share ⇨ share a

해설 vision은 이때 가산명사로 쓰여 '미래상, 전망'이라는 의미로 쓰였기 때문에 ④ 뒤에 쓰인 common vision 앞에 부정관사 a를 써야 한다. 부정관사가 들어가야 할 적절한 자리는 ④이다.

해석 우리는 많은 공통점을 가지고 있다. 우리는 신세계의 국가로서 같은 역사를 가지고 있다. 우리는 제국들에 의해 성립되었지만 자유민주국가로 성장했다. 우리는 지리적으로 통합되어 있다. 우리는 같은 반구 내의 21세기 비전을 가지고 있다.

21 Mideast diplomats will be pressing Syria ① to stop backing Hezbollah. As the guerrillas fired more deadly rockets onto Israel's ② third-largest city Sunday, things have worsened. Israel faced ③ tougher-than-expected ground battles and ④ bombard targets in southern Lebanon.

정답 ④ bombard ⇨ bombarded

해설 faced 과거동사 다음에 and 이하의 동사 또한 과거 시제로 써야 한다. ④의 현재형인 bombard를 bombarded로 고쳐야 문법적으로 맞다.

해석 중동 외교관들이 헤즈볼라에 대한 지원을 중단하라고 시리아에 압력을 넣을 것이다. 게릴라들이 이스라엘에서 3번째로 큰 도시에 미사일을 쏨에 따라 사정은 악화되고 있다. 이스라엘은 예상보다 어려운 지상전을 겪게 됨에 따라 남부 레바논 목표지역에 폭판을 퍼붓고 있다.

22 Breathing ozone can trigger ① <u>variety of</u> health problems including chest pain, coughing, throat irritation, and congestion. It can ② <u>worsen</u> bronchitis, emphysema, and asthma. "Bad" ozone also can reduce lung function and ③ <u>inflame</u> the linings of the lungs. Repeated exposure may permanently ④ <u>scar</u> lung tissue.

정답 ① variety of ⇨ a variety of

해설 다양한 의미로 쓰이는 표현은 'a variety of 또는 varieties of'가 되어야 한다. 따라서 정답은 ①이다. ②, ③, ④은 모두 동사로 쓰였고, 시제, 태 모두 문법적으로 오류가 없다.

해석 오존을 들이마시는 것은 가슴통증, 기침, 후두염 및 출혈을 유발할 수 있다. 이것은 기관지염, 기종, 그리고 천식을 악화시킬 수 있다. 나쁜 오존은 폐기능을 약화시키며 폐세포의 염증을 유발한다. 반복적인 오존에 대한 노출은 폐조직에 영구적인 상처를 남길 수 있다.

23 She suffered from severe emotional disturbance, the most remarkable symptom ① <u>which</u> was compulsive stealing from the home, the staff, other children and from families ② <u>that</u> would take her ③ <u>in for</u> brief home stays. However, she was able to overcome these difficulties and is now pursuing her goal of working with the disabled and ④ <u>is engaged to</u> get married.

정답 ① which ⇨ of which

해설 첫 문장은 She suffered ~ disturbance까지가 '주어 + 동사 ~'에 해당한다. 그런데 뒤에 연결사 없이 the most remarkable symptom으로 연결되기 때문에 which는 of which가 되어야 한다. 이때 which의 선행사는 emotional disturbance다. 그러므로 '명사 of which'의 기본구조를 갖춰야 한다.

해석 그녀는 심각한 감정적 장애로 고통받았다. 가장 심했던 것은 집, 직원, 다른 아이들, 또는 홈스테이를 제공했던 가정으로부터 충동적으로 물건을 훔치는 것이다. 그러나 그녀는 이러한 어려움을 극복하고 이제 그녀의 목표였던 장애인을 돕는 일을 하고 있으며 약혼까지 한 상태이다.

24 He was noted ① <u>as being crossed</u> and disagreeable because he was not happy, and he was not happy because he wanted to ② <u>go down</u> the mountain and visit the big world below and his father ③ <u>wouldn't let</u> him. No one paid any attention to Kiki Aru, because he didn't ④ <u>amount to</u> anything, anyway.

정답 ① as being crossed ⇨ as being cross

해설 cross가 타동사일 경우에는 '교차시키다, 엇갈리게 하다'라는 의미다. 주어진 문장에서는 논리적으로 적합하지 않은 어휘다. 따라서 형용사형인 cross를 써야 '시무룩한, 화난, 언짢은'이라는 의미로 자연스럽다. 따라서 정답은 ①이다.

해석 그는 행복해하지 않았기 때문에 불만이 많고 동의하기 힘든 존재로 알려져 있었다. 그가 행복하지 않은 이유는 그가 산을 내려가 아래의 넓은 세상을 만나고 싶어 하나 아버지가 이를 허락하지 않아서이다. 그는 아무런 존재도 아니었기 때문에 키키 아루에 대해 아무도 신경을 쓰지 않았다.

10

25 The utilization of ① <u>state-of-the-art</u> Internet technology ② <u>is allowing</u> thousands more Americans to engage in public policy debates on ③ <u>the most pressing</u> issues of today. ④ <u>With an advent of</u> the virtual dialogue, citizens are infinitely closer to the policy issues that affect their lives.

정답 ④ With an advent of ⇨ With the advent of

해설 of의 한정을 받고 '~의 출현, 도래'와 같은 표현에서는 부정관사가 아니라 정관사와 함께 쓰여야 하므로 정답은 ④이 된다. of 이하의 구조가 '특정한 대상을 서술하며 지칭'하고 있기 때문에 불특정을 나타내는 부정관사와 함께 쓰면 어색하다.

해석 첨단의 인터넷 기술사용은 수천만 미국인들이 현안들에 대한 정책토론에 참여할 수 있도록 만든다. 가상대화의 등장으로 시민들은 자신들의 생활에 영향을 미치는 정책이슈들을 밀접히 접할 수 있다.

26 ① <u>Many as</u> 1,200 people die a day in violence in the Democratic Republic of Congo and more than ② <u>half of them</u> are children. The United Nation's children's fund UNICEF reports ③ <u>will have publicized</u> that more children under the age of five die in the war-battered African nation each year than ④ <u>do</u> in China, which has a population 23 times larger, it said in a report.

정답 ① Many as ⇨ As many as 또는 Many

해설 many 다음에 수사를 동반한 복수 명사가 쓰여야 하므로 as를 삭제하거나 '~만큼이나 많은'이라는 말이 필요하면 as many as와 같은 표현이 와야 한다.

해석 콩고민주공화국에서 1,200명이 하루에 죽었으며 이중 절반이 어린이였다. UN 어린이 기금재단인 유니세프의 보고서에서는 전쟁에 휩싸인 아프리카 국가들에서 매년 죽는 5세 미만의 어린이들의 사망자 수가 인구가 23배 많은 중국보다도 많다고 내용을 발표할 것이라고 한다.

27 If the reviewer feels ① <u>unqualified</u> to review a part of a patch, they can ② <u>delegate</u> part of the review to another party who ③ <u>needs</u> not be a blessed reviewer. If the reviewer feels unqualified to review any of the patch, and feels there is a better ④ <u>blessed</u> reviewer, they should attempt to notify a better reviewer.

정답 ③ needs ⇨ need

해설 '~할 필요가 없다'라는 의미를 나타낼 때에는 조동사 need를 이용해서 'need not + 동사원형'으로 써야 하기 때문에 needs가 아니라 need가 와야 한다.

해석 검토자가 패치의 일부분을 검토할 자격이 없다고 느껴질 경우 다른 검토자를 지정할 수 있으며 그 경우 뛰어난 검토자일 필요는 없다. 검토자가 보다 뛰어난 검토자가 있다고 느낄 경우 그들에게 연락을 하도록 노력해야 한다.

28 American investigators ① <u>were given</u> the first name and telephone number of one of the Sept. 11 ② <u>hijackers</u> two and a half years before the attacks ③ <u>on</u> New York and Washington, but the United States appears ④ <u>to fail</u> to pursue the lead aggressively, American and German officials say.

정답 ④ to fail ⇨ to have failed

해설 appears는 현재 시제로 쓰였다. 그 다음에 연결되는 부정사는 의미적으로 '그 이전에 실패했음'을 나타내야 하기 때문에 완료부정사가 와야 한다. 따라서 ④의 to fail은 to have failed라고 고쳐야 한다.

해석 미국 조사단은 9/11 납치범들의 이름과 전화번호를 뉴욕과 워싱턴에 대한 공격이 있기 2년 반 전에 받았었다. 그러나 미국은 그러한 단서를 적극적으로 추적하지 않은 것으로 보인다고 미국과 독일 관료들은 밝혔다.

29 Landfills take up valuable space and emit methane, a potent greenhouse gas ; and ① <u>although</u> incinerators are not as ② <u>polluted</u> as they once were, they still produce noxious ④ <u>emissions</u>, so people dislike ④ <u>having them around.</u>

정답 ② polluted ⇨ polluting

해설 ②의 polluted는 polluting으로 바꿔야 옳다. 소각로가 오염되는 것이 아니라 (환경) 오염시키기 때문에 능동의 뜻으로 써야 한다. ①은 'although + S + V ~, S + V ~, so + S + V ~'의 구조로 맞게 쓰였다. ④의 dislike는 동명사를 목적어로 취하는 동사로 맞게 쓰였다.

해석 매립지는 귀중한 장소를 차지해 버리고 강력한 온실 가스인 메탄가스를 배출한다. 비록 소각로가 이전보다는 오염도가 덜하지만, 여전히 유독가스 배출량이 많다. 그래서 사람들은 주변에 매립지가 있는 것을 싫어한다.

30 Harmful bacteria can survive ① <u>for</u> as long as 24 hours on computer keyboards, a study released yesterday showed, ② <u>highlighting</u> what could be a growing threat as hospitals increase investment in technology. The study carried out at Northwestern Memorial Hospital in Chicago found that keyboards can contaminate the fingers, ③ <u>bare</u> or gloved, of a nurse or ④ <u>doctor</u>, who could then transfer bacteria to patients.

정답 ① for ⇨ 삭제

해설 survive는 자동사로 쓰였다. 'survive long'이 자체로 부사의 수식을 받아 자동사의 역할을 할 수 있다. 그러므로 ①의 전치사 for는 없어야 한다. ②은 현재분사 구문으로 의미상의 주어는 a study가 된다. ③의 bare는 형용사로 '벌거벗은, 알몸의' 의미로 주어진 문장에서는 '맨손의'라는 뜻으로 쓰였다. ④의 doctor 앞에 굳이 부정관사가 없어도 a nurse에 연결되는 구조라서 생략이 가능하다.

해석 어제 발표된 연구에 따르면, 병원이 기술에 대한 투자를 늘리는 상황에 과연 증가하는 위협이 무엇일지를 강조하면서, 해로운 박테리아는 컴퓨터 키보드에서 24시간 동안이나 생존할 수 있다고 밝혔다. 시카고의 노스웨스턴 메모리얼병원에서 수행된 연구는 장갑을 끼고 있건 아니건 간에 간호사나 의사의 손가락을 오염시킬 수 있고, 환자들에게 박테리아를 옮길 수 있다고 밝혔다.

홍준기 교수

주요 약력

現. 박문각편입학원 총괄 디렉터 겸 대표 교수
코리아중앙데일리 객원(중앙일보 영문신문) 해설위원
Korea JoongAng Daily 독해 연재 매주(토요일) (2013. 1. ~ 현재)
前. 시설관리공단 공채 시험 영어과 출제 위원
KBS 굿모닝팝스 독해 연재

주요 저서

- 박문각편입 문법 시리즈 (박문각출판 刊)
- 박문각편입 독해 시리즈 (박문각출판 刊)
- 박문각편입 논리 시리즈 (박문각출판 刊)
- 박문각편입 어휘 시리즈 (박문각출판 刊)
- 박문각편입 적중 모의고사 (박문각출판 刊)
- 공무원 VOCA 마스터 (박문각출판 刊)
- 석세스 편입독해/편입논리 (종합출판Eng 刊)
- 스타영문법사전(공저) (종로편입아카데미 刊)
- 영문법 Restart(공저) (종합출판Eng 刊)
- 중앙데일리 리딩 스펙트럼(Ⅰ – Ⅳ) (종합출판Eng 刊)
- 시사독해 실렉션 (종합출판Eng 刊)

동영상 강의
www.pmg.co.kr

박문각 편입
실전 문법

초판 인쇄 2020년 9월 1일 | **초판 발행** 2020년 9월 10일
편저 홍준기 | **발행인** 박 용 | **발행처** (주)박문각출판
등록 2015년 4월 29일 제2015-000104호
주소 06654 서울시 서초구 효령로 283 서경 B/D
팩스 (02)584-2927 | **전화** 교재 주문 (02)3489-9400

저자와의
협의하에
인지생략

정가 12,000원
ISBN 979-11-6444-744-2